Behind Wooden Walls: Neolithic Palisaded Enclosures in Europe

Edited by

Alex Gibson

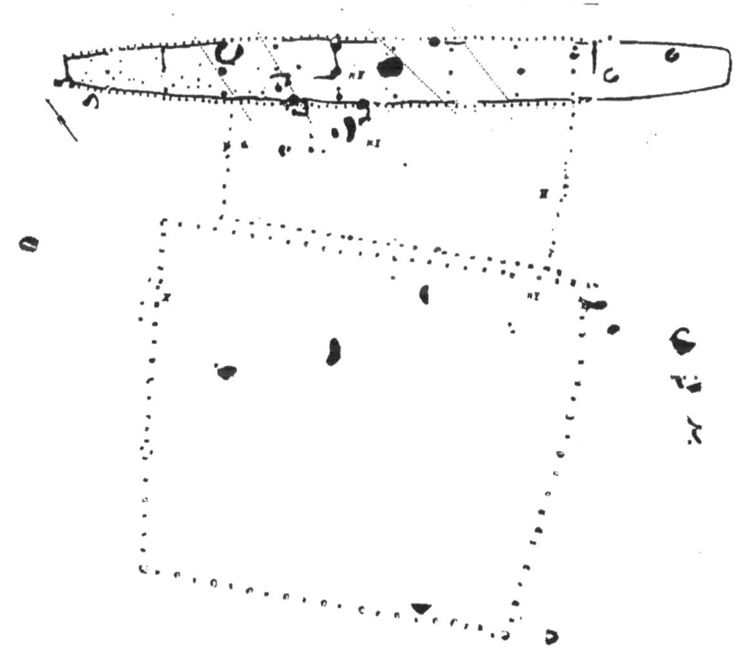

BAR International Series 1013
2002

Published in 2016 by
BAR Publishing, Oxford

BAR International Series 1013

Behind Wooden Walls: Neolithic Palisaded Enclosures in Europe

ISBN 9781841712932 paperback
ISBN 9781407323954 e-format
DOI https://doi.org/10.30861/9781841712932
A catalogue record for this book is available from the British Library

BAR Publishing is the trading name of British Archaeological Reports (Oxford) Ltd. British Archaeological Reports was first incorporated in 1974 to publish the BAR Series, International and British. In 1992 Hadrian Books Ltd became part of the BAR group. This volume was originally published by Archaeopress in conjunction with British Archaeological Reports (Oxford) Ltd / Hadrian Books Ltd, the Series principal publisher, in 2002. This present volume is published by BAR Publishing, 2016.

BAR titles are available from:

BAR Publishing
122 Banbury Rd, Oxford, OX2 7BP, UK
EMAIL info@barpublishing.com
PHONE +44 (0)1865 310431
FAX +44 (0)1865 316916
www.barpublishing.com

CONTENTS

List of Contributors ii

List of Figures iii

1 Introduction 1
Alex Gibson

2 The Later Neolithic Palisaded Sites of Britain 5
Alex Gibson

3 Irish Palisade Enclosures – A Long Story 24
Eoin Grogan & Helen Roche

4 Palisade Enclosures – The Second Generation Of Enclosed Sites In The Neolithic oif Northern Europe 28
Mac Svensson

5 Palisaded Enclosures in the German Neolithic 59
Michael Meyer

6 On Palisades, Houses, Vases and Miniatures: the Formative Processes and Metaphors of Chalcolithic Tells 93
Dragos Gheorghiu

LIST OF CONTRIBUTORS

Dragos Georghiu
Centre of Advanced Studies in the Visual Arts
University of Arts
10 Budisteanu
Bucharest
Romania

Alex Gibson
Department of Archaeological Sciences
University of Bradford
Bradford
BD1 7DP

Eoin Grogan
The Discovery Programme
34 Fitzwilliam Place
Dublin 2
Republic of Ireland

Michael Meyer
Lehrstuhl für Ur- & Frühgeschichte
Insitut für Geschichtswissenschaften
Humboldt-Universität zu Berlin
Hausvogteiplatz 5-7
D-10117 Berlin
Germany

Helen Roche
The Discovery Programme
34 Fitzwilliam Place
Dublin 2
Republic of Ireland

Mac Svensson
Riksantikvarieämbetet
Åkergränden 8
226 60 Lund
Sweden

LIST OF FIGURES

Chapter 2
Fig 2.1. Radiocarbon dates from British Later Neolithic Palisaded Enclosures

Fig 2.2. View corridors from outside the entrances of palisade enclosures

Chapter 4
Fig 4.1. Distribution of causewayed enclosures in the northern group of the Funnel Beaker Culture (after Hassman 2000).

Fig 4.2. Schematic survey plans of six south Scandinavian causewayed enclosures (after Madsen 1988). Scale 1:5000.

Fig 4.3. Distribution of the palisaded sites and the other Scandinavian sites referred to. 1. Dösjebro, 2. Hyllie, 3. Bunkeflo, 4. Vasagård, 5. Grødbygård, 6. Rispebjerg, 7. Sigersted I, 8. Östra Torn, 9. Helgeshøj, 10. Bakkegård, 11. St. Herrestad, 12. Büdelsdorf, 13. Sarup, 14. Stävie, 15. Hindby mosse, 16. Markildegård.

Fig 4.4. Schematic survey plans of five south Scandinavian palisade enclosures (Vasagård and Rispebjerg after Nielsen, F. O. 1998, 2000, 2001. Bunkeflo after Jonsson 1995). Scale 1:5000.

Fig 4.5. Axe knapping area at Dösjebro during excavation in the cold autumn of 1998. Photo: H. Pihl.

Fig 4.6. Flint axes deposited at the palisade enclosure at Dösjebro. Photo: B. Almgren.

Fig 4.7. Structured deposition of scrapers and flakes in a small pit (before excavation) at Dösjebro. Photo: K. Lund.

Fig 4.8. Section of the posthole (A68723) with a large deposition of flakes.

Fig 4.9. The western entrance of the palisade enclosure at Hyllie.

Fig 4.10. Deliberately deposited flint axe in the western entrance of the enclosure at Hyllie. Drawing: E. Rudebeck. (from Svensson 1991 Fig. 5). Scale 1:2.

Fig 4.11. Plans of two circular structures at Rispebjerg (from Nielsen 2000 Fig. 8).

Fig 4.12. Axes and chisels from Rispebjerg. The two in the middle are fire cracked – probably deliberately. Photo: K. Rasmussen (from Nielsen, F. O. 2001 Fig. 9).

Fig 4.13. Location map of Šventoji.

Chapter 5
Fig 5.1 Fences in settlements of the older (♦) and middle Neolithic (▲) in Germany mentioned in the text. Open symbols uncertain. See Appendix1,Table 1.

Fig 5.2 Examples of Neolithic fences. 1 – Gerlingen, LBK (Appendix1,Table 1,4); 2 – Bochum-Hiltrop, Hillerberg, Rössen (Appendix1,Table 1,10; the northwestern part of the building is reconstructed). Different scales.

Fig 5.3 Examples of circular palisades in Germany and France. 1 - Wittenheim (Haut-Rhin), Rössen III (Appendix1,Table 2,6); 2 - Künzing-Unternberg, MN (Appendix 1,Table 2,3); 3 - Schkölen-Räpitz, Kr. Leipziger Land, Late Bronze Age (Steinmann 1999, Abb. 12).

Fig 5.4 *Kreispalisadenanlage* (circular palisaded enclosure) from Quenstedt, Schalkenburg (Appendix1,Table 2,4)..

Fig 5.5 *Kreispalisadenanlagen* (circular palisaded enclosures) and similar features of the middle Neolithic (◆) and the younger Neolithic (▲) in Germany and France. See Appendix 1,Table 2. No. 4 and 6: only palisade; No. 1, 2 and 3: the palisades are presumed not to be contemporary with the ditches because of a difference in plan, 1 and 2 are uncertain; No. 5: the ditch is stratigraphically later than the palisade.

Fig 5.6 Length and width of Neolithic palisaded enclosures (in meters). 1 - Kreispalisadenanlagen (circular plisaded enclosures) of the late middle and early later Neolithic from Germany and France (see Appendix 1,Table 2); 2 - Non-circular palisade enclosures of the German Neolithic (see Appendix 1,Table 3-5). In some cases the measurements are estimated (for the data see lists 2-5).

Fig 5.7 Palisaded enclosures of the LBK in Germany. Open symbols uncertain. See Appendix 1,Table 3.

Fig 5.8 Examples of LBK palisades in Germany: 1 - Meindling (Appendix 1,Table 3,8); 2 - Köln-Lindenthal: phases according to Bernhard 1986 (not to scale). The palisade was erected in phase 12 and it is assumed that it did not enclose any contemporary houses.

Fig 5.9 Diagram showing the number of palisades with associated settlements and with an earlier or later ditch system in the different periods. As far as it can be said the settlement traces inside the *Kreispalisadenanlagen* are not contemporary. *Kreis* = *Kreispalisadenanlagen*.

Fig 5.10 Palisade enclosures of the middle Neolithic in Germany. Open symbols uncertain. See Appendix 1,Table 4.

Fig 5.11 Examples for MN palisades in Germany: 1 - Hambach 260: the excavator presumes that the palisade existed alone in the first phase; 2 - Inden; 3 - Meisternthal: the palisade encloses settlement features and an ellipsoid ditched enclosure. 3 grids = 20m.

Fig 5.12 Palisaded enclosures of the younger Neolithic (◆) and the late- and final Neolithic (●) in Germany. Open symbols uncertain. See Appendix 1,Table 5. ★: final Neolithic/early Bronze Age timber circle from Pevestorf, Kr. Lüchow-Dannenberg.

Fig 5.13 Enclosures of the later Neolithic with the palisade enclosure presumed to be an initial phase. 1 - Mayen (Appendix1,Table 5,4); 2 - Urmitz (Appendix 1,Table 5,7), transition middle to later Neolithic (Bischheim). Different scales.

Fig 5.14 Timber circle of the final Neolithic/early Bronze Age from Pevestorf, Kr. Lüchow-Dannenberg with recorded sections of the posts (Meyer 1993, plan 1 and pl. 96).

Black: posts of the circle; cross filling: Graves of the Únětice culture (K 8, K 10); filled with lines: inhumation of the globular amphorae culture. KbK - cremation graves of the gobular amphorae/Schönfeld culture; SK - concentration of sherds belonging to this cemetery; unfilled features are undated. Scale: 1:100, post-sections 1:50.

Chapter 6

Fig 6.1 The Radovanu tell, southern Romania.

Fig 6.2 Plan of the Poljanica tell, level I (after Todorova 1982), showing the plan of the palisade. The black lines represent a continuous wooden palisade made of posts bedded within a trench. The grey lines within the pattern of the palisade represent trenches without wooden posts, while those inside the perimeter of the palisade represent megaron or common houses.

Fig 6.3 Plan of the Poljanica tell, level VIII (after Todorova 1982), showing the plan of the palisade.

Fig 6.4 Plan of the Ovcarovo tell, level I (after Todorova 1982), showing the plan of the palisade.

Fig 6.5 Plan of the Ovcarovo tell, level XII (after Todorova 1982), showing the plan of the palisade.

Fig 6.6 Barn from Uzunu village, southern Romania. The house was made with material taken from a Boian-Gumelnita tell.

Fig 6.7 Detail of a window showing the many layers of repair with clay and painting.

Fig 6.8 Detail of a wall of a barn made of wattle, Uzunu village, southern Romania.

Fig 6.9 Detail showing the clay filling of the wattle work.

Fig 6.10 The rotation of houses on the east-west axis at Poljanica levels I - VIII.

Fig 6.11 Lid from Pietrele tell, after Berciu 1956: 46, fig. 58.

Fig 6.12 Lid from Goljamo Delcevo tell, after Todorova 1982: 105, fig. 58/12).

Fig 6.13 Clay model from Cascioarele tell on the island.

Fig 6.14 Clay model from Gumelnita tell (after Serbanescu 1997: 249, fig. 3/5).

Fig 6.15 Gumelnita vase with a lid with an architectural handle from Pietrele tell (after Berciu 1956: 42, fig. 51).

Fig 6.16 Adding faces to the archaeological reconstruction: an ethnological example from 1900 Romania (Hebbelynck 1905: 386).

CHAPTER 1

INTRODUCTION

Alex Gibson

The early forests of Europe have long been exploited by human groups. They were the habitats of hunted animals. They were the sources of edible roots and fruits. They also provided raw materials for tools and utensils, weapons, shelter and protection. Wood was important to early humans yet the rarity, over large areas of Europe, of surviving wooden objects from prehistoric contexts and the extraordinary conditions necessary for the long term preservation of wood mean that it is a rarely studied and often ignored medium. With regard to the Neolithic, the first 'Age of Monuments' in the accepted sense, early finds-dominated archaeological attention has understandably focussed on earthwork monuments, the tangible remains of which can still be seen, surveyed and, of course, excavated. These monuments, usually defined by a variety of forms of banks and ditches, also partly comprise the degree of negative features (ditches) which is necessary for the accumulation of artefacts. The recovery of these objects was the principal aim of the early archaeologists, who were more concerned with collection than stratigraphic detail, and yet it was on these finds that chronological frameworks came to be constructed.

With the refinement of archaeology and the development of remote sensing techniques, the corpora of known monument types increased in numbers but there was also the discovery of hitherto unknown (and undated) types of site. In Britain, timber circles represent a case in point. The first to be excavated was Woodhenge in Wiltshire which, coincidentally, was also the first major site to have been discovered using aerial photography. Despite the international fame of Woodhenge, lying so close to its stone counterpart, timber circles remained largely unstudied despite the high-profile excavation of some comparable sites in the latter half of the twentieth century (see Gibson1998 for a summary). This is hardly surprising. The lack of surface features at these sites means that their study is regarded as unrewarding by many archaeologists and they do not share in the romantic imagery and neo-pagan reverence bestowed upon their stone counterparts. They remain hidden, largely unknown, uninspiring and certainly not understood. Indeed, their existence is such a generally well kept secret that when a rare, water-logged example of a timber monument came to light on the tidal flats off the Norfolk coast, general ignorance caused its significance to be exaggerated out of all proportion by professional archaeologists, neo-pagans and practitioners of alternative religions alike. But that is another story.

Wooden monuments tend to be chance discoveries. They may be found during the excavation of more visible sites. For example, the palisades at Knowth, Co. Meath (Eogan 1984; 1986) lay below the passage grave and the palisade at Mount Pleasant, Dorset (Wainwright 1979) lay within the large Wessex henge monument. At Balfarg, Fife (Mercer 1981) the timber circles were situated within a henge and were unsuspected prior to the excavation of the site in advance of housing development. At Oddendale in Cumbria (Turnbull 1990) the timber circle was below the cairn They may be found during geophysical survey at other monuments. For example, there are the multiple post circles within the stone circle at Stanton Drew, Somerset (inf Andrew David), and a possible palisaded enclosure at Tara, Co. Meath (Condit 1999).

I would also include aerial photography in this category of chance discoveries since so much chance is involved in this type of survey: the weather conditions must be right, the ground-water conditions must be right, the growth cycle of the crops must be right and there must be an aerial photographer in the right place at the right time. The discovery of the Hindwell palisaded enclosure in Powys, mid-Wales is just such an example (Gibson 1999). It was discovered in 1994 during a flight to photograph an excavation nearby. The weather conditions were not ideal for aerial photography, but the excavation had reached a crucial stage and was ready for photographing. Low cloud forced us to fly into the Walton Basin from the south instead of from the north, as would have been more direct, and had this not happened we would not have flown over the site. The discovery of the dark, curving cropmark was immediately reported (and the exact field pinpointed) to Chris Musson of the Welsh Royal Commission on Ancient and Historical Monuments. At that time, Chris had responsibility for aerial photography within the Commission and knew the area well having flown over it on many occassions. He took to the air two days later but found that the cropmark had disappeared. Two days of rain had been sufficient to alter the growing conditions of the cereal and the cropmark had 'washed out'. Other areas of the perimeter of this site were found during flying in subsequent years but I suspect that they were only found because we were looking for them. Had we located these later cropmarks without the benefit of hindsight we might just have interpreted them as relict field boundaries or even animal tracks.

I suspect that the size of these sites has hampered their recognition. The whole perimeter at Hindwell has never shown in the ground cover and this may be true of other sites in similar agricultural regimes. If only arcs of ditch are recorded, then they may not be recognised as forming parts of the circumference of an enclosure and instead they may be recorded or catalogued as field boundaries (or pit alignments in the case of the pit-defined palisades). It is the hidden nature of these sites that has ensured their lack of study and it is clearly difficult to design a programme of active survey. Where does one start to look? What (non-excavation) criteria will distinguish an arc of palisade from a curving field boundary? How can these sites be dated other than by active intervention?

There is also another aspect of invisibility which has had an equally detrimental effect on the study of these wooden sites and that is the invisibility of the original above ground appearance. With other monuments, particularly those composed of stone and earth, architectural elements survive. Passage graves may still be entered and the visual experience of the modern visitor is likely to be *broadly* similar to that of the monuments' creators. Similarly, stone circles will look much today as they did to their prehistoric users. Enough survives of earthen long barrows for us to be able to reconstruct their original appearance with a fair degree of accuracy. This is not the case with timber monuments whether they be houses, mortuary structures, palisades or timber circles. Occasionally freak survivals will be encountered such as the lake villages of France and Switzerland, the pile-built structures at Flag Fen, Cambridgeshire, or the waterlogged shrine at Bargeroosterveld in the Netherlands but these are exceptions that prove the rule. Generally speaking, all that survives are the postholes and these may be capable of providing the bases for several equally plausible reconstructions.

Chris Musson's architectural feasibility study of the multiple timber circles at Woodhenge, the Sanctuary and Durrington Walls is a case in point (Musson in Wainwright & Longworth, 1971). Musson set out, from an architect's point of view, to explore the likelihood of whether these circles might have been roofed. He was able to propose several equally plausible reconstructions for each site but despite this concluded that they probably were <u>not</u> originally roofed. Despite this, Musson's roofed reconstructions were seized upon indiscriminately by subsequent archaeologists because they were attractive hypotheses and the grandeur of their scale served to demonstrate that Neolithic populations were far from 'primitive'. Unfortunately few archaeologists paid due regard to Musson's actual conclusions.

It must be readily admitted, however that the reconstruction of the above ground appearance of timber circles and palisaded sites is largely a matter of personal preference. One can adopt a conservative stance and view them as freestanding posts or logs: the palisaded sites constructed using contiguous posts looking rather like a US cavalry fort in some John Ford movie. The more adventurous might also use a north American analogy and look at the scant archaeological (as opposed to pictorial or ethnographic) evidence for totem poles. The realist will admit that we might never know. However, the squared off timbers below ground in the early Neolithic palisade at Etton in Cambridgeshire and above ground at the peculiar timber shrine at Bargeroosterveld suggest that there must be a good chance of at least some of these posts having been carved, or at least trimmed or shaped, to some degree.

From the papers contained in this volume, it can be seen that there is a common concern across Europe and that is our lack of understanding regarding these enclosures. Little large-scale excavation has been undertaken. Where sites have been excavated, there are problems with horizontal stratigraphy and phasing. The lack of dating evidence at many sites also presents obvious problems as does the general paucity of internal features and the difficulty in proving the degree of contemporaneity (if any) between any internal features and the perimeter walls. Therefore questions such as 'what were they for?' are likely to remain unanswered for a considerable time.

Despite this pessimism, an increasing amount of work is taking place across Europe on Neolithic palisade enclosures and the result of this is that more enclosures are being recognised and the numbers of known sites are being increased. In recognition of this, a session was organised at the European Association of Archaeologists' annual conference in Lisbon in September 2000. The aim of this lecture session was to draw together some of this new data from Europe and to discuss and formulate some common trends and approaches. This volume arises from that conference and provides an overview on the current state of knowledge regarding palisaded enclosures. The paper by Eoin Eogan and Helen Roche was not presented at the conference and their presence is especially welcome here. The paper given in Lisbon by Josh Pollard does not appear in these proceedings as the West Kennet sites have now been fully published (Whittle 1997). It was originally intended to include a paper discussing the French sites but in the end this was not forthcoming. Nevertheless readers are directed to a paper by Chris Scarre (2001) for a general over view of western France though in this article early as well as later Neolithic enclosures are discussed.

Perhaps it is too early to ask the question 'what were these sites for?' and indeed it may prove impossible to answer. Palisaded enclosures may have played a number of different roles within their societies and these roles may have changed or varied through time and space. A question we can ask is 'what did these sites mean to the people that built them?' and here we can glean more. It is hoped that the papers constituting this volume, as well as presenting a large body of data, go some way to shedding some light on the answer to this question.

BIBLIOGRAPHY

Condit, T. 1999. Beneath the ground at Tara, *Archaeology Ireland,* 47, 29.

Eogan, G. 1984. *Excavations at Knowth* 1, Royal Irish Academy Monographs in Archaeology, Dublin.

Eogan, G. 1986. *Knowth and the passage tombs of Ireland*, Thames and Hudson, London.

Gibson, A.M. 1998. *Stonehenge and Timber Circles.* Stroud: Tempus Publishing.

Gibson, A.M. 1999. *The Walton Basin Project: Excavation and Survey in a Prehistoric Landscape 1993-97.* Research Report 118, London: Council for British Archaeology.

Mercer, R. J. 1981. The excavation of a late neolithic henge type enclosure at Balfarg, Markinch, Fife, Scotland, 1977-8. *Proceedings of the Society of Antiquaries of Scotland,* 111, 63-171.

Scarre, C. 2001. Enclosures and related structures in Brittany and Western France. In T. Darvill & J. Thomas (eds), *Neolithic Enclosures in Atlantic Northwest Europe*, 24-42. Oxford: Oxbow Books.

Turnbull, P. 1990. *Excavations at Oddendale, Cumbria, 1990: Interim Report*. Cumbria County Council Planning Dept.

Wainwright, G.J. 1979. *Mount Pleasant, Dorset: Excavations 1970-71.* Research Report 37, London: Society of Antiquaries.

Wainwright, G.J. & Longworth, I. H. 1971. *Durrington Walls Excavations: 1966-68.* Research Report 29, London: Society of Antiquaries.

Whittle,A.W.R. 1997. *Sacred Mound Holy Rings. Silbury Hill and the West Kennet Palisade Enclosures: A Later Neolithic Complex in North Wiltshire.* Monograph 74, Oxford: Oxbow Books.

CHAPTER 2

THE LATER NEOLITHIC PALISADED ENCLOSURES OF THE UNITED KINGDOM

Alex Gibson

INTRODUCTION

As in Scandinavia, there appear to be two generations of palisaded enclosure in Neolithic Britain and Ireland (Gibson 1998a; Grogan & Roche this volume). The older generation can be assigned to the earlier Neolithic, dating broadly to the fourth millennium, and these tend to have an association with causewayed enclosures. The palisades at Orsett (Hedges & Buckley, 1978), Haddenham (Evans, 1988) and Donegore (Mallory, 1993), for example, have been excavated and have proved to have been broadly contemporary with the ditched perimeters. Detailed aerial photographs suggest the presence of palisades at other sites such as those at Norton or Corntown in Glamorgan (Burrow *et al.* 2001), Freston in Suffolk (Oswald *et al.* 2001, fig 3.14) and Haddenham in Cambridgeshire (Oswald *et al.* 2001, fig 4.11). While it is obvious that these earlier palisades are perfectly suited for defensive or protective purposes, they do tend to appear to be *comparatively* modest in proportions. The postpits average some 0.6m deep and rarely exceed 1m. The post diameters, as extrapolated from the postpipes, are remarkably uniform at some 0.3m. This suggests that timbers the size of telegraph poles may have stood between about 2 and 3m high. Though these are substantial posts, weighing between an estimated 150kg and 250kg, and though clearly they would have formed a significant barrier to any unwelcome visitors seeking access, nevertheless these posts are quite modest when compared with the later Neolithic examples. The posts of these second generation enclosures are estimated to have weighed up to several tonnes. A review of these first generation palisaded causewayed enclosures has recently been published (Oswald *et al.* 2001)

The later Neolithic sites, the 'second generation' enclosures as Mac Svensson so aptly calls them (chapter 5, this volume), may well develop from the earlier palisades though this is difficult to prove. But certainly one does not need to look outside of the UK for the origins of these insular timber enclosures. The native population would have behind them a long tradition of enclosing space with wooden walls. There is enough overlap in the chronology of the earlier and later sites to suggest that some first generation palisades may have still been standing while the later ones were being constructed (see Gibson 1998a, fig.6.4: 1999, Table 55). The second generation sites, however, are markedly more monumental than their predecessors. They are not so overtly defensive/protective in character and they tend to be associated with other types of ritual monument. Furthermore, the palisaded sites are also found outside of the main distributions of causewayed enclosures for example in Scotland and mid-Wales.

DESCRIPTION

Three types of palisade were identified in an earlier review (Gibson 1998a). These consisted of:

- Type 1 palisades made up by individual posts each set in their own postpit (such as Meldon Bridge),
- Type2 close set but not contiguous posts set in closely spaced pits (as at Hindwell) and
- Type3 contiguous posts set within a palisade trench (such as at Mount Pleasant).

This typology still seems to be valid and no site yet known combines the different construction techniques. This suggests that each site may have been planned as a single entity though later modifications may have been made to the internal arrangements as well as the perimeters. This typology may also have a chronological implication as has been proposed earlier (Gibson 1998a, fig 6.4) and is discussed again below.

The Type 1sites are united in having entrances marked by avenues of posts. These avenues are generally short, roughly measuring about 40-50m, and are consistent in two respects. Firstly they are not radial to the enclosures (though they are more or less radial at Dunragit) and secondly, they project outwards from the enclosures. As will be discussed below, these entrances do not suggest that these enclosures had a primarily defensive role.

The sizes of the enclosures vary with the majority averaging just under 5ha. Ballynahatty encloses less than 1ha while Hindwell encloses a massive 34ha making it the largest late Neolithic enclosure so far recorded. The areas of Meldon Bridge, Walton and the total area of Dunragit are similar at about 7-8ha while Forteviot encloses slightly less than 5ha. Mount Pleasant and the two West Kennet enclosures also cover about 5ha. Too little of the perimeter of Dorchester is known to calculate the area accurately but if the arc is projected then the site will have enclosed a minimum of 11ha. If it was oval rather than circular, this area may have been much more. Hindwell clearly stands out as unique, being over twice the size of the imposing henge at Avebury, but I do not see it as necessarily particularly singular. More sites doubtless wait to be discovered since the obvious problems of detecting such large sites have already been identified in the introduction to this volume.

DATING

Type 1 enclosures may be the earliest type (fig 2.1). The recent excavations at Dunragit may support this as finds of Grooved Ware have been produced from secondary contexts (Thomas 2001). This enclosure also seems to have had a long and complex history suggesting that an origin of perhaps as early as 3000 Cal BC may be possible. The outermost perimeter at Dunragit also has a scalloped effect which suggests that it was constructed in distinct lengths or segments. In this respect the enclosure strongly resembles the ditches of causewayed enclosures. This may again suggest an early origin for the type 1 palisades but admittedly dating on morphological grounds alone is at best unreliable and at worst foolhardy. Radiocarbon dates from primary contexts sampled during the excavation will ultimately sustain or demolish this hypothesis. The recently published radiocarbon dates from Meldon Bridge, however, If taken at face value may suggest that the type 1 palisades were long-lived, perhaps being constructed over a period of as much as 1000 years.

The dates from the Type 2 sites of Dorchester and Hindwell form a remarkably uniform group clustering within a date range of approximately 2800-2600 Cal BC. Unfortunately no artefacts were recovered from the excavations at Hindwell but the dates are exactly comparable with those recovered from the Grooved Ware phase of pre-barrow activity at Upper Ninepence less than 1km to the North and overlooking the site of the enclosure (Gibson 1999). Grooved Ware was associated with the postholes at Greyhound Yard, Dorchester and Irish Grooved Ware was recovered in large quantities from the timber circle and double palisade enclosure at Ballynahatty (inf Barry Hartwell). Work continues at this fascinating site and the publication is eagerly awaited.

The Type 3 enclosures are once again problematic not least because of the curious mix of date ranges from West Kennet 2 where it would appear that old materials were finding their way into primary contexts. The dates from West Kennet 1 and Mount Pleasant are more helpful, however and the Beaker associations from the latter site support the hypothesis that this type of solid-walled enclosure is possibly the latest in the sequence.

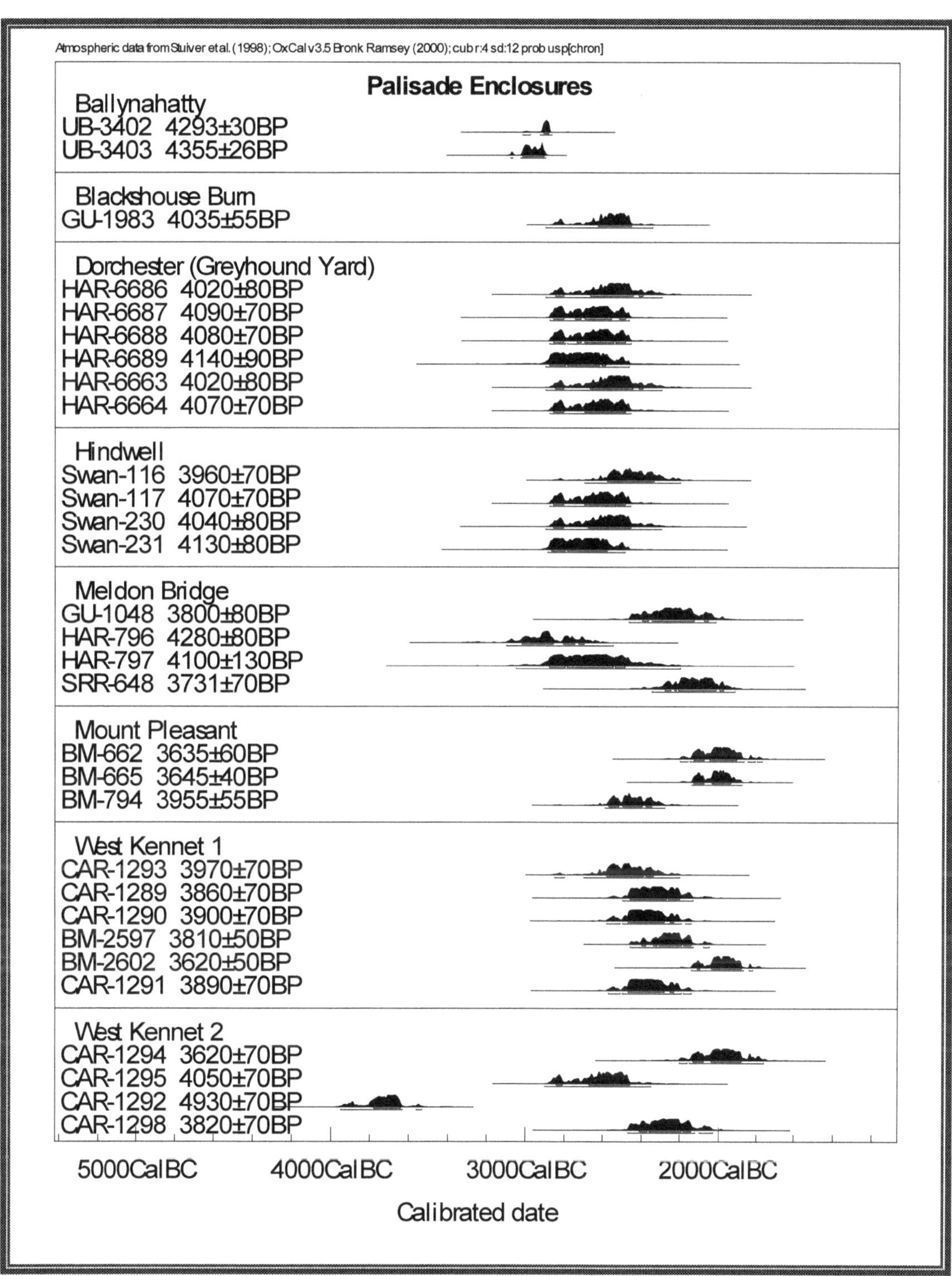

Fig2.1: *Radiocarbon dates from British Later Neolithic Palisaded Enclosures*

RECONSTRUCTION

It has already been argued that despite the morphology, all these sites may have originally presented the onlooker with a solid perimeter. The two smaller posts between the larger uprights at Meldon Bridge are crucial to this argument but it must be remembered that these medial posts were not located between every pair of main uprights. Thomas's (2001) comment that the innermost freestanding posts at Dunragit were 'more a timber circle than a true palisade' is therefore puzzling. While on the one hand there does not appear to be any evidence for median posts at Dunragit nevertheless it appears that Thomas has not considered the possibility of horizontal pegged timbers nor has he considered the evidence for closed perimeters at many timber circles (Gibson 1998b). However, it must be acknowledged that the reconstruction of the superstructures of such organic, perishable monuments must rely almost totally on personal preference and hypothesis.

It is the preference of the present writer to envisage these enclosures as having closed perimeters. This can clearly be demonstrated at the type 3 sites but is less easy to prove at those of type 1 and 2. The arguments in favour of this hypothesis are, to my mind, the medial posts at Meldon Bridge and the recurring presence of fomalised entrance avenues at all type 1 sites. The entrance avenues do not, of course mean that the rest of the perimeter had to be *necessarily* closed. Arenas formed by freestanding posts may also have had formalised approaches just as there appear to have been portal stones at some circles of freestanding stones. But taken with the evidence for median posts at Meldon Bridge and given that there appears to be some evidence for visual and physical exclusion at these enclosures, then it may be that the entrances are indeed proscribed routes through otherwise solid barriers.

This discussion of perimeter form is, of course, related to our perceptions of how high these posts might originally have stood. Enough has been written on the reconstructions of timber circles over the last quarter century for the conservative below:above ground ratio of 1:3.5 to have become accepted in the archaeological literature. This assumes that for every unit below ground, at least three and a half units *could* have stood above ground. The depths of the postholes therefore give a possible clue as to the potential of the original heights of the timbers. A 2m deep posthole, as at Hindwell for example, could have supported a post standing some 7m above ground giving the post a total length of 9m. This ratio was calculated empirically by Roger Mercer (1981, 149-150) who used the posthole ramps at Neolithic sites to estimate the length of the post. This assumes that the function of the postramp is to topple the post into the hole and therefore the outer edge of the postramp represents the point of gravity of the post. A postramp 4m long (including the posthole diameter) would be designed to unbalance a post 8m long. However this assumes a long, straight post. Trees, to the contrary, tend to thicken towards their bases and in fact the point of balance may be nearer to a third of the way up the length of the post. Therefor the same postramp and posthole may have been sufficient to unbalance a post not 8m long but 12m. In short, these estimations are beset with problems due to the large number of unknown variables involved in the calculations. Despite this, less than empirical research by the present writer who asked over 10 farmers and as many architects/builders in mid-Wales during the early 1990's the simple question, 'how deep would you bury a post to make it stable?' came out with roughly the same figure. The ratio 1:3.5 can then be regarded as a useful guide though it may be conservative.

This calculation is hypothesis not fact. While these postholes could certainly *have* been dug to certain specified depths in order to provide stability for monumental posts, however it is also possible that it was the act of *burying* the post that was important. In support of this hypothesis, we can recall the central 'posthole' at the timber monument of Holme-next-the-Sea (Pryor 2001). Dug to over 1m deep, this posthole did not support a post 4.5m long but an up-turned tree-stump which did not stand more than 1m above the ground. Waterlogging preserved the data at this site so that we can be certain of the nature of the central upright. On a terrestrial site only the posthole would have survived and one might have assumed that the central focus was a large, free-standing post. The inversion of the tree-stump at Holme and the reversing of the normal world order that this act symbolises must serve as a cautious reminder of the range of possibilities when we attempt to reconstruct postholes, particularly large postholes.

There may also be a case for uniting the two hypotheses. It has been demonstrated elsewhere (Gibson 1998b) that Stonehenge should be regarded as a timber circle made out of stone. The use of woodworking techniques in its construction and the multiple rings and horseshoes in its groundplan are better paralleled amongst timber circles than stone ones. If one reconstructs timber circles as lintelled structures then it considerably aids our understanding of the peculiar and otherwise unparalleled arrangement of uprights that make up this unique pile of stones on Salisbury Plain. If, however, tree trunks stood inverted in the postholes of timber circles, their skyward roots would have reached across to their neighbours to form ready made lintels and entry to the circle would have been through natural wooden arches. Thus timber circles might represent a world turned upside down, an arena in which normal order is reversed. By so doing this world is united with the underworld and timber circles may thus provide areas where the world of the present and the world of the ancestors come together. The hypothesis is, as yet, unprovable but not necessarily implausible.

But are we correct to draw upon timber circles to help us understand palisade enclosures? The two types of monument are, after all, united only in their being made of wood and their enclosing of space. The answer is probably not. I mention these other reconstructions simply to raise awareness of alternative hypotheses and to remind archaeologists of the ambiguity of the data as far as reconstructing the original form of the perimeter is concerned. I however have already nailed my colours to the post choosing in favour of solid perimeters: barriers containing the space within and excluding the world without.

The outwardly protruding entrance avenues of the Meldon Bridge type (type 1) enclosures have previously been mentioned. It has already been argued that these are not ideally suited to defence as was originally suggested (Burgess 1976). They do not force attackers to 'run the gauntlet'. To do this the avenues would have to have projected inwards so that the defenders had access to the sides. Instead, they only offer the would-be attacker the opportunity to set a fire at the entrance and burn the avenue down. These avenues, therefor, must be regarded as channels to ensure the controlled and ordered entry of individuals either in single file or, at most, two abreast. They also ensure that the entrants' view into the enclosure is restricted. This device is seen elsewhere, such as, for example at Avebury where the avenue turns at the last moment to directly approach the entrance. This turn ensures that the gazes of those walking down the avenue is directed away from the monument and only in the last few metres are they channeled directly towards the entrance. Their view of the interior is still obstructed, however, by the two large stones immediately within the bank and ditch.

The avenues of the type 1 enclosures and indeed the narrow entrances at the type 2 and 3 sites (Hindwell and Mount Pleasant) may similarly be designed to restrict access and vision. Fig 2.2 gives an indication of what may been seen inside enclosures if the theory of controlled access and vision is correct. These examples would be rendered more accurate if contours were included and computer-generated viewshed analysis employed. Neither has been undertaken here and the view corridors suggested must be regarded as illustrative rather than definitive. They illustrate the field of vision of someone standing about 10m outside the monument, directly in front of the entrance. It is interesting to note the restricted nature of these fields of vision, particularly at the type 1 enclosures. What is also noteworthy is that in the case of those sites with known internal monuments (Hindwell and Forteviot), the internal features lie to one side of the view corridor. Only at Mount Pleasant does this not seem to be the case with the internal hengiform monument and timber circle lying within the view corridor particularly from the eastern entrance, and roughly at the junction of the view corridors from the North and East gates. Despite this, the bank around the inner monument, its distance from the entrances and the multiple nature of the timber circle, would still deny a clear view of the monument from outside.

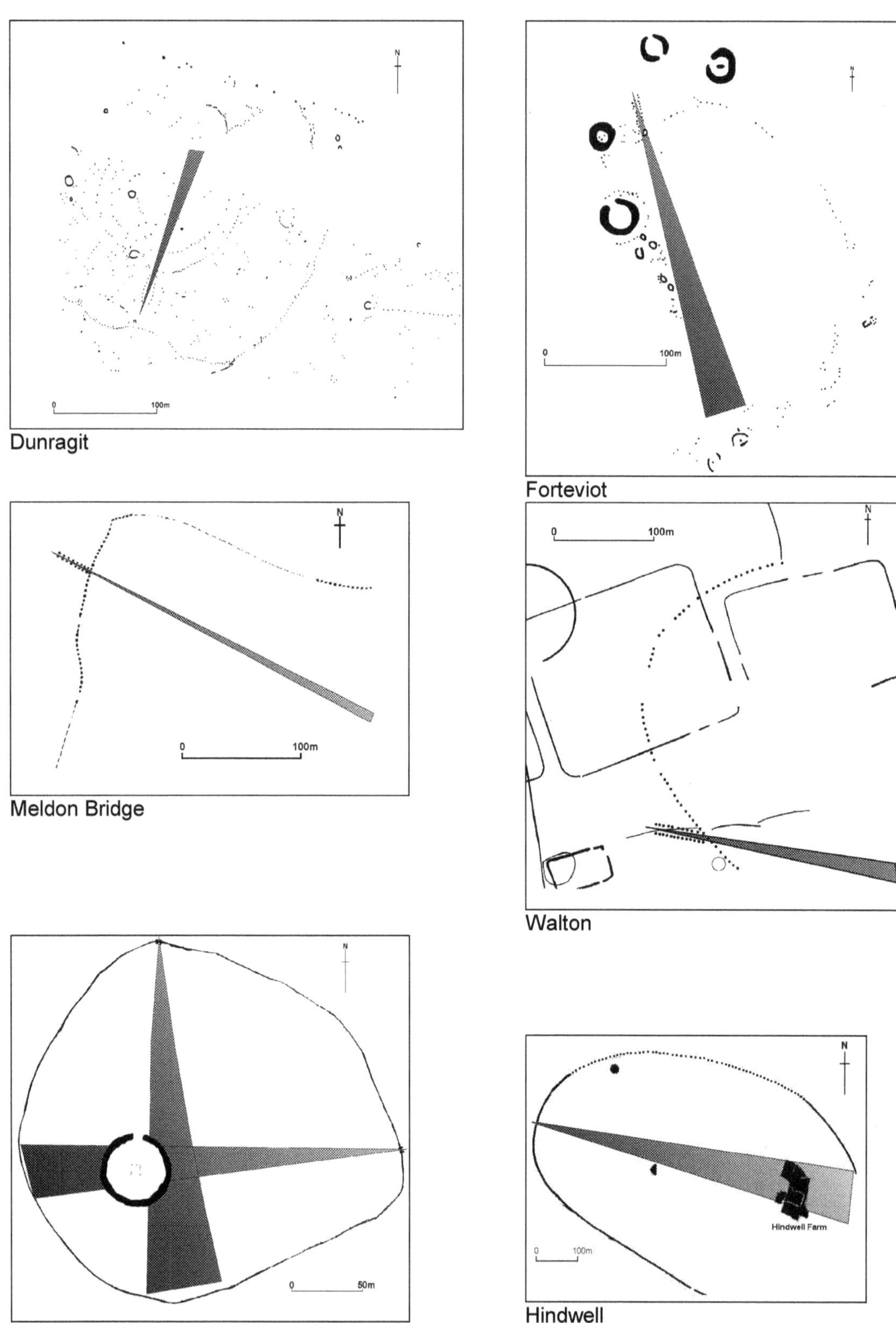

***Fig 2.2**: View corridors from outside the entrances of palisade enclosures*

PERMANENCE OF PLACE

The life span of many of these sites is not yet understood. Insufficient excavation has taken place at any palisaded enclosure to identify any real sequences of activity. Nothing is known of the internal arrangements at Hindwell, for example, despite undertaking 20Ha of close-interval caesium-vapour magnetometry (Gibson 1999b). The internal features photographed from the air at Forteviot are undated, other than by analogy, and the monument types identifiable are long-lived, spanning most of the third and second millennia BC. At West Kennet 2, the internal circular monuments do appear to be broadly contemporary with the perimeter but the construction of radial walls and other activities suggest that the monument, once constructed, was not static. Work at Dunragit has also already identified the erection, removal and replacement of posts and it is hoped that the results of this project will greatly illuminate the nature of activities and sequences at the enclosure. Interim statements at Ballynahatty suggest a similar pattern of building and rebuilding activity.

At Mount Pleasant, a spread of charcoal associated with sherds of plain bowl were located beneath the bank. This material was C14 dated 2880-2460 Cal BC (at two standard deviations) and was associated with over 1000 flint artefacts and small quantities of sheep and cattle bones. It was interpreted as representing the traces of rather transitory pre-enclosure settlement (Wainwright 1979). Subsequent to this, the henge was constructed and within this the palisade perhaps as much as 800 (or as little as 200) years later. Substantial barrows were constructed over the bank of the henge in the second millenium.

At Blackshouse Burn there had been pre-enclosure activity in the form of stakeholes and flat laid slabs beneath the bank in Trench A. The double postholes represented the first phase of construction of the enclosure. The bank was then constructed between the lines of posts and was possibly revetted by planking or hurdling. This bank was later augmented by the addition of more stones and was augmented again, once the posts had decayed. The bank was then finally capped by a layer of flat slabs. This 'sealing' of the monument has been noted at other sites, particularly cairns (Gibson 1993) and prolonged activity has been documented at many other types of monument, especially barrows.

At Meldon Bridge activity on the site seems to have started around 3000 BC with the digging of pits and the deposition of middle Neolithic Impressed Ware. The timber perimeter seems to have been constructed some time after 2600 BC. Speak and Burgess (1999) estimate that the perimeter may have stood for nearer 50 than 100 years. Sometime later, presumably in the early second millennium, standing stones were erected on site and a linear cremation cemetery attests the continued importance of the site around 1700-1050BC.

Of course the palisades themselves may have lasted for a considerable time (assuming that systematic and periodic destruction were not part of the grand design). Wainwright (Wainwright & Longworth 1971, 224-5) has estimated that the rate of decay of an oak post was approximately some 15 years for each inch (25mm) of radius. If this is accepted, then the posts at Hindwell might have lasted for about 200 years or about 8 generations. The entrance posts at Mount Pleasant may have lasted for over 500 years or 20 generations. The actual life of the monument may, however, have been much longer as the earth-bound sections of the posts at Hindwell had been charred prior to their erection and the resulting carbonised 'skin' would have acted as a most efficient water repellant. The geophysical survey also appears to show that the palisade was double in some areas but not everywhere (Gibson 1999b). High magnetic anomalies in the NE and SSW arcs suggest that parts of the outer and inner palisades respectively had burned down. We may be witnessing signs of a complex and possibly prolonged duration of construction, destruction and possibly reconstruction over an unspecified period. Such a process is already being suggested for Dunragit and Ballynahatty. At the latter site, some posts of the complex appear to have been levered out and the resulting voids filled with cultural material including Grooved Ware. The few centuries over which these palisades may have stood are nothing archaeologically but in terms of human timescales mean that people could have lived with these monuments for a considerable time before their demise. The monuments themselves would have taken on an antiquity of their own. They may have attracted their own histories, lore and mythology well before their collapse or destruction.

There is also circumstantial evidence to suggest that the sites of some of the palisade enclosures remained important after the palisades themselves had disappeared. For example, at Dorchester, a Roman settlement later occupied the site. At Meldon Bridge, a marching camp was constructed over the site of the enclosure. Dorchester might be explained in terms of the suitability of the area for settlement and Meldon Bridge might be coincidental (except that a fort was later constructed on the plateau above the enclosure) but in the Walton Basin something different appears to be happening. Both the Walton and Hindwell enclosures are superimposed by Roman camps. Three small practice camps overlie the Walton enclosure while a substantial pre-Flavian marching camp capable of housing some 12-13,000 men, a smaller, possibly equally early camp and a later Flavian fort overlie the Hindwell site. Given that there are large tracts of the Walton Basin suitable for stationing an army on the march, it seems more than pure coincidence that the only major Roman activity overlies the two palisade enclosures.

Jeff Davies (in Gibson 1999b) has commented on the unusual arrangement of the three camps overlying the Walton enclosure. While it must remain a possibility that they represent three successive visits by the Roman army, Davies considers this unlikely preferring the theory that they are practice camps constructed by the garrison of the Hindwell fort during its occupation in the Flavian campaigns. The chosen location for the construction of these camps by the army of occupation may not be entirely fortuitous.

Surface traces of the Hindwell enclosure probably survived as late as the Roman period because the Roman road that passes through the valley curves to follow the outline of the northern perimeter of the enclosure. This later became fossilised as a well-defined holloway and is now followed by a modern lane. It must also be remembered that the fort at Hindwell, and probably also the large marching camp, belong to the Flavian advances. This was an army of occupation and subjugation. The policy of assimilation with which Rome is generally credited had not been implemented in Wales as she was not yet part of the Empire. It makes great sense therefore that locally important places would have been deliberately slighted by this imperialistic power out to stamp its authority on the local population. Leaving aside the politics of imperialism, it also suggests that the place was still important to the inhabitants of the Walton Basin some two and a half millennia after the construction of the palisade. The significance of the place will undoubtedly have changed but the important observation is that a special meaning remained. It is also likely that an (albeit slight) earthwork remained at Hindwell. A slight ditch marking the outline of the former palisade may still have demarcated the important area. Tradition and the oral record may also have combined to preserve the significance of the areas of the former palisades. Taking this into account, then the Roman settlement at Dorchester and the marching camp at Meldon Bridge may take on a significance beyond coincidence. There is also a large marching camp to the NW of the Forteviot enclosure (Speak & Burgess 1999, fig 49) though in this case the Roman monument does not encroach on the Neolithic site.

ASSOCIATIONS

Associations at these sites are difficult to prove because they rely on the identification of cropmarks of monuments presumed to be Neolithic or Bronze Age in date. The later Neolithic and early Bronze Age however span 2 millennia and therefore association, sequence or exact contemporaneity and coexistence cannot be proved without excavation. Furthermore, some features such as pits which may be revealed on aerial photographs are undatable and, as mentioned above, excavation at Meldon Bridge has suggested that the pit digging activity predated the enclosure. Monuments revealed on aerial photographs, therefor, may demonstrate a sequence and add to the permanence of place debate mentioned above rather than association in the strict archaeological sense.

In terms of direct artefactual association, Grooved Ware was found at Dorchester, Ballynahatty and West Kennet 1 and 2. Grooved Ware and Beaker pottery was associated with Mount Pleasant. Grooved Ware has been mentioned as coming from secondary contexts at Dunragit. At Hindwell and Walton there were no finds at all from the excavated features and fieldwalking over the interior of Hindwell produced only a very few flints in contrast to the dense flint scatters in the fields around. This negative evidence is itself of interest suggesting that the interior may have been reserved in some way, kept apart from the world beyond.

At Forteviot a small single-entranced henge monument surrounded by a circle of pits (presumably a timber circle) seems to be the main internal monument though there are other ring-ditches and pits within and without the perimeter. At Dunragit there appear to be pit circles, alignments, ring-ditches and penanular ring-ditches within the three lines of enclosure. Small ring-ditches, pits and a penanular ring-ditch lie within the Leadketty site and there is a large interrupted ring-ditch, 100m in diameter to the NNE. A similarly large ring-ditch lies outside the Walton site but there are no known internal features. Within the Hindwell enclosure, two springs rise and there are two substantial round barrows of presumed Bronze Age date. The northern of the two has revealed aerial photographic and geophysical evidence for a triple ring-ditch suggesting a complex sequence of development. Some pits were also identified during the geophysical survey but clearly their contemporaneity with the enclosure can only be demonstrated by excavation and also, given the nature of the local gravel, these pits need not be anthropogenic. The timber circle and ring ditch at Mount Pleasant may predate the palisade slightly but similar features within West Kennet 2 were shown to be broadly contemporary.

There also appear to be large empty areas within the enclosures. The eastern halves of the Leadketty and Forteviot enclosures appear to be largely devoid of features while it is the western halves of the West Kennet 2 and Ballynahatty palisades that appear empty. Even if we assume that some of the pits in the Hindwell enclosure are contemporary, large tracts of the interior are empty. This is despite Roman period features being clearly visible as cropmarks. There are some pits visible within the Walton enclosure but these may be natural given that this site lies on the same mudstone gravel subsoil as Hindwell. These pits aside, the arable, cropmark-producing western half of this enclosure appears to be empty. Whatever was happening within these enclosures does not seem to have left any visible archaeological traces and the emptiness of the majority of sites is remarkable.

RESOURCES

Whatever their function, whatever mysteries, rituals or social relationships they were designed to preserve or maintain, palisaded sites involved their builders in considerable effort and use of resources, both material and human. A problem with any attempt to estimate the resources involved in the construction of the palisade enclosures must necessarily be how we reconstruct the sites as well as the accuracy of our calculations of post dimensions. These problems have already been outlined above. Similarly, the area of woodland required to supply the timber needed for the enclosures will have depended on the type of woodland available; sparse tree cover, light mixed woodland, climax oak forest and so on. At Hindwell we have no palaeoenvironmental data from which to reconstruct the immediate contemporary environment. There are no deep bogs nearby and soil pollen did not survive. At the Upper Ninepence site nearby the charcoal was almost entirely oak but given the broad contemporaneity of this site with the Hindwell enclosure it could possibly be that the people at Upper Ninepence were burning the branch timbers that were the by-products from the building of the palisade.

Despite these uncertainties, various archaeologists, including the present writer, have attempted to reconstruct the resource implications for palisade enclosures. At Mount Pleasant, the calculations were based on a 1:2 below/above ground ratio for the posts thus a post bedded 3m deep would 'have stood 6m high and on average 40cm thick' (Wainwright 1979, 237). This would mean that each post would have weighed just under 1 tonne. In fact, posts buried 3m deep *may* have been sufficiently stable to have stood as much as 10-12m high and although this may be at first sight hard to envisage, nevertheless timbers of this length and over would have been readily available in climax or dense oak forest. If this latter estimate is correct, then each post would have weighed in the region of 1.6 tonnes. Wainwright claims that 1600 posts would have been needed involving the exploitation of 900 acres (approximately 350ha). The basis of Wainwright's estimate is not given but it is unlikely to be accurate for it assumes that fewer than two trees would have been growing in each acre (fewer than 5 trees per hectare) of woodland.

At West Kennet, the palisade ditches were at least 2m deep and reached up to 2.7m (Whittle 1997). Whittle uses Mercer's (1981) 1:3.5 ratio and estimates that the posts may have stood 6-8m high. Whittle further estimates that 2800 posts would have been needed for the double enclosure West Kennet 1 and 1600 at West Kennet 2 (this assumes that the two palisades at West Kennet 1 were contemporary and that the enclosures were complete circuits). Whittle rightly points out that two posts could be obtained from a single tree if we are dealing with dense forest and therefore calculates that about 15ha would have been felled assuming that there were some 100-200 trees of less than 0.5m diameter per hectare. This figure is likely to be more accurate than those used by Wainwright at Mount Pleasant.

At Hindwell, the posts were 0.8m thick and may have stood over 6m high therefor having had a total length of 8-9m. Each might have weighed some 4.8 tonnes. About 1400 posts would have been needed and perhaps 700 trees. These figures are simply for the uprights, any planking used to form a solid perimeter would clearly have far more resource and logistical implications. The trees used were larger in diameter than those at Mount Pleasant and West Kennet, averaging 0.8m in diameter, and so there may have been fewer of these trees per hectare in which case selection would have to have been undertaken. If there were 50-100 such large trees per hectare, then some 7-14 hectares may have been exploited. The smaller trees in this area may have been used for any horizontal elements. Even the largest estimate for woodland exploitation is well below the area (34ha) enclosed by the palisade.

Speak and Burgess (1999) also use the 1:3.5 ratio for their calculations at Meldon Bridge but they take the ratio to calculate the total length of the post rather than the above ground ratio. Thus for the western perimeter postholes, estimated at being 1.5m deep, the total length of the post is given as 5.25m with 3.75m being above ground. Correct use of this convention, however, would calculate the posts as *standing* 5.25m high and having a total length of 6.75-7m. A similar mis-calculation affects the given sizes of the larger posts in the north-west angle which may have stood some 7m high (5m in Speak & Burgess 1999) and had a total length of 9m (7m in the report). These mis-calculations persist throughout the report and also affect the estimates of resources. They can be 'corrected' as follows (table 2.1) (correct is in inverted commas because it assumes the 1:3.5 as used by other authors to be 'correct').

Locations of posts	**Speak & Burgess**			**Recalculation according to accepted convention.**		
	Height (m)	**Total length**	**Weight (tonnes)**	**Height (m)**	**Total length**	**Weight (tonnes)**
W perimeter	3.75	5.25	0.39	5.25	6.75	0.5
NW perimeter	5	7	1.26	7	9	1.9
N perimeter	4	5.6	0.75	5.6	7.2	1
Total tonnage of wood			92.08			126

Table 2.1: *Revised calculations for Meldon Bridge.*

There were only *c.*135 posts used at Meldon Bridge although this excludes the smaller interval poles between the main posts. Therefore, for the main elements of the perimeter, as few as 70 trees might have been needed or less than 1ha of dense woodland.

Site	Type	Average height of posts above ground	Tonnes of timber needed	Area enclosed	Area of woodland exploitation
Meldon Bridge	1	4.25m	290	8 ha	2 ha?
Hindwell	2	7m	6330	34 ha	7-14 ha
West Kennet 1	3	7m	1480	4 ha	7-14 ha
West Kennet 2	3	7m	850	6 ha	4-7 ha
Mount Pleasant	3	11m	2800	4.5 ha	4-8 ha

Table 2.2: *Natural Resources need for the construction of some palisade enclosures.*

These comparisons suggest that the type 2 palisades may have been more monumental than the type 1 and 3. This is especially so when one considers the Greyhound Yard site at Dorchester with its posts capable of standing over 10m high and weighing some 11 tonnes each. Unfortunately so little of the perimeter of this site is known that other estimates cannot be reliably made.

These estimates may be totally wrong. They are based on so many assumptions. But to them must be added the wood for the horizontal elements, where there were any, estimated as some 160 tonnes for Meldon Bridge. What they do, however, is allow comparisons of scale to be made and the degree of varying monumentality between ostensibly similar monuments to be made. These comparisons can be summarised in Table 2.2.

CONCLUSION

So much remains to be discovered regarding their function and role within the communities that constructed them but what is clear is that they involved their builders in considerable effort and had a serious resource implication (both human and material). They must have been monumental constructions, dominating the landscapes in which they were sited yet they seem to have been secretive places with restricted access and closed off from the outside world. This is in contrast to the openness of the causewayed enclosures which preceed them but not dissimilar to the henges and timber circles with which they are chronologically and often physically associated.

The corpus of later Neolithic palisade enclosures in Britain is a small one, but one which is growing and I have every expectation that it will continue to grow as archaeologists have now come to recognise them. One danger is that now that archaeological attention is being paid to these sites, aerial photographs may be over-interpreted so that lengths of field ditch or later prehistoric pit alignments may all be interpreted as Neolithic by over-enthusiastic aerial archaeologists.

GAZETTEER

Site Name Ballynahatty
County Co. Down
NGR J327677
Description Small oval monument comprising a double perimeter of spaced posts enclosing approximately 1ha. The entrance appears to be an elaborate post-built structure. A double timber circle lies within the enclosure and the enclosure itself lies within a ritual landscape to the N of the Giant's Ring henge and chambered tomb. The postpits average 1.8m deep and the posts averaged 0.3m in diameter.
Dating 4293±30 BP (UB-3402), 4355±26 BP (UB-3403).
Both dates from charcoal from the posthole packing.
References Hartwell 1998 & pers comm.

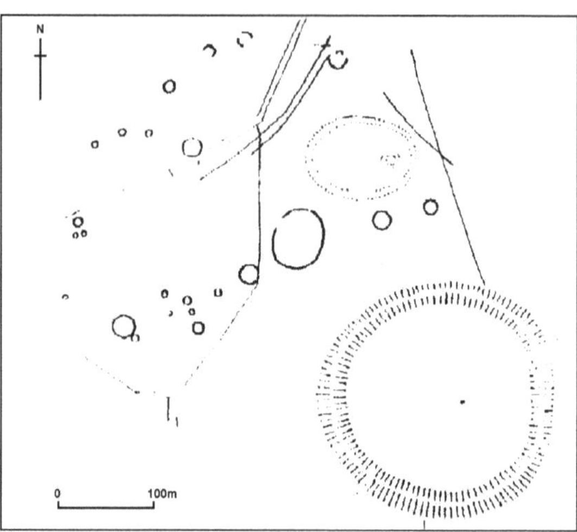

After Hartwell 1998

Site Name Blackshouse Burn
County Lanarkshire
NGR NS952404
Description Roughly circular double palisade enclosure approximately 300m across and with a stone bank between the palisades. Inner and outer palisades are c.9m apart. Post pipes suggest post of 0.2-0.4m across and the postholes were up to 0.8m deep. The postholes of the inner perimeter were spaced at between 0.8-1.4m apart and those of the outer perimeter1.4-2.7m apart. Entrance in the NW with a circular banked enclosure immediately outside.
Dating Outer rings of oak post 4035±55 BP (GU-1983).
References Lelong & Pollard 1998

Site Name Bridge of Keltie
County Perthshire
NGR NN649067
Description pit defined enclosure defined on 2 sides by a right-angled bend in the Keltie Water. Possible avenue.
Dating Tentative analogy
References Burgess & Speak 1999, 112.

Site Name Broadclyst
County Devon
NGR Not available
Description Site visible as a well-defined double-ditched enclosure on aerial photographs. It measures some 300m across. The inner crop mark is narrower than the outer suggesting the possibility of a palisade within a ditch.
Dating Tentative analogy
References Griffith 2001.

Site Name Dorchester (Greyhound Yard)
County Dorset
NGR
Description Represented by a 40m long arc of large postholes possibly enclosing over 10ha. The postpits measured some 3-6m long (including the access ramp each pointing to the exterior) by 2-3m wide and averaged 2.8m deep. The posts varied between 0.8m and 1.2m in diameter. No entrance or internal features have yet been identified. Associated with Peterborough Ware and Grooved Ware in the backfill of the postholes.
Dating 4020±80 BP (HAR-6686), 4090±70 BP (HAR-6687), 4080±70 BP (HAR-6688), 4140±90 BP (HAR-6689), 4020±80 BP (HAR-6663), 4070±70 BP (HAR-6664).
References Woodward et al. 1993.

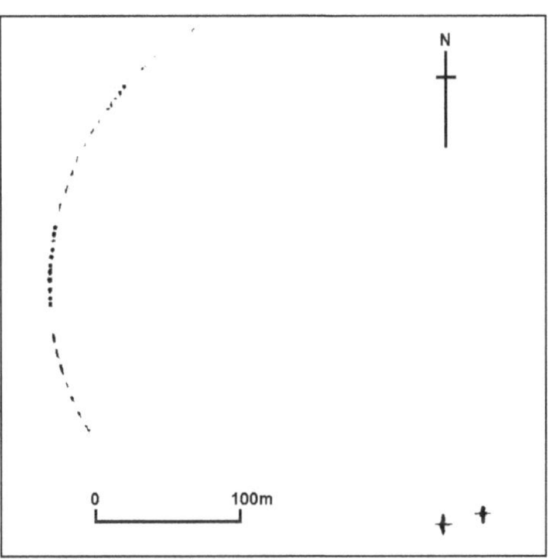

After Woodward et al. 1993

Site Name Dunragit
County Dumfriess
NGR NX148574
Description A triple, roughly circular enclosure of well-spaced posts enclosing an area of about 7ha. The innermost enclosure has a diameter of c.110m, the middle enclosure has a diameter of c.140m and the outermost enclosure has a diameter of c.300m. A double post avenue with slightly bowed sides leads from the middle palisade to the S. The outermost palisade in particular has a scalloped appearance as if constructed in a series of short, irregular lengths. The monument is set within a palimpsest of pits, pit alignments and ring-ditches.
Dating Grooved Ware.
References Mercer 1993: Thomas 2001.

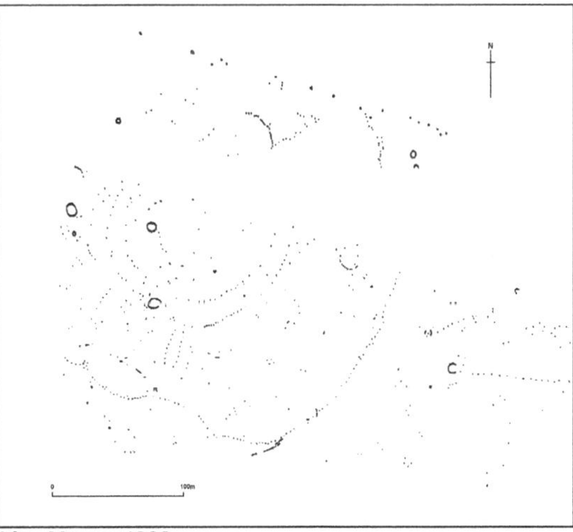
After Mercer 1993

Site Name Ferrybridge
County West Yorkshire
NGR SE476241
Description A series of short lengths of pit alignments surround an area occupied by a henge and two timber circles. Excavated parts of the pit alignments suggests that they did not hold posts or that the posts had been removed. There is also a double pit avenue to the NW of the henge.
Dating Tentative analogy
References Wainwright 1990: Turner 1992: Inf J. Hedges.

Site Name Forden Gaer
County Powys
NGR SO207991
Description Double line of post pits, 40m long and aligned NE-SW. Ends in a pair of larger posts at the SW. The similarity of this feature to the entrance passages at Meldon Bridge and Walton is worthy of comment but there is no trace of a perimeter. However, there is a curved linear cropmark to the N and NE. The pits were 8.5m apart, averaged just over 1m in diameter and 0.9m deep. Both had clearly held posts c.50cm in diameter (though 1 timber had been squared). Excavated in 1987, there were no finds and, due to the presence of two parallel slots 'outside' the avenue, the feature was interpreted as a Dark Age hall.
Dating Tentative analogy
References Blockley et al. 1990.

Site Name Forteviot
County Perthshire
NGR NO053169
Description Near circular enclosure of spaced individual postholes enclosing an area of c.6ha. The E side appears to have been formed by the edge of a natural terrace. The entrance is formed by a double avenue of posts leading off just to the W of N. Internal features comprise a penannular ring-ditch surrounded by a circle of pits, grouped and isolated pits and 3 small ring ditches. Three ring diitches are grouped around the entrance avenue to the N and 3 smaller ring ditches lie outside of the enclosure to the S.
Dating Analogy
References St Joseph 1976: Harding & Lee 1987: Gibson 1998a: Speak & Burgess 1999.

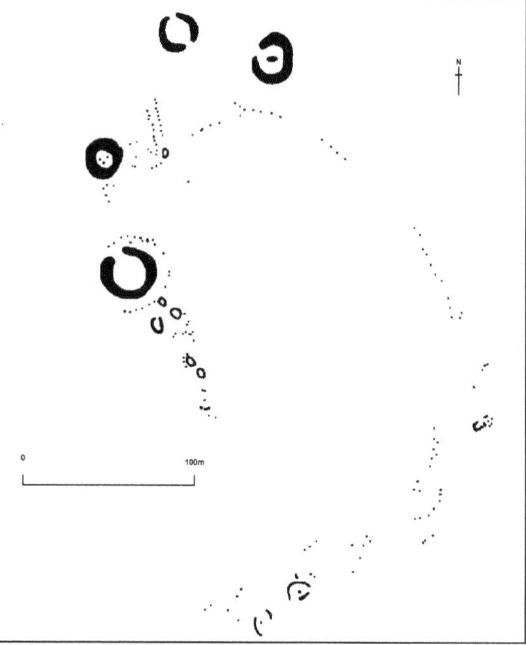

After St Joseph 1976

Site Name Hindwell
County Powys
NGR SO2560
Description Large oval enclosure formed of close-set but not contiguous posts each set in its own posthole. The oval measures c.800m NW-SE by 500m NE-SW. The perimeter measures 2.35km and the area enclosed is c.34ha. Postholes were 2m deep and each contained a post 0.8m diameter. They were accessed by a ramp from the exterior. Geophysical survey has highlighted some possible internal pits and linear areas of burning parallel with the palisade and outside the enclosure on the NE and SE arcs. Entrance marked by large postholes in the NW arc. Two round barrows survive as earthworks in the interior. Two springs rise within the monument.
Dating 3960±70 BP (Swan-116), 4070±70 BP(Swan-117), 4040±80 BP (Swan-230), 4130±80 BP (Swan-231); combined date range c.2800-2500 Cal BC. Samples from the outer rings of the oak posts.
References Gibson 1999a; 1999b.

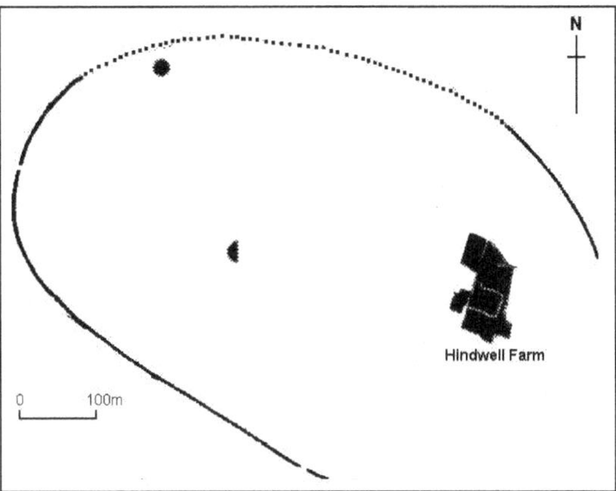

After Gibson 1999b

Site Name Leadketty
County Perthshire
NGR NO 020 161
Description Arc of postholes and skewed double post alignment entrance similar to Meldon Bridge and Walton. The ends of the arc measure some 300m across and the base of the arc to the northern perimeter is approximately 130m. The entrance corridor leads to the NE. There are traces of pits and 3 possible ring-ditches within the monument. A ring-ditch lies outside the monument to the NE and there is a large, circular ditched enclosure, over 100m in diameter, to the NNE.
Dating Analogy
References Barclay 2001.

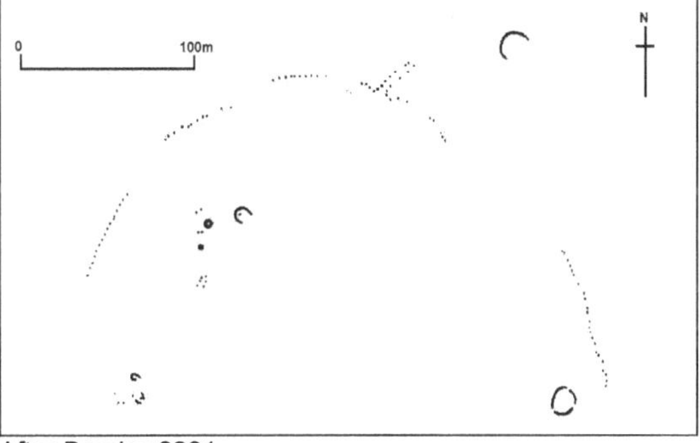

After Barclay 2001

Site Name Meldon Bridge
County Peeblesshire
NGR NT205404
Description Curved enclosure formed of spaced posts with smaller posts between the larger uprights. The enclosure cuts off the confluence between two streams, the Lyne Water to the S and the Meldon Burn to the E. This area measures approximately 8ha.Postholes of the NW perimeter measured 1.4m deep and contained posts 0.5m in diameter. The pits of the W perimeter were slightly smaller. Entrance marked by a double

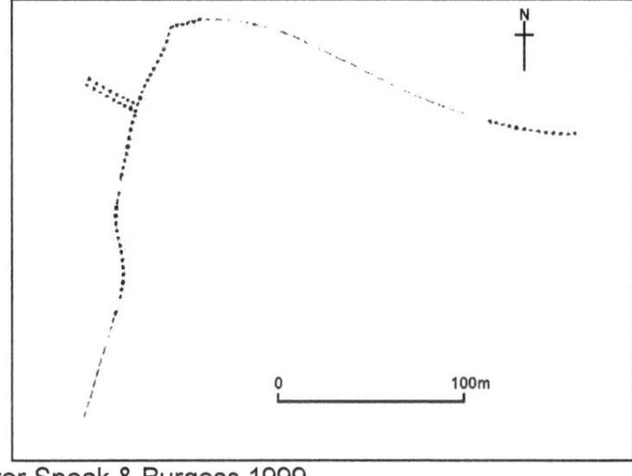

After Speak & Burgess 1999

post avenue externally to the NW. Interior occupied by a long sequence of deposition and burial from middle Neolithic Impressed Ware to Bronze Age Cordoned Urn

Dating 3800±80 BP (GU-1048),
4280±80 BP (HAR-796),
4100±130 BP (HAR-797),
3731±70 BP (SRR-648).

Dates from oak charcoal. GU-1048 comes from the packing of a perimeter posthole, the other dates are from the weathering cones of the perimeter post pits.

References Speak & Burgess 1999.

Site Name Mount Pleasant
County Dorset
NGR SY710900
Description Roughly oval palisade measuring c.270m by 245m. Posts contiguous and set within a palisade trench. The trench was 1-2m wide and 2.5-3m deep. The posts were 0.3-0.5m diameter. Two entrances, one in the N and one in the E flanked by much larger posts 1.7m in diameter. Set within a hengiform enclosure and enclosing a multiple timber circle within a penannular ditch.
Dating Grooved Ware and Beaker associations. Antler in palisade trench, 3635±60 (BM-662), charcoal from palisade trench 3645±40 BP (BM-665), bone from palisade trench 3955±55 BP (BM-794)
References Wainwright, G.J. 1979.

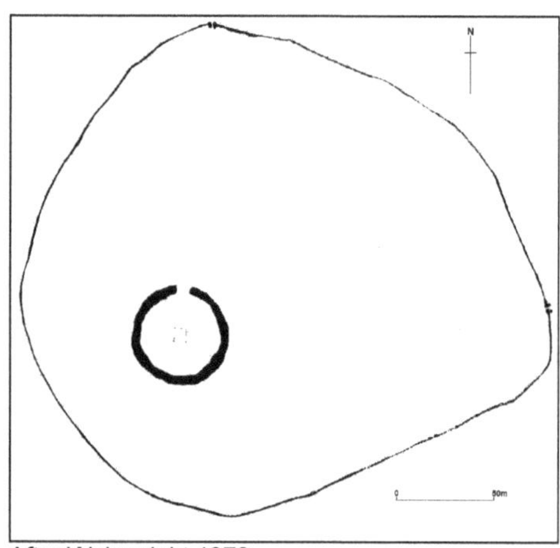

After Wainwright 1979

Site Name Nether Exe
County Devon
NGR Not Available
Description Oval enclosure visible on aerial photographs measuring some 550m NW-SE by 370m NE-SW. Some breaks in the ditch may be possible entrances. Three ring-ditches lie within the enclosure and there is a further concentration of two ring-ditches and 2pits to the NW.
Dating Analogy
Refernces Griffith 2001.

Site Name Selvie Wood
County Angus
NGR NO280483
Description Arc of irregularly-spaced pits close to a possible pit circle.
Dating Analogy
References Speak & Burgess, 1999, 112.

Site Name Stonehenge
County Wiltshire
NGR SU122422
Description Length of palisade ditch traceable for over 1300m to the W of Stonehenge. The exact nature, date and extent of this ditch is not known. It may represent a boundary or part of an enclosure.
Dating Context
References Cleal et al. 1995.

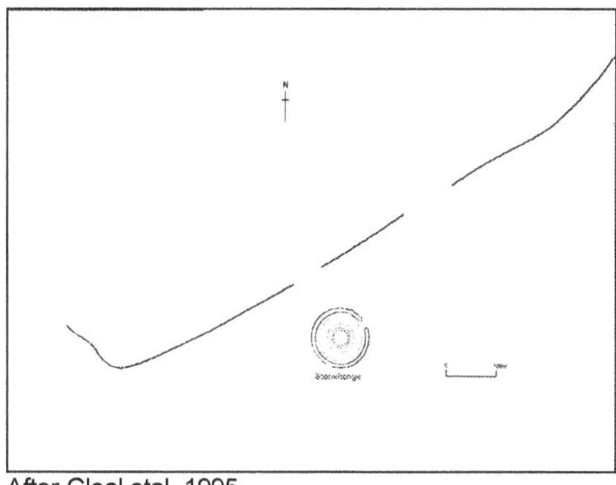
After Cleal etal. 1995.

Site Name Walton
County Powys
NGR SO253598
Description Cropmark of a sub-circular enclosure defined by spaced individual pits. This may cut off a former confluence of the Riddlings Brook to the S and a cropmark palaeochannel (possibly the former channel of the Hindwell or Summergill Brook) to the E. Area enclosed estimated at 8ha. Entrance marked by a skewed double avenue of posts leading to the W. Excavation of a posthole in 1998 suggested that the posts were of oak, 0.6m in diameter and the posthole was c.1.25m deep. There is a large ring-ditch, 100m in diameter, outside the enclosure 80m to the WNW and a smaller ring ditch immediately outside the enclosure to the SW.
Dating Analogy
References Gibson 1999a; 1999b: St Joseph 1980.

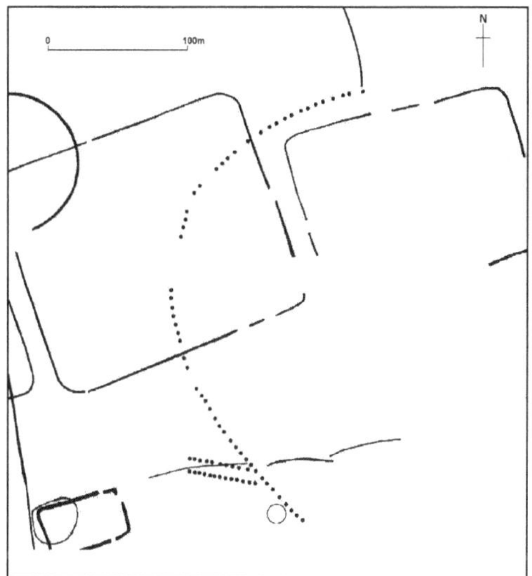

After Gibson 1999a

Site Name West Kennet 1
County Wiltshire
NGR SU112682
Description Sub-circular enclosure with double circuit traced S of the R. Kennet. NW arc has not been located. The outer enclosure measures approximately 240m in diameter. In the S arc, the inner and outer palisades are separated by c.30m. The palisade trenches are over 2m deep (up to 2.7m) and contained posts measuring c.0.6m in diameter.
Dating Grooved Ware ceramics. Outer perimeter: Bone from post packing 3970±70 BP (CAR-1293), 3860±70 BP (CAR-1289), 3900±70 BP (CAR-1290), Antler from post packing 3810±50 BP (BM-2597), 3620±50 BP (BM-2602). Inner perimeter, bone from post packing 3890±70 BP (CAR-1291).
References Whittle, A. 1993; 1997.

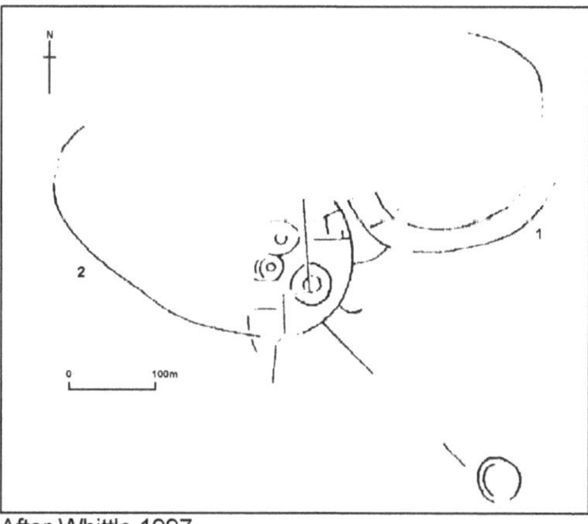

After Whittle,1997

Site Name	West Kennet 2 (see above for plan)
County	Wiltshire
NGR	SU110682
Description	Oval single circuit palisade measuring c.340m NW-SE by c.210m SW-NE. Three internal double timber circles within the SE end of the enclosure. Linked by a curving radial ditch, c.50m long, to enclosure 1 and by a straight palisade, c.230m long to a 4th double enclosure c.50m in diameter.
Dating	Grooved Ware associations. Bone from backfill, 3620±70 BP (CAR-1294), 4050±70 BP (CAR-1295). Bone from backfill of radial ditch, 3930±70 BP (CAR-1292), 3820±70 BP (CAR-1298).
References	Whittle, A. 1993; 1997.

BIBLIOGRAPHY

Barclay, G. 2001. Neolithic enclosures in Scotland. In T. Darvill & J. Thomas (eds), *Neolithic Enclosures in Atlantic Northwest Europe*, 144-154. Oxford: Oxbow Books.

Blockley, K. with Owen G & Owen W. 1990. Excavations in the vicinity of Forden Gaer Roman Fort, Powys, 1987. *Montgomeryshire Collections*, 78, 17-46.

Burgess, C.B. 1976. Meldon Bridge: a Neolithic defended promontory complex near Peebles. In C.B. Burgess & R. Miket (eds), *Settlement and Economy in the Third and Second Millennia BC*, 151-79. BAR 33, Oxford: British Archaeological Reports.

Burrow, S., Driver, T.& Thomas, D. 2001. Bridging the Severn Estuary: two possible earlier Neolithic enclosures in the Vale of Glamorgan. In T. Darvill & J. Thomas (eds), *Neolithic Enclosures in Atlantic Northwest Europe*, 91-100. Oxford: Oxbow Books.

Cleal, R.M.J., Walker, K.E. & Montague, R. 1995. *Stonehenge in its Landscape: Twentieth Century Excavations*. English Heritage Archaeological Report 10. London: HMSO.

Evans, C. 1988. Excavations at Haddenham, Cambridgeshire: a 'planned' enclosure and its regional affinities. In C. Burgess, P. Topping, C. Mordant & M. Maddison (eds), *Enclosures and Defences in the Neolithic of Western Europe*, 127-48. BAR S403, Oxford: British Archaeological Reports.

Gibson, A.M. 1993. The Excavation of Two Cairns and Associated Features at Carneddau, Carno, Powys, 1989-90. *Archaeological Journal*, 150, 1-45.

Gibson, A.M. 1998a. Hindwell and the Neolithic Palisades of Britain and Ireland. In A. Gibson & D. Simpson (eds), *Prehistoric Ritual and Religion: Essays in Honour of Aubrey Burl* 68-79. Stroud: Sutton publishing.

Gibson, A.M.1998b. *Stonehenge and Timber Circles.* Stroud: Tempus Publishing.

Gibson, A.M. 1999a. *The Walton Basin Project: Excavation and Survey in Prehistoric Landscape, 1993-7.* Research Report 118, York: Council for British Archaeology.

Gibson, A.M. 1999b. *The Walton Basin, Powys, Wales: Survey at the Hindwell Neolithic Enclosure.* Welshpool: Clwyd-Powys Archaeological Trust.

Griffith, F. M. 2001. Recent work on Neolithic enclosures in Devon. In T. Darvill & J. Thomas (eds), *Neolithic Enclosures in Atlantic Northwest Europe*, 66-77. Oxford: Oxbow Books.

Harding, A.F. & Lee, G. E. 1987. *Henge Monuments and Related Sites of Great Britain.* BAR No.175, Oxford: British Archaeological Reports.

Hartwell, B. 1998. The Ballynahatty complex. In A. Gibson & D. Simpson (eds), *Prehistoric Ritual and Religion: Essays in Honour of Aubrey Burl* 32-44. Stroud: Sutton publishing.

Hedges, J. & Buckley, D. 1978. Excavations at a Neolithic Causewayed enclosure, Orsett, Essex. *Proceedings of the Prehistoric Society*, 44, 219-308.

Lelong, O. & Pollard, T. 1998. The excavation and survey of prehistoric enclosures at Blackhouse Burn, Lanarkshire. *Proceedings of the Society of Antiquaries of Scotland*, 128, 13-53.

Mallory, J.P. 1993. A Neolithic ditched enclosure in Northern Ireland. *Actes du XIIe Congrès International des Sciences Préhistorique: Bratislava, 1-7 Septembre 1991,* 415-17. Bratislava: UISPP.

Mercer, R.J. 1981. The excavation of a late Neolithic hengetype enclosureat Balfarg, Markinch, Fife, Scotland. *Proceedings of the Society of Antiquaries of Scotland*, 111, 63-171.

Mercer, R.J. 1993. Secretary's Report. *Monuments on Record: Annual Review 1992-3,* 6-13. Edinburgh: RCAHMS.

Oswald, A., Dyer, C. & Barber, M. 2001. *The Creation of Monuments. Neolithic Causewayed Enclosures in the British Isles.* Swindon: English Heritage.

Pryor, F.M. 2001.*Seahenge*. London: Harper Collins.

Speak, S. & Burgess, C. 1999. Meldon Bridge: a centre of the third millennium BC in Peeblesshire. *Proceedings of the Society of Antiquaries of Scotland*, 129, 1-118.

St. Joseph, J.K. 1976. Air reconnaissance: recent results, 40. *Antiquity*, 50, 55-7.

St. Joseph, J.K. 1980. Air reconnaissance: recent results, 49. *Antiquity*, 54, 47-51.

Thomas, J. 2001. Neolithic enclosures: reflections on excavations in Wales and Scotland. In T. Darvill & J. Thomas (eds), *Neolithic Enclosures in Atlantic Northwest Europe*, 132-143. Oxford: Oxbow Books.

Turner, R. 1992. Field Services. *West Yorkshire Archaeology Service Review 1991-2.* Wakefield: West Yorkshire Archaeology Service.

Wainwright, G.J. 1979. *Mount Pleasant, Dorset: Excavations 1970-71.* Research report 37, London: Society of Antiquaries of London.

Wainwright, G.J. 1990. Archaeology Review 1989-90. London: English Heritage.

Whittle, A. 1993. The Neolithic of the Avebury area: sequence, environment, settlement and monuments. *Oxford Journal of Archaeology*, 12(1), 29-53.

Whittle, A. 1997. *Sacred Mound Holy Rings. Silbury Hill and the West Kennet Palisade Enclosures: a Later Neolithic Complex in North Wiltshire.* Monograph 74, Oxford: Oxbow Books.

Woodward, P.J., Davies, S.M. & Graham, A.H. 1993. *Excavations at Greyhound Yard, Dorchester 1981-4.* Monograph 12, Dorchester: Dorset Natural History & Archaeological Society.

CHAPTER 3

IRISH PALISADE ENCLOSURES – A LONG STORY

Eoin Grogan and Helen Roche

INTRODUCTION

A comparatively small number of palisaded sites have been identified in Ireland a few of which date to the Neolithic (Condit and Simpson 1998). These all appear to be domestic enclosures, such as the double palisade at Knowth, Co. Meath (Eogan 1984; 1986) that belongs to the pre-passage tomb phase on the site. Palisades also occur at Donegore and Lyles Hill, Co. Antrim (Mallory and Hartwell 1984; Gibson and Simpson 1987; Simpson and Gibson 1989), Tara, Co. Meath (M. O'Sullivan pers comm.) and Thornhill, Co. Derry (Logue 2001; Anon. 2000). A few ditched sites, such as Goodland, Co. Antrim (Case 1973), or Langford Lodge, Co. Antrim (Waterman 1963), may also have supported palisades. Towards the end of the Neolithic, timber circles and enclosures of a ceremonial nature may, in part, continue this tradition. These have been excavated at Ballynahatty, Co. Down, Knowth, Newgrange and Bettystown, Co. Meath (Hartwell 1998; Eogan and Roche 1997; Sweetman 1985; 1987; Eogan, J. 1999), and Balgatheran, Co. Louth (Ó Drisceoil 2000). A palisade and ditch also surround the embanked stone circle at Castleruddery, Co. Wicklow (Grogan and Hillery 1993), while a new post enclosure has been identified at Tara (Condit 1999). Stone palisades, contiguous circles of upright stones, occur as the inner element of a number of embanked stone circles and may equate to timber palisades on related sites.

NEOLITHIC FENCED ENCLOSURES

These sites seem to have palisades with a domestic or farming role; they are similar in size and construction and Gibson (1998, 73) has referred to them as fenced sites to distinguish them from the sacred or ritual enclosures defined by (usually) much larger freestanding posts. The most extensively investigated palisades are those at Knowth (Eogan 1984; 1986). There are two concentric arcs of palisade trench, evidently part of an oval or circular enclosure about 70-100m in diameter on the west side of the hilltop. The western side of the site has been eroded to the underlying shale bedrock and no trace survives here. The trenches held closely spaced upright posts that may have been up to 2.5m in height. There is no surviving evidence for an entrance. A large roughly cobbled 'yard' occurred towards the north-eastern side of the interior; this may suggest the use of the site as a stock enclosure. Despite the absence of stratigraphic evidence it is possible that the outer palisade, which cuts across an earlier rectangular house, is later, built as a replacement for the inner one. The house, and two others found to the north and east beneath the large tomb (Eogan and Roche 1997), produced the same Western Neolithic cultural assemblage. Other activity of this date includes a small ancillary building and a flint working area, also outside the palisade enclosure. The Knowth evidence suggests a stockade for cattle beside the domestic settlement consisting of houses, other smaller buildings and work areas. This phase dates to the end of the Early Neolithic period around 3500-3300 cal. BC.

Excavations at Thornhill revealed at least five houses and what appear to be several phases of palisade construction dating to the Early Neolithic (Logue 2001; Anon. 2000). The complex covers an area about 100m in diameter and both rectangular and circular structures appear to have been identified. The artefactual and other structural evidence indicate a wide array of domestic activities.

At Donegore an area measuring 200m by 150m on the hilltop is enclosed by a double ditch and double palisade, although it is not certain that all were contemporary (Mallory and Hartwell 1984; Mallory and McNeill 1991, 36-6, 78-9). A twin palisade, one dating to around 3000 cal. BC and the other to *c.*2600 BC, also surrounded the nearby hilltop at Lyles Hill (Gibson and Simpson 1987; Simpson and Gibson 1989). Estyn Evans (1953) had previously identified extensive Neolithic activity on the hilltop. Part of a palisade trench, perhaps enclosing a substantial portion of the hilltop, was identified during excavations at Tara in the 1950s. This appears to pre-date a small passage tomb and belongs to the Irish Early Neolithic (3800-3400 BC). The function of the palisade is unknown but the size of the palisade suggests a secular role (M. O'Sullivan pers comm.). It is possible that during the Neolithic settlement enclosures were occasionally sited on hilltops; one such site has been identified at Knocknarea, Co. Sligo (Berg 2000), while it has been suggested that the so-called hillfort on Turlough Hill, Co. Clare, could also date to this period (Grogan forthcoming).

A second enclosure has recently been discovered on the north edge of the summit at Tara through geophysical survey (Condit 1999; Newman forthcoming). The evidence suggests that this consists of a substantial palisade flanked inside and out by rings of large freestanding posts enclosing an area 200m by 180m in diameter. In the centre is the Rath of the Synods, a multi-period site with significant activity of Iron Age and early historic date. Although the new enclosure could be Iron Age there is an even more intriguing possibility that it could be earlier because the earliest phase at the Rath of the Synods (Grogan *et al.* forthcoming) is a circular ditched enclosure belonging to the Neolithic or Early Bronze Age. This ditch had been levelled before the Iron Age. At present it does not appear that the new enclosure is defensive in nature.

LATE NEOLITHIC TIMBER CIRCLES

A number of small ritual structures have been identified at Knowth, Ballynahatty, Bettystown and Balgatheran. These are *c.* 6.5m to 16m in diameter and consist of large upright posts that may have been up to 4m in height. The Knowth, Bettystown and Balgatheran circles consist of single post rings. Two principal phases were recognised at Ballynahatty (BNH5; Hartwell 1998). In the first, a circle of posts 11m diameter was erected around a setting of four larger posts. The posts of both the circle and inner uprights were then replaced with much more substantial timbers with the inner four being up to 7m in height. A second, outer, circle of uprights 16m in diameter was added and this may have had a cladding of timber planks. The Knowth (E) and Ballynahatty (SE) circles had well-defined entrances; at Ballynahatty settings of posts about 10m from the entrance served to funnel the approach to the circle.

A second larger circle (BNH5) surrounds the timber circle at Ballynahatty. This consisted of a double ring of upright timbers (Hartwell 1998) enclosing a circular area up to 90m in diameter. Each ring consists of at least 180 posts that could each have been as much as 6m in height. Although the entrance to this enclosure may have maintained the same orientation as the earlier circle the approach to the site was altered slightly to the north to take greater account of the local topography. The similar large multiple pit circle at Newgrange encloses an area of 80m in diameter (Sweetman 1985). At least one of the rings of pits held large upright freestanding timbers probably at least 3m in height. A second multi-ring structure at Newgrange may be a domestic building (Sweetman 1987).

The sites and complexes at Newgrange, Ballynahatty, Knowth, Bettystown and Balgatheran have all produced Irish Late Neolithic Grooved Ware and the dates suggest they were constructed within a relatively short period around 2600 BC. Ballynahatty and the two Boyne Valley sites (Knowth and Newgrange) occur within extensive ritual landscapes that include both earlier passage tombs and contemporary embanked enclosures ('henges'). Possibly related to these is the Castleruddery embanked stone circle that is surrounded by a crop mark ditch measuring 80m by 70m (Grogan and Hillery 1987). Within this is a second narrow ditch, probably a palisade trench, which encloses an area about 60m in diameter. Although the date of the enclosure is unknown it probably predates the circle. At Longstone Cullen, Co. Tipperary, and extensive Grooved Ware assemblage occurred within a circular enclosure defined by an inner ditch and outer bank (P. Danaher and H. Roche pers comm.).

LATER PREHISTORIC REVIVAL

In the Iron Age large ceremonial timber circles, including palisade enclosures and post circles, were erected at several regional centres, such as Emain Macha, Co. Armagh, Dún Ailinne, Co. Kildare,

Rathcroghan, Co. Roscommon and Tara, Co. Meath (Fenwick *et al.* 1999; Cooney and Grogan 1994; Cooney 2000). While separated from the Neolithic examples by a lengthy chronological gap these may be a conscious reflection of the earlier monuments (Gibson 2000) and recent re-assessment of some ceremonial enclosures indicates that related sites, such as the embanked stone circles at Grange, Co. Limerick, and Castleruddery, Co. Wicklow, and other ritual enclosures like Johnstown South, Co. Wicklow, were also being erected in the Middle-Late Bronze Age (Roche 1995; Grogan forthcoming; Fitzpatrick 1998).

CONCLUSIONS

Enclosures, whether of ritual or settlement purposes, were not a feature of the Irish Neolithic. Two forms of circles or palisades were, however, erected in small numbers during the period. The first consist of apparently domestic sites where stockades for defence or to control cattle were constructed on hill or ridge tops in the Early Neolithic. These are quite different in form and construction to the circles of very large freestanding posts constructed for ritual purposes in the Late Neolithic. The latter are part of an important period of change in ceremonial and funerary traditions. These sites form part of a range of new monuments, including embanked enclosures ('henges'), and are found in close association with Middle Neolithic passage tombs and related settlements.

BIBLIOGRAPHY

Anon. 2000. Spectacular evidence for Neolithic at Derry development site, *Archaeology Ireland,* 53, 5.

Bergh, S. 2000. Transforming Knocknarea – the archaeology of a mountain, *Archaeology Ireland,* 52, 14-18.

Case, H. J. 1973. A Ritual Site in North-East Ireland, in G. Daniel and P. Kjaerum (eds), *Megalithic Graves and Ritual*, 173-96, Jutland Archaeological Society, Moesgård.

Condit, T. 1999. Beneath the ground at Tara, *Archaeology Ireland,* 47, 29.

Condit, T. & Simpson, D. 1998. Irish Hengiform Enclosures and Related Monuments: a Review, 45-61, in A.Gibson and D. Simpson (eds) *Prehistoric Ritual and Religion*, Sutton, Stroud.

Cooney, G. 2000. *Landscapes of the Irish Neolithic,* Routledge, London.

Cooney, G. & Grogan, E. 1994. *Irish Prehistory. a social perspective*, Wordwell, Dublin.

Eogan, G. 1984. *Excavations at Knowth* 1, Royal Irish Academy Monographs in Archaeology, Dublin.

Eogan, G. 1986. *Knowth and the passage tombs of Ireland*, Thames and Hudson, London.

Eogan, G. & Roche, H. 1997. *Excavations at Knowth* 2, Royal Irish Academy Monographs in Archaeology, Dublin.

Eogan, J. 1999. Recent Excavations at Bettystown, Co. Meath, *Irish Association of Professional Archaeologists Newsletter* 30, 9.

Evans, E. 1953. *Lyles Hill: A Late Neolithic Site in County Antrim*, Archaeological Research Publications 2, HMSO, Belfast.

Fenwick, J., Brennan, Y., Barton, K. & Waddell, J. 1999. The magnetic presence of Queen Medb, *Archaeology Ireland,* 47, 8-11.

Fitzpatrick, M. 1998. Johnstown South Enclosure, *Excavations* 1997, 199-200, Wordwell, Dublin.

Gibson, A. 1998. Hindwell and the Neolithic Palisaded Sites of Britain and Ireland, 68-79, in A. Gibson & D. Simpson (eds) *Prehistoric Ritual and Religion*, Sutton Publishing, Shroud.

Gibson, A. 2000. Circles and henges: reincarnations of past traditions? *Archaeology Ireland,* 51, 11-14.

Gibson, A. & Simpson, D. 1987. Lyles Hill, Co Antrim, *Archaeology Ireland* 5, 72-5.

Grogan, E. forthcoming. *The North Munster Project. The later prehistoric landscape of south-east Clare*, Discovery Programme Monographs.

Grogan, E. & Hillery, T. 1993. *A Guide to the Archaeology of County Wicklow*, Ross Enterprises, Greystones.

Grogan, E., Velzian, C. & Caulfield, S. forthcoming. *Excavations at Tara, Co. Meath by Seán P. Ó Ríordáin: the Rath of the Synods*, UCD Archaeological Monographs .

Hartwell, B. 1998. The Ballynahatty complex, in A. Gibson & D. Simpson (eds), 32-44, *Prehistoric Ritual and Religion*, Sutton:Stroud.

Logue, P. 2000. A Neolithic Settlement at Thornhill, Co. Londonderry, *Neolithic Settlement in Ireland and Western Britain*, The Prehistoric Society/School of Archaeology and Palaeoecology, Queen's University, Belfast, Unpublished Conference Summaries, Belfast.

Mallory, J. & Hartwell, B. 1984. Donegore Hill, *Current Archaeology* 92, 271-74.

Mallory, J. & McNeill, T. 1991. *The Archaeology of Ulster*, Institute of Irish Studies, Queen's University, Belfast.

Newman, C. forthcoming. Discovery Programme Reports 6, The Discovery Programme/Royal Irish Academy, Dublin.

Ó Drisceoil, C. 2000. Louth timber circle, *Archaeology Ireland* 56, 6.

Roche, H. 1995. Style and Context for Grooved Ware in Ireland with special reference to the assemblage at Knowth, Unpublished MA Thesis, National University of Ireland.

Simpson, D. & Gibson, A. 1989. Lyles Hill, *Current Archaeology* 114, 214-15.

Sweetman, D. 1985. A Late Neolithic/Early Bronze Age pit circle at Newgrange, Co. Meath, *Proceedings of the Royal Irish Academy* 85C, 8-221.

Sweetman, P. 1987. Excavation of a Late Neolithic/Early Bronze Age site at Newgrange, Co. Meath, *Proceedings of the Royal Irish Academy* 87C, 283-98.

Waterman, D. M. 1963. A Neolithic and Dark Age Site at Langford Lodge, Co. Antrim, *Ulster Journal of Archaeology* 26, 43-54.

CHAPTER 4

PALISADE ENCLOSURES – THE SECOND GENERATION OF ENCLOSED SITES IN THE NEOLITHIC OF NORTHERN EUROPE

Mac Svensson

INTRODUCTION

Neolithic enclosed sites have been found on the Continent and the British Isles since the end of the nineteenth century. They have been used by several Neolithic cultures over a time span of between 6000 and 2000 BC (Andersen 1997). Different types of enclosures are known in most of Europe with the exception of the northernmost parts, but a distinctive western and central European distribution has emerged according to present knowledge. The actual number of such sites is not known but can be estimated at more than two thousand (Raetzel-Fabian 2000).

The term enclosure actually embraces a heterogeneous group of Neolithic monuments, for which an extremely wide range of terminology is used in the archaeological literature. The common theme is the enclosed area, which often is of considerable size. That the sites are referred to in such different ways reflects partly factual differences in design and construction, but also, and not leastly, the great variety of interpretations held by scholars concerning the importance and function of these places.

It is obvious that the monumental enclosures were of significant importance to Neolithic society, but the actual function(s) of the Neolithic enclosures is still a controversial question. Probably no other prehistoric structure has been interpreted in so many and different ways. Nearly every possible function has been discussed: cemeteries, astronomical structures, settlements, mythical settlements, defences, cattle-kraals, marketplaces, manufacturing places, cult centres and central gathering places. The list could have been longer but it includes the most frequently occurring proposals.

How the enclosures have been interpreted has varied considerably depending on several factors as the dominant paradigm of the time, national traditions, historical and political situations and of course the subjective notions of the scholars. The discussion has often been based on fragmentary and fragile foundations since only a few sites have been uncovered and excavated to their full extent and the quality of studies and publications are extremely varied between different areas (Andersen 1997). But the varied range of interpretations also emphasises the fact that the enclosures are very complex and difficult to interpret. Just as they had an extensive distribution in time and space and different design, it is also likely that they served various purposes. In a way every enclosure is unique and has its own history since no such place seems to be quite like any other. But there are also some recurrent general themes as Andersen has shown in his study of the causewayed enclosures in north western Europe (Andersen 1997), even if these themes were used or emphasised in varied ways. Archaeologists have always created types and categories, and probably always will. But we have to avoid single explanations for why a specific category appeared. One and the same monument or object can be taken up, used and transformed in various ways in different social situations and regions. The challenge is to consider and try to combine the particular and general in approaching these fascinating places.

CAUSEWAYED ENCLOSURES. THE FIRST GENERATION OF ENCLOSED SITES IN NORTHERN EUROPE

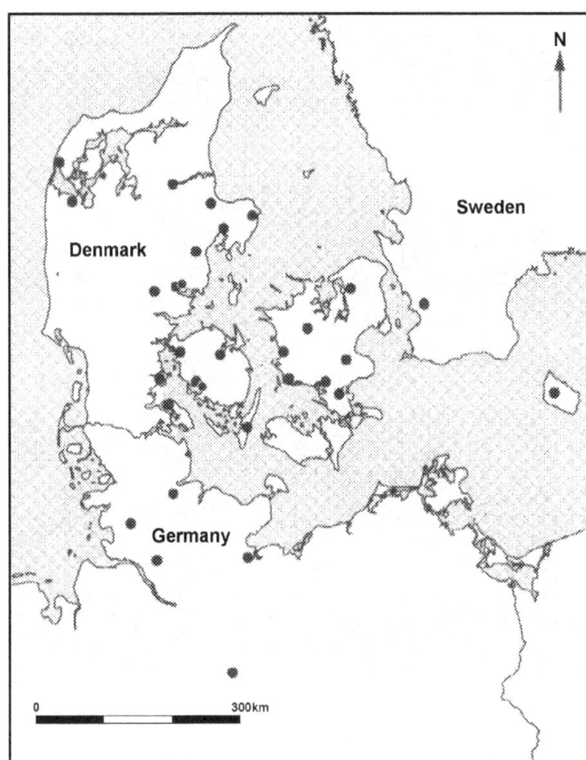

***Fig 4.1**. Distribution of causewayed enclosures in the northern group of the Funnel Beaker Culture (after Hassman 2000).*

The fact that enclosures also formed a part of the northern group of the Funnel Beaker Culture has been established quite recently. The first enclosure was found in 1968 at Büdelsdorf in northern Germany (Hingst 1971) and later on through the well known structures at Sarup on the Danish island of Fyn (Andersen 1997, 1999a-b). To date, nearly 30 causewayed enclosures of the Sarup type are known within the northern Funnel Beaker Culture, mainly in Denmark (fig 4.1) (Andersen 1997, Hassmann 2000). The form and the content of these places match especially the enclosures of north western Europe, in the Michelsberg, Chasséen and Windmill Hill Cultures (Andersen 1997). Sites of the Sarup type in Denmark cover extensive areas (c.1.6 – c.20 ha.) and they are characterised by, from a topographical point of view, strategic arranged ditch systems sometimes combined with palisades (fig 4.2).

The sites seem to have been erected during quite a limited period of time between 3500 and 3200 BC, which corresponds to the archaeological phases ENII (Fuchsberg & Virum-phase), MNAI and MNAII. This is also a period that displays many other new ideas and innovations expressed for example by the building of large numbers of megalithic graves, the introduction of the ard and the appearance of the first imported metal objects. The enclosures at Sarup are almost completely excavated and exhaustively published (Andersen 1997, 1999 a-b) but most other sites have only been the subject of minor excavations.

A common opinion generally held by Scandinavian scholars is that the sites were regional centres and assembly places with a considerable ritual element (Madsen 1988, Andersen 1997). In the latest publications – the Sarup monographs – the cemetery theory has achieved renewed interest since the sites are thought to have been places for temporary burials (Andersen 1997).

It is notable that there is only one convincing piece of evidence for the existence of Sarup sites in south Sweden, in spite of the fact that several large-scale excavations have taken place within main occupation areas of the Funnel Beaker Culture. Even the dating of this site is uncertain. The enclosure at Stävie in western Scania is situated on a promontory close to the Kävlinge River and consists of a single ditch system and internal votive pits. Larsson has dated the ditch system to the final phase of the Funnel Beaker Culture (MNAV) (Larsson 1982). But according to Madsen this dating is not relevant to the lower part of the stratigraphy and therefore the primary phase of construction has not been established (Madsen 1988). This problem can only be solved through further excavations. The situation in southern Sweden might indicate that the demand for enclosures varied in time and space even within a limited and quite homogenous region such as the southernmost part of Scandinavia (Karsten 1994).

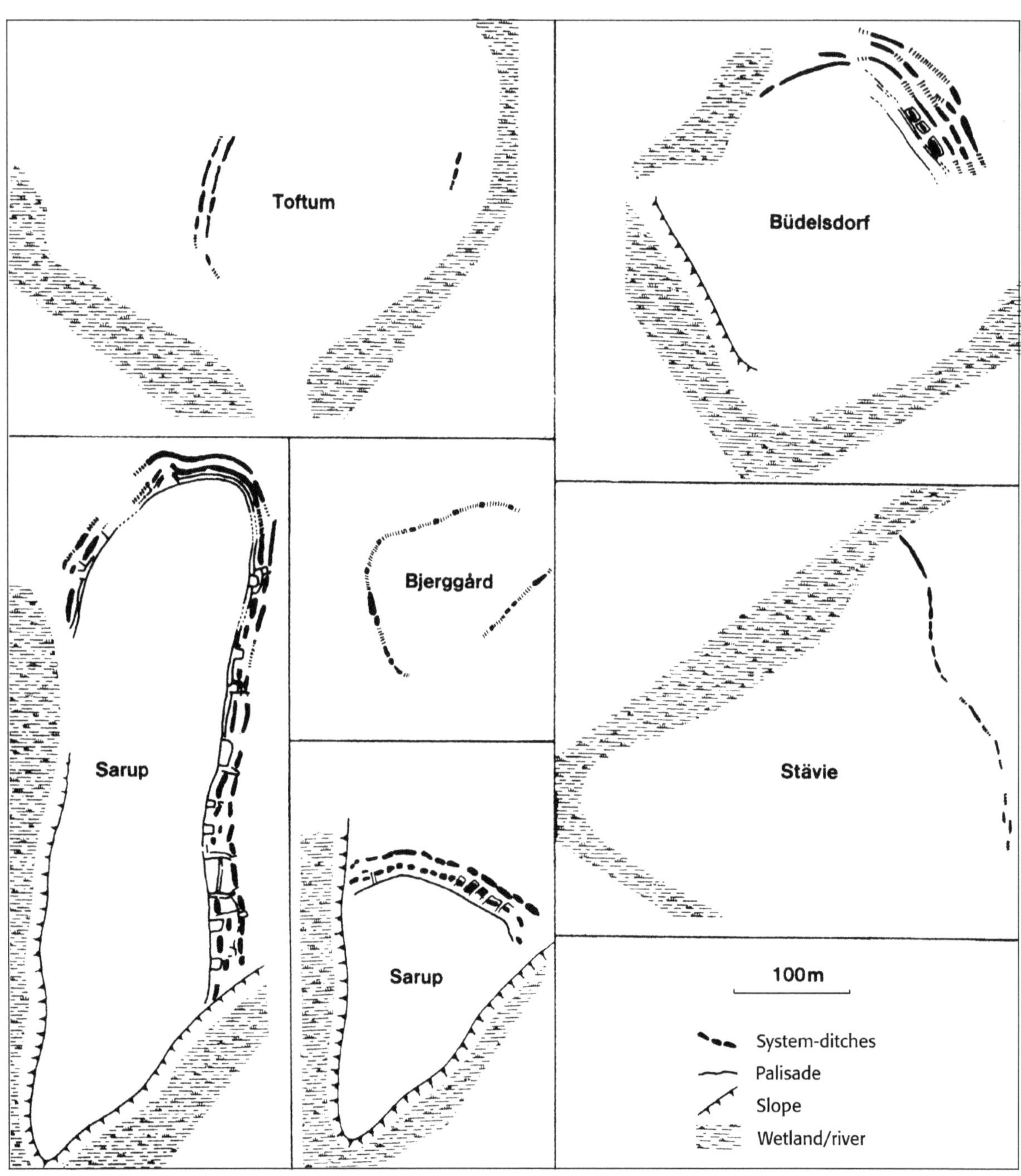

Fig 4.2. *Schematic survey plans of six south Scandinavian causewayed enclosures (after Madsen 1988). Scale 1:5000.*

Central Settlements – From Ditch Systems To Palisades

In the early part of the Neolithic the settlements were small and scattered but during the later part of the Funnel beaker Culture (MNAII-V) extensive sites – central settlement places - were established. These places usually cover several hectares and sometimes considerably more (Skaarup 1985). Some are extremely rich in finds and a few have produced evidence for internal structures. Like Sarup several causewayed enclosures in Denmark were transformed into central settlements (Andersen 1997). These places contain internal features and artefact assemblages indicating a more domestic and persistent presence. But several sites, similar to the site at Hindby mosse discussed below, show that these central settlements did not mark the end of ritual activities. No contemporary ditch systems or palisades are recorded but frequent recuttings and depositions in older ditch systems, especially during the final phase of the Funnel Beaker Culture, are also documented at many places (Andersen 1997, Larsson 2001). The establishment of these extensive places marked a change in the settlement pattern and probably in the social order from small dispersed segmentary settlements to a concentration of in any case parts the population to fewer and larger units (Svensson 1986, Andersen 1997). The central settlement sites play a key role in the understanding of the course of events that led the way from the causewayed enclosures to the palisade enclosures in southern Scandinavia.

Hindby mosse in south western Scania represent one example of a central settlement (Svensson 1986). It was located on a promontory in a small lake and was mostly surrounded by water. Whether there was an artificial barrier on the landward side was unfortunately not established by the excavation that took place in the early seventies. The site consisted of an almost circular cultural layer with various features spaced around a large open area measuring 80 x 60 m. Only about 15% was excavated but the finds assemblage is still by far the largest from the Funnel Beaker Culture in Sweden. Much of the data suggests ordinary domestic tasks – like the tons of flint waste and the almost eight thousand scrapers scattered throughout the cultural layer. But there are also bones from at least twenty humans, deliberately burnt flint axes and structured deposits of axes, pots and animal bones – finds which clearly witness activities connected with the ritual aspects of social life. Altogether the data suggests an interweaving of the living and the dead, the practice of domestic and ritual activities at the same place.

THE PALISADED SITES

In recent years a new type of enclosed Neolithic site - palisade enclosures – has been discovered in southern Scandinavia (fig 4.3). They have not yet been subjected to detailed studies. None are published in detail but reports are available for the south Swedish sites and some have been published in short articles. Except for the palisade at Sigersted I, which is reinterpreted in this article, the Danish material is still mainly published in notices and in brief articles. Therefore it is not possible to analyse and interpret these sites and their finds in detail.

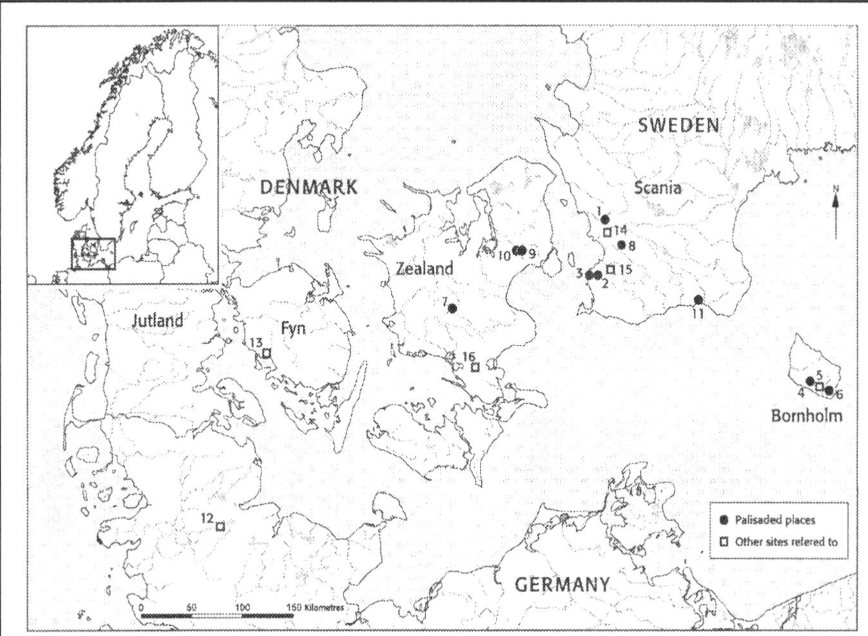

Fig 4.3. Distribution of the palisaded sites and the other Scandinavian sites referred to. 1. Dösjebro, 2. Hyllie, 3. Bunkeflo, 4. Vasagård, 5. Grødbygård, 6. Rispebjerg, 7. Sigersted I, 8. Östra Torn, 9. Helgeshøj, 10. Bakkegård, 11. St. Herrestad, 12. Büdelsdorf, 13. Sarup, 14. Stävie, 15. Hindby mosse, 16. Markildegård.

The discovery of the palisade enclosures is one of the most important contributions to Scandinavian archaeology made by contract archaeology. With a few exceptions the enclosures in southern Scandinavia can not be traced on aerial photographs. We have to use the more patient method of excavation. Palisades can be located and dated by trenching but large-scale excavations are necessary to achieve a deeper understanding. Contract archaeology provides these conditions but is not free to decide where to dig, and a major problem when studying and comparing these extensive sites is the fact that only minor parts of them have been excavated. At Dösjebro for example, where the most extensive excavations have taken place, the area with Middle Neolithic remains cover about 30 ha of which the palisade has enclosed a little more than 3 ha. About 15 % of these 30 ha have been investigated. We have so far only made keyhole excavations into these extensive and complex sites.

Despite these critical problems regarding the source data, which by no means is unique for southern Scandinavia, it seems appropriate to present an overview and sum up the present state of knowledge. A synthesis of the material is in preparation by the author. In this article I will briefly present the sites, their dating, construction, as well as some ideas about their function and their cultural and wider context.

Dösjebro

(Svensson 1998 a-b, Karsten & Svensson 1998, Andersson & Svensson 1999, 2000, Månsson & Pihl 1999, Svensson, Pihl & Andersson 2001)

Between 1995-1998 the Swedish National Heritage Board carried out extensive archaeological investigations in western Scania in advance of the construction of a new high-speed railway. The archaeological project is one of the largest ever to have been undertaken in Sweden and included large-scale excavations at a well-preserved system of Neolithic sites – wetland deposits, settlements, graves and a palisade enclosure in the Saxå/Väla river. The sites constitute a substantial continuous sequence from the earliest to the latest phase of the Funnel Beaker and Battleaxe Cultures. The analysis of the extensive data is under way and the results presented here are still to be vied as preliminary.

A Middle Neolithic site with a palisade enclosure is situated on each side of the Väla River in the bottom of the valley near the village of Dösjebro, 6 km from the coast. In spite of the fact that the site it self is not exposed, it has a strategically and central location by the confluence of two rivers and is flanked by two ridges – the highest and most distinct "land marks" on the surrounding plain. Numerous barrows are still clearly to be seen on these ridges. A passage grave is situated a few hundred metres eastwards. Several other megalithic graves and wetlands with votive depositions are still present or have been recorded in the close vicinity. The votive finds from Dagstorps mosse 2 km to the east constitute one of the largest collections of bog artefacts to have been found in Sweden (Karsten 1994). A sequence from the Early Neolithic (ENII) to the Late Neolithic is represented and the depositions include single artefacts as well as hoards. Except for one hoard of Late Neolithic bronzes it was mainly axes that were deposited (or collected?). The causewayed enclosure at Stävie is situated just 6 km to the south (Larsson 1982). Several settlements from the Funnel Beaker period and the Late Neolithic have been excavated in the vicinity.

The Middle Neolithic site at Dösjebro is very extensive and several activities and structures have been identified: a palisade enclosure, domestic debris, structured depositions, large-scale flint axe production and a cemetery of the late Funnel Beaker and the Battleaxe Cultures.

The palisade

The palisade lies low on sandy ground immediately to the south of the river and consists of a single palisade, which described an almost U-shaped structure (fig 4.4). Today the palisade and the present river enclose an area of about 3 ha. But the extent of the palisade along by the river poses some problems, since the northern parts of the palisade were destroyed when the river flow was altered about one hundred years ago. The enclosed area could very well have been completely surrounded by a palisade, since both the western and the eastern parts of the palisade appear to be turning inwards as if to converge. About one half of the palisade has been excavated, but only minor and peripheral parts of the internal area were investigated and just a few structures contemporary with the palisade were found.

Several components in the construction of the palisade have been identified: the main palisade, a circular structure, supporting posts, entrances and radial rows of posts. The majority of the posts have been set

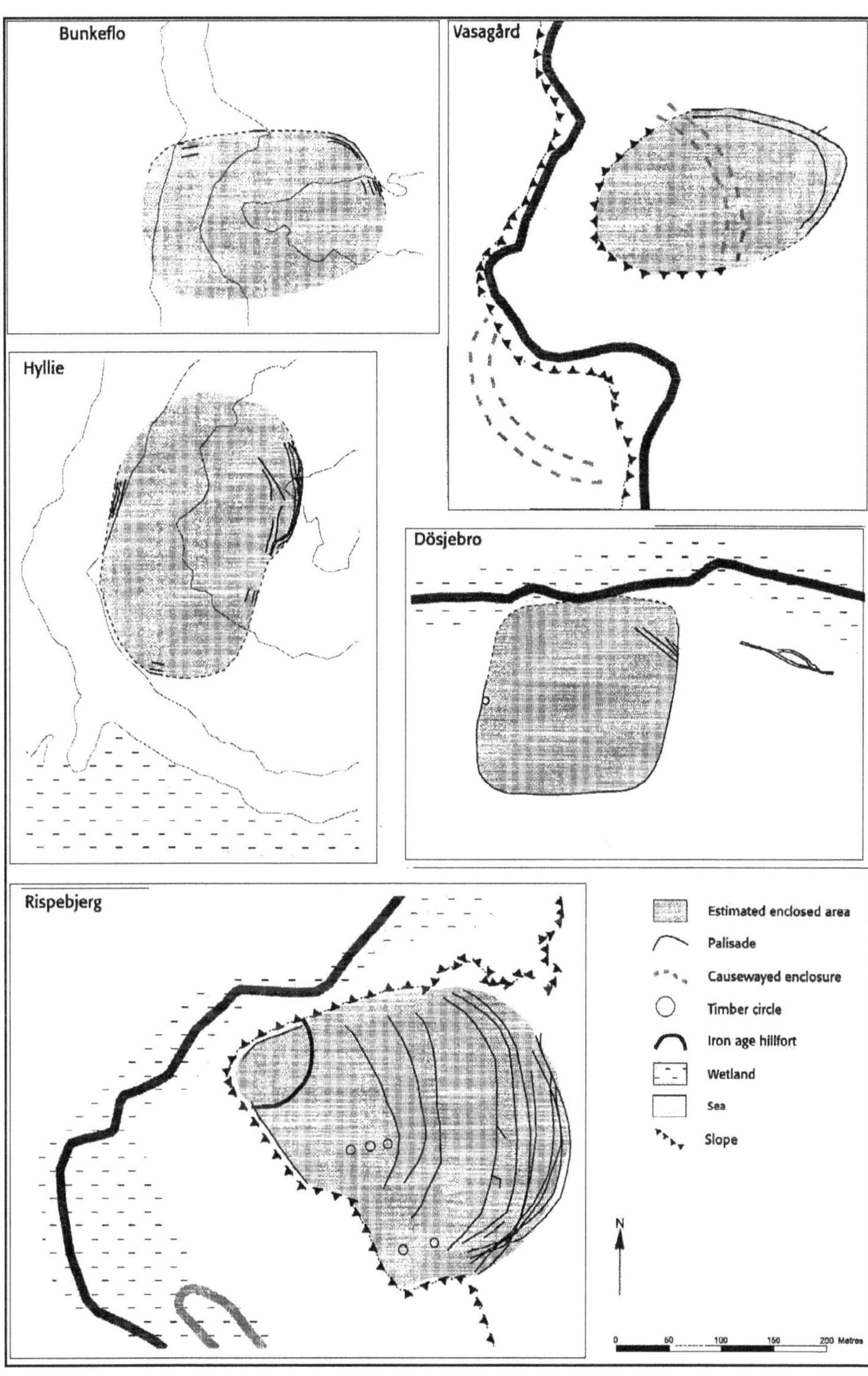

Fig 4.4. Schematic survey plans of five south Scandinavian palisade enclosures (Vasagård and Rispebjerg after Nielsen, F. O. 1998, 2000, 2001. Bunkeflo after Jonsson 1995). Scale 1:5000.

about one metre apart. About 500 such posts were recorded. However some segments consisted of ditches where the posts had been placed close to each other. The form and dimension of the post pipes indicate that the posts were of round timber with diameters of 0.15-030 m. The posts in the ditches were the smallest. The depth of the postholes varied between *c*.0.30-0.70 m., but the upper parts have been reduced considerably by cultivation. Packing stones were found in some postholes. Most of them were fire-cracked. Some posts on the inside of the palisade have probably functioned as supporting posts since they were leaning towards the palisade. This also indicates a certain height for the palisade and it seems that originally, the palisade has probably reached at least head height.

A circular shaped structure was partially connected with the palisade in the western part of the enclosed area. This structure with a diameter of 7m was defined by 16 postholes. It didn't form a closed circle since there was an opening to the north east where two postholes placed in extended positions may have constituted an entrance. The design of the palisade makes it hard to identify entrances, but some of the gaps in the ditches and between the postholes in the palisade may possibly be interpreted as entrances/exits. Some of these were combined with larger postholes, perhaps some kind of gateway. A flint axe was deposited at one of the entrances. Charcoal and soot were present throughout the post pipes, but only in the upper part and this shows that the palisade enclosure was burnt down rather than that the posts were charred before they were put into the ground. Fragments of burnt clay occurred in some of the postholes, which could indicate that the gaps between the wooden uprights have been filled with wattle and daub or that the timber construction was plastered in some way. Both the finds and the radiocarbon dates assign the palisade to the early part of Battleaxe Culture. Sherds from spherical beakers with horizontal cord decoration typical of the Battleaxe Culture (Malmer 1962) were recovered from the postholes. Three radiocarbon dates obtained from charcoal from the burnt posts in the palisade gave very similar values of between 2880-2590 BC, which correspond to the transition between MNA and MNB.

Parts of a complex system of four undulating rows of postholes were documented to the east of the palisade enclosure. These extended for at least 100m along the river course, but the eastern part is cut by a modern crayfish pond. No post pipes or charcoal were present and the postholes were not as deep as those of the palisade enclosure. But several contained stone packing, which indicate that they had supported quite substantial uprights. What kind of structure this post system represents has not been established. The fact that it points towards or leads to the palisade enclosure might indicate a connection between the two - perhaps some kind of passage towards an opening in the enclosure. But the striking differences in construction and design between the two structures do not give confidence to such an interpretation. In the Neolithic of Scandinavia such extensive systems of posts are, as far as we know, associated with enclosures and therefore the rows may represent parts of such a structure, probably slightly older than the palisade. At any rate, the design of the western part of the post system does not support an idea of a completely enclosed structure.

Several sherds from a single vessel, typical for the final phase of the Funnel Beaker Culture (MNA), were found in one of the postholes. These sherds probably also date the rows of posts because it does not seem reasonable to suggest that these sherds found their way into the postholes by chance. If this is the case, then this post system is associated with a different and probably slightly older cultural context than the palisade. Structured depositions of scrapers in a small pit situated quite close by suggest connections with ritual activities. The association between the post system and this deposition is supported by the recovery of a sherd from a late Funnel Beaker Culture clay disc that formed a part of the deposition.

The Cemetery

North of the palisade, on the opposite side of the Väla River, a cemetery with nine inhumation graves of the Battleaxe Culture was excavated. Yet another grave, which belonged to the cemetery, had been found earlier in 1920. Cemeteries of the Battleaxe Culture typically consist of just a few graves and the cemetery at Dösjebro is one of the largest in Sweden. One particular grave stands out by the nature of its rich grave goods. Bone fragments and skeleton colourings of three or four individuals were recorded. Five pots, two battleaxes, flint axes, blades and amber beads were found. At least one of the graves had a wooden construction, which had been visible above ground. The details of the individual graves are beyond the scope of this article. Deposits of Middle Neolithic Funnel Beaker pottery and a few sherds of Battleaxe pottery formed a concentration close to the cemetery. The character of the pottery resembles the finds from megalithic graves. It is possible that the deposit represents the offering horizon in front of a destroyed tomb situated just outside the excavation area. Further investigations are planned. Datable finds and construction details assign six of the inhumation graves to a late part of the Battleaxe Culture. Five radiocarbon dates obtained from charcoal associated with these graves gave values within the sequence of 2870-2190 BC. Some of the radiocarbon dates indicate an overlap in time between cemetery and palisades but the typological dates suggests that at least parts of the cemetery are slightly later than the palisade enclosure.

Most of the graves are placed in a straight line, which is characteristic of the period. It has been proposed that linear cemeteries have been located along communication routes (Müller 1904, Malmer 1962, Jørgensen 1977). The line of graves at Dösjebro is arranged in a right angle to the river near by. This location and orientation might indicate the presence of a former river crossing point. There is, however, no empirical data regarding Neolithic communication structures. We can also note that the present bridge is situated in this vicinity, as was the Medieval one and, according to the reconstructions of the road network during the Viking period and the Middle Ages, one of the main roads in western Scania passed just to the south of the cemetery and the palisade enclosure (Blomquist 1951, Stenholm 1986).

***Fig 4.5**. Axe knapping area at Dösjebro during excavation in the cold autumn of 1998. Photo: H. Pihl.*

Fig 4.6. Flint axes deposited at the palisade enclosure at Dösjebro. Photo: B. Almgren.

Flint axe manufacturing

Extensive areas for the manufacture of flint axes have been documented near by but outside the palisade. Several axe workshops were excavated and one of these was especially well preserved. It formed a distinct, large oval (*c*.3.0 x 2.3m) composed of a compact layer of *c*.100,000 flints weighing a total of 118 kg (fig 4.5). A larger fragment from a type B thick-butted axe from this workshop provides a MNB (Battleaxe Culture) date (Nielsen 1979). The abundant waste material from the manufacturing areas, which mainly consist of splinter and small flakes from the two final steps of the knapping process, reflects extensive production. But the large numbers of small polished flint fragments also show that the manufacturing included the reshaping of axes or chisels. Smaller tools, especially transverse arrowheads, were also produced on site. Senon flint and two types of Danien flint have been utilised and in this respect it is also notable that material from stone (as opposed to flint) axes is completely absent. The lack of coarse primary flakes and grinding stones indicates that the first as well as the final steps of the production were undertaken somewhere else and indicate a specialised mode of production. The assemblage is the largest of this category to have been found in Scandinavia so far, in spite of the fact that the site is situated away from the primary sources of flint. Considerable quantities of flint, probably several tons, have been transported. The nearest known flint source with nodules large enough for axes is situated along the coastal cliffs about 10km away. No settlement remains were associated with the workshops and this indicated that the production was undertaken outside the daily domestic sphere. There is a close association in space between the workshops and the enclosure. This connection is further stressed by the structured depositions of knapping waste resulting from axe manufacturing in the postholes of the palisade, which suggests that the palisade and at least some of the axe production are contemporary.

Structured depositions

Several finds are interpreted as deliberate deposits. These occurred at the time of the palisade construction and are found both inside as well as outside the enclosed area. A few rough outs for flint axes occurred in the fossil sediments along the river. They may represent wetland offerings (Karsten 1994). Postholes and small shallow pits with deposited artefacts were recorded both inside and outside the palisade. The deposits consist of axes, tightly packed flakes from axe manufacturing, smaller tools, especially scrapers, and some pottery in various combinations (fig 4.6). A single axe was deposited in a small pit just inside the palisade by one of the entrances. The axe is small, unpolished, thick-butted almost thin-bladed and with an asymmetrical edge. This type can be dated to the later part of MNA and MNB (Vang Petersen 1993). The axe was placed exactly vertical with the edge facing upwards close to a head sized stone (cf. Winther 1935). The find material from another pit was entirely dominated by scrapers. On the surface the artefacts formed a circle along the edge of the pit (fig 4.7). The excavation demonstrated that the bottom and the sides of the shallow dish-shaped feature were properly lined with scrapers and flakes before the pit was back filled.

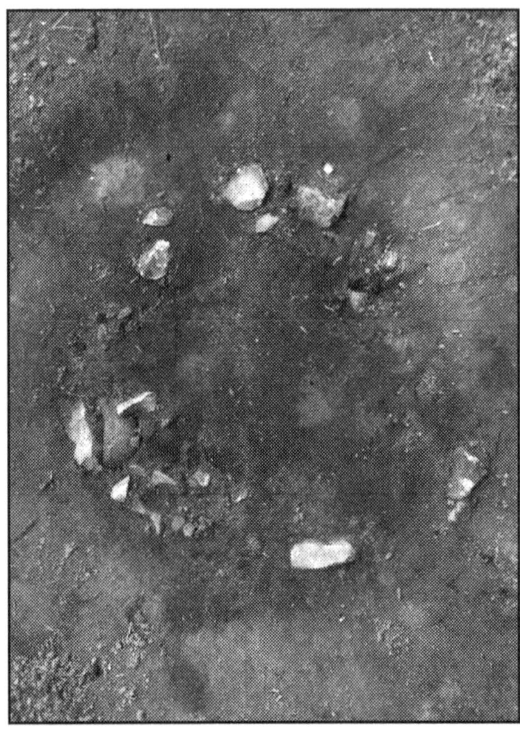

***Fig 4.7**. Structured deposition of scrapers and flakes in a small pit (before excavation) at Dösjebro. Photo: K. Lund.*

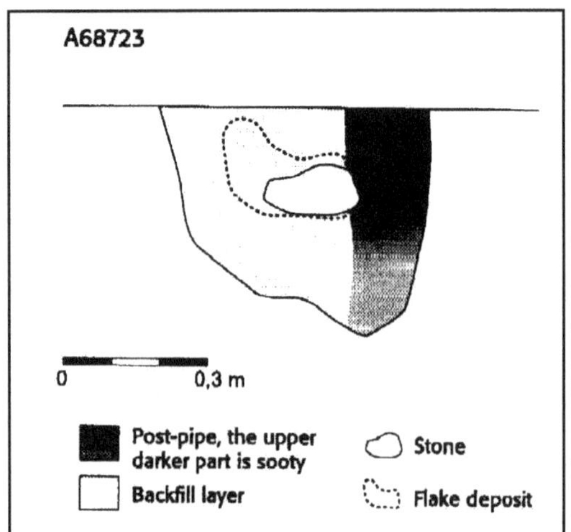

***Fig 4.8**. Section of the posthole (A68723) with a large deposition of flakes.*

The excavation provides reliable data regarding the composition of the finds and how they had been deposited in the postholes and trenches of the palisade. Mainly flint but also pottery, burnt clay and some burnt bones were found. Apart from some artefacts (3 axes and a few scrapers, knives, borers, transverse arrowheads and hammer stones) the flint assemblage is completely dominated by small flakes and splinters. One posthole contained 1640 flakes deposited around a packing stone (fig 4.8). In some cases the flakes were tightly packed in cone-shaped concentrations, and it is clear that they had been placed close by the posts in some kind of organic container. Several of the flakes can be classified as unmistakable waste products from the two final knapping steps of axe or chisel manufacture. It is notable that the amount of burnt flint is considerably larger (*c.*30%) inside the palisade compared to the other features of the site and most Neolithic structures in general. This large percentage of burnt flint, when combined with the find context and stratigraphy, shows that the majority of finds were present in the postholes when the palisade was burnt down. The fact that almost every find came from the upper part of the filling around the post-pipes and in distinct concentrations demonstrates that the artefacts are primary and had been deliberately deposited. The stratigraphic position demonstrates that the deposition of material took place during the refilling of the postholes when the postholes were packed and the posts stabilized. The many splinters found in some deposits may indicate that flint knapping was practised close to the features where the material was deposited. Several flakes in one and the same posthole are chipped from the same nodule. However, flakes from several axe blanks or nodules are represented in the larger deposits. This demonstrates that these are derived from not just one knapping process but from several knapping episodes gathered together in one deposition. Axe manufacturing was clearly important at this site and emphasises a temporal, spatial and functional association between the enclosure and axe production.

Hyllie

(Almquist & Svensson 1990, Svensson 1991)

The enclosure was discovered in 1989 during a rescue excavation in south western Scania. It was the first palisade enclosure to be identified in the whole of Scandinavia. The site is situated on the western slope of a low hill close to a wetland. Present knowledge suggests that the enclosure formed a large oval or egg shaped structure, enclosing *c.*4.5ha and probably completely surrounded by palisades (fig 4.4). About 20% of this area was excavated. Due to further threats, major parts of the site will probably be excavated in the near future.

Several palisades of closely set postholes were observed in two sectors of the excavation area. In the western part, the palisade system consisted of three parallel rows of postholes. The middle and the outer rows consisted of about 8m long undulating segments. However, the inner row was absolutely straight. The distance between the postholes on the inner and middle row was consistently 0.20m. With regard to reduction through cultivation the depth of the majority of postholes is estimated to have originally been about 0.50m. Post-pipes with a diameter of between 0.10 and 0.50m were recorded. The largest posts were associated with the narrow gate-like western entrance, which led at right angels through the outer and middle, but not through the inner palisade. About 10m to the north a narrow gap in the innermost fence line formed the entrance to the interior of the enclosure (fig 4.9).

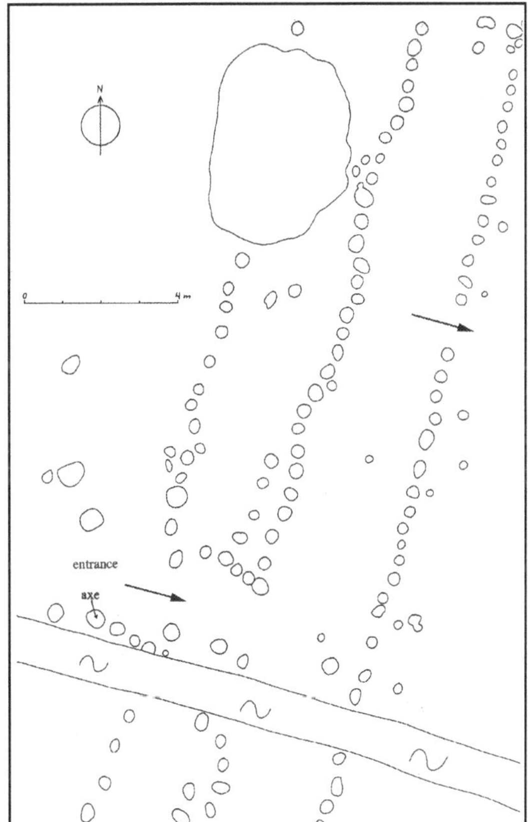

***Fig 4.9**. The western entrance of the palisade enclosure at Hyllie.*

At least five rows of palisades formed the eastern part of the enclosure. The outermost palisade consisted of undulating segments like the western part of the enclosure, each about 8m long. Such segments were also found in the other rows, but more irregularly. The inner palisades were straighter and formed some kind of polygonal enclosure. With a few exceptions, the posts in the palisades were set 0.20m apart. The outer palisades were partly constructed in such a way that there were narrow paths or corridors through the palisades. They probably functioned as entrances. Wide openings also occurred, but only in the inner fences.

One problem concerns the relative chronology of the palisades. Stratigraphic relationships between the post rows were not observed, but on the other hand they were integrated and adapted to each other and gave the impression that they have been parts of a fairly contemporary structure.

The finds from the postholes are extremely few. They consist of a few flint flakes and waste, a small polished flint fragment, two flake scrapers, a retouched blade, a flint axe and two decorated potsherds. The potsherds are decorated with a toothed stamp and can be dated to the later part of the Battleaxe Culture (Malmer 1962). Deep in the filling of one of the postholes from the gate-like entrance in the western part of the enclosure, a flint axe was deposited in a vertical position with the edge facing downwards (fig 4.10). The axe is a secondary worked, thick-bladed, hollow-ground type, and represents one of the most typical artefacts of the Battleaxe Culture (Malmer 1962). Some additional finds can also be interpreted as deliberate depositions. The two flake scrapers and the retouched blade were found in the postholes flanking another entrance. Even though there was no chance of excavating all the postholes in the enclosure, it seems like it was the postholes of the entrances, or at least some of them, that were subject to deliberate depositions of artefacts. A radiocarbon date is available from a posthole in the gate-like entrance. Charcoal from the structure gave the date 2865-2470 BC, which agrees very well with the cultural material from the postholes.

Longhouses, postholes, pits and hearths were found beside the palisades and in the interior however most of these features are dated to the Iron Age. In the eastern part three Early Neolithic pits occurred. One contained a complete funnel beaker, which can be interpreted as a ritual deposit. One of the palisades cut one of this pits and is consequently later in date.

It is remarkable that there were no structures or finds from the Battleaxe Culture either inside or outside the enclosure. This situation makes an interpretation of the site as an enclosed settlement very unlikely. It is even more remarkable that contemporary settlements are also completely absent in the neighbourhood. But intensive agriculture at the enclosure has completely eroded all Neolithic layers and shallow features. At comparable sites where these structures are preserved activities like flint axe production (Svensson 1998, Månsson & Pihl 2000) and the deliberate destruction of axes by fire (Nielsen 1998, Larsson 2000) have been recorded. If such activities also were undertaken at this enclosure the traces are likely to be found in the plough soil, which has still not been investigated.

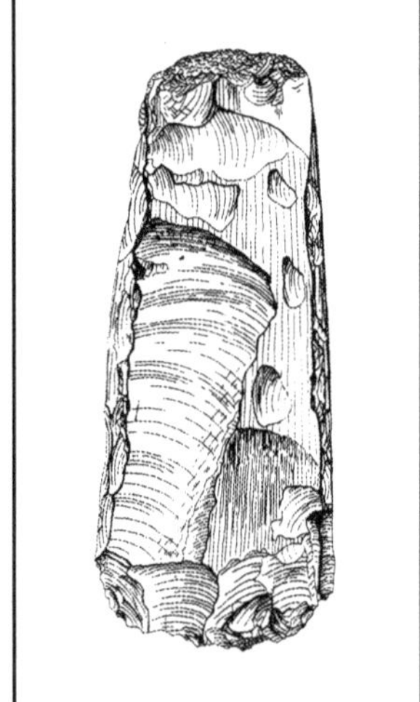

Fig 4.10. *Deliberately deposited flint axe in the western entrance of the enclosure at Hyllie. Drawing: E. Rudebeck. (from Svensson 1991 Fig. 5). Scale 1:2.*

There are indications of the existence of megalithic graves a few kilometres to the east and west (Sandén 1995). A grave from the Battleaxe Culture has recently been excavated *c.*1.5km to the south and a small cemetery is situated 2.5 km to the east (Winge 1976). The extensive central settlement of Hindby mosse, from the later part of the Funnel Beaker Culture, has been excavated about 5km to the east (Svensson 1986). Another palisade enclosure at Bunkeflo is located only 4km to the west (Jonsson 1995).

Bunkeflo

(Jonsson 1995)

This palisade enclosure was discovered in 1995 during trial excavations by the Malmö museum in south western Scania. Only a minor excavation has been undertaken but in combination with plough soil survey, phosphate and magnetic susceptibility (MS) analysis. The palisade system is located around a low hill within a flat landscape close to the Neolithic coastline.

Minor parts of the northern and eastern parts of the enclosure have been recorded but only a few features were excavated. Present knowledge suggests a concentric system of palisades. If the enclosure was constructed fairly symmetrically around the hill it constituted an oval, closed structure enclosing *c.*3.5ha. Three to five parallel palisades have been identified in the excavation trenches (fig 4.4). The posts were set quite close to each other with a distance of usually less than half a metre between them. The depth of the 17 postholes that were excavated varied between 0.26-0.58m, but these features have been much reduced by ploughing. Post-pipes with a diameter of between 0.10-0.20m were recorded (Jonsson personal communication). Two 2-4 m wide gaps in the palisades can be interpreted as entrances. The narrower one is situated in the outer palisade and the wider gap was in one of the inner palisades. It is notable that the gaps are not placed in front of each other. A peculiar aspect of this site is a 19m long and straight posthole arrangement in the middle of the outer corridor. The structure resembles a two aisled longhouse but none of the features were excavated which makes the interpretation problematic. A tempting thought is that parts of the palisade system were roofed. The magnetic susceptibility produced high values, especially in the western part of the enclosure. These high values indicate the former presence of fire but low phosphate values indicate that the burning was not associated with domestic activities (Engelmark & Linderholm 1997). Several postholes also contained charcoal, which may imply that the palisades, or parts of them, had been burnt.

A flint axe was deposited in one of the postholes close to the inner entrance. The axe is unpolished, thin bladed with an asymmetrical edge, an oblique butt and corresponds to a Malmer type 1 axe of the Battleaxe Culture (Malmer 1962, Jonsson 1995, Högberg 2000). Apart from a borer, a few flint flakes and waste this was the only artefact found in the palisades during the limited excavation. Two radiocarbon dates from charcoal from the postholes in the enclosure gave the values 2880-2500 BC and 3735-3510 BC. The latter date is from the axe deposit and must be regarded as too old. The material for dating is apparently not extensive but can be assigned to the Battleaxe Culture.

No structures or finds contemporary with the palisade enclosure were found in the large-scale excavation immediately to the north of the enclosure (Thörn 1998) but several artefacts of later Middle Neolithic date (MNB) have been collected in the vicinity (Bunkeflo 9:4). A few hundred metres north of the enclosure an axe deposit (hoard) comprising two rough outs for hollow ground axes, a rough out for a thick bladed axe and a chisel was found under a large stone (Karsten 1994).

Of special interest is a later cemetery located on the top of the low hill within the enclosure. Four flint daggers from the Late Neolithic (SNA), a bracelet and a bronze sword of the Early Bronze Age were found (Jonsson 1995). Some additional graves from the Late Neolithic and the early Bronze Age have also been excavated nearby (Söderberg 1884, Salomonsson 1971, Lindhé et al 2000). An extensive settlement with several longhouses from the Late Neolithic and early Bronze Age was recently excavated about 500m east of the enclosure. Radiocarbon dates indicate that the history of occupation may be traced back to the later part of the Middle Neolithic (MNB) (Lindhé et al 2000). Two megalithic graves are situated along the coast a few kilometres to the south. There are also indications of other destroyed megaliths both in that area and *c.*1km inland (Sandén 1995). A Battleaxe Culture burial has been found about 3km to the south.

Of particular interest are the rough outs for flint axes collected on several occasions from the beach ridge (Kjellmark 1903, Salomonsson 1971). The rich find spot near Sibbarp is situated a few hundred metres north of the enclosure. From this site at least 500 rough outs have found their way into various museums, but the original number has probably been much higher (Salomonsson 1971). These finds are by far the largest of this category so far discovered in Sweden and it was the local Danien flint that had been utilised. Considering that it was probably only the discarded products that were left behind by the Neolithic axe knappers these finds probably represent extensive production. The axes are difficult to classify in detail because the rough outs are coarse, some of them are fragments and the majority have been washed and rolled by waves. The material has not yet been re-examined but according to Salomonsson the majority consists of rough outs for small thick butted axes, some of them hollow-edged, of the Middle Neolithic (Salomonsson 1971). The presence of these types of axes indicate that at least part of the axe manufacturing may very well have taken place at the same time as activities connected with the palisade enclosure.

Recent excavations have revealed a small axe knapping area (Högberg 1999) some 500m to the east of the palisade and investigations of the plough soil nearby produced large amounts of axe production waste. The excavation report is not published so detailed information such as the exact date within the Neolithic is not yet known. No knapping areas were preserved there but the character of the material indicates extensive production (Sarnäs 2000).

To sum up there is not much known about associated activities within the enclosure, but the place is situated in a social landscape clearly made up by graves and especially axe manufacturing areas.

Vasagård

(Nielsen, F. O. & Nielsen, P. O. 1989, 1990, 1994, Nielsen, F. O. 1996, 1997, 2000, 2001)

Two sites with palisade enclosures dating to the final phase of the Funnel Beaker Culture are known so far at Vasagård and Rispebjerg on the small Danish island of Bornholm in the southern part of the Baltic Sea. They are situated 8km from each other but share similar settings in the landscape at topographically pronounced positions beside rivers and springs *c.*4km from the coast.

The palisade enclosure at Vasagård is preceded by two almost identical causewayed enclosures. They consist of two parallel circuits of ditches located opposite to each other on either side of the Læse River. The enclosures have been placed where the valley is especially wide and form a low lying, basin-shaped arena surrounded by steep slopes between the two causewayed arcs. They are connected as well as separated by this arena and the most impressive way of entering this area is by river when the dramatic scenery can be appreciated to the full.

A megalithic grave is situated directly to the north of the western part of the enclosure. Votive finds from the Funnel Beaker Culture, the Battleaxe Culture and the Late Neolithic are known within 2km from Vasagård, but they are not as frequent as around Rispebjerg (Nielsen, F. O. 1996). Settlements of a permanent character with several longhouses from the MNAV have been excavated only a few kilometres from the enclosure (Nielsen, F. O. & Nielsen, P. O. 1985, 1991. Nielsen, P. O. 1999).

The site at Vasagård was discovered in 1988 and excavations were also undertaken 1993-4. It is mainly the eastern part of the enclosure system (Vasagård East) that has been investigated. The following presentation is based on the brief reports that have been published so far. The finds from Vasagård East indicate that the site had been continuously in use from the later part of the Early Neolithic (ENII) to the final phase of the Funnel Beaker Culture (MNAV). The final phase is especially well represented by abundant finds in the ditches in both the western and the eastern part. A double system of palisade ditches was also constructed during this phase (fig 4.4). The ditches have held close-set posts measuring 0.25-0.4m. in diameter. Palisades have so far only been recorded on the eastern side. They formed a reversed double C like the older ditch systems, but the palisade enclosed a larger area of c.3ha.

Three timber circles have been identified within the enclosure (Nielsen, F. O. personal communication). There also surviving culture layers contemporary with the palisades. These layers contain abundant material of a domestic nature and have been interpreted as signs of permanent occupation (Nielsen, P. O. 1999) although no houses have been found despite active searching (Nielsen, F. O. & Nielsen, P. O. 1994). The second enclosure period is characterised by more finds of a ritual nature than were recorded in the previous phases. Both complete as well as burnt flint axes and chisels, pottery, clay discs and carbonised grains were deposited in the palisade ditches and in pits. Four radiocarbon dates from carbonised grain from a pit with finds from MNAV are available. One of the dates is Mesolithic but the others range between 2910-2460 BC (Heinemeier et al 1996).

Rispebjerg

(Nielsen, F. O. 1996a-b, 1997a-b, 1998a-b, 2000, 2001, Straunsbjerg Thorsen 1999, 2000)

The site at Rispebjerg has been known for a long time but the presence of palisades was first discovered in 1995. Since then, this spectacular site has been excavated on several occasions by Finn Ole Nielsen from Bornholms Museum. The information presented here is based on the brief accounts that have been regularly published.

The palisade enclosure has a dramatic and strategic setting in the landscape being located on a meander promontory with steep slopes leading down to Øle River. The topography has clear defensive advantages and this is emphasised by the Iron Age fort that occurs within the Neolithic enclosure. The enclosed area and the amount of finds are greater than at Vasagård. An area of about 10ha contained finds and structures from the final phase of the Funnel Beaker Culture, and these represent the main period of occupation although there are also finds from the earlier phases of the Funnel Beaker Culture as well as the Battleaxe Culture. Only minor parts of the site have been investigated, mostly by long and narrow trial trenches, though some smaller areas have also been stripped. Due to favourable geological conditions it has also been possible to document the palisade system as crop marks on aerial photographs.

A complicated system of at least 14 concentric palisade ditches has enclosed *c.*6ha of the promontory (fig 4.4). The stratigraphy between the ditches demonstrates that the palisade system represents several phases of construction. According to the latest hypotheses the palisades were arranged in three or four zones around an inner, low lying, flat arena-like space. The palisade system appears to represent at least three phases all with a similar layout and all dated within the MNAV (Nielsen 2000). However, the complexity of the site is illustrated by the discovery of some east-west oriented and completely divergent palisades in the north-eastern part of the site (Straunsbjerg Thorsen 1999). Whether these palisades belong to a different enclosure system or represent some kind of radial palisades like those at West Kennet in southern England (Whittle 1997) is not yet known. Further and more large-scale excavations are needed to solve the details in the complex history of occupation and construction at such an extensive site as Rispebjerg.

The depth of the palisade ditches varies a greatly from 0.7m to just a few centimetres. These differences can at least partly be explained by variations in the conditions of preservation. Some structures have been well protected below the later fortifications, while others have been reduced by modern deep ploughing. The numerous stones in the ditches have served as packing around the wooden posts which were of round timber 0.2-0.3m in diameter and set so close that it would not have been possible for an adult person to pass through. In spite of the huge area covered by the enclosure system only one entrance have been identified. This is located in the south western part of the enclosure and consists of a narrow gap with stone paving in the outermost palisade, but there are no corresponding gaps in the inner palisades.

So far five circular structures or timber circles have been located and it is possible that the site encloses a large number of such structures (fig 4.11). The two circles in the southern part of the enclosure had diameters of 7.5m and 8m. They consisted of eight post-pipes each with a diameter of *c*.0.4m. The larger of these timber circles was actually a double circle with an inner ring, also of eight postholes, but of smaller dimensions. These timber circles were most likely burnt down since they were associated with charcoal and burnt clay, flint and bone. A deliberately crushed stone axe was interpreted as a ritual deposit (Straunsbjerg Thorsen 1999). Parts of three other circles have recently been identified in the western part of the enclosure. One of these had a diameter of *c*.10m and had a centrally placed posthole. Two ditches were located about 25m to the south and a slightly trapezoid post-built structure extended from the timber circle towards one of the ditches. Connecting rows of postholes can also be observed beside one of the timber circles in the south western trench. The timber circles at Rispebjerg have not been radiocarbon dated but an identical structure from the site Grødbygård has been dated to 2900-2670 BC (Heinemeier et al 1996), which corresponds to the transition between MNAV and MNB.

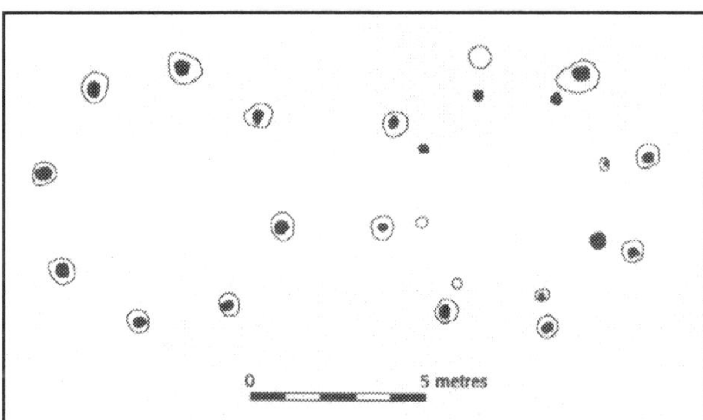

Fig 4.11. *Plans of two circular structures at Rispebjerg (from Nielsen 2000 Fig. 8).*

The palisade ditches contain abundant finds of pottery, which include deposits of complete pots. A lot of fragments from deliberately fire cracked flint axes and chisels have been collected on the ground surface at Rispebjerg (fig 4.12). Characteristic at the site is also the unusually high amount of grinding stones for the production of flint axes and stone tools, the small decorated slates with shallow geometric patterns (Kaul 1997) and the large number of tanged blade arrowheads. The presence of cultural layers with finds of a domestic nature within the enclosed area has been interpreted as evidence of regular settlement (Nielsen, P. O. 1999a, Nielsen, F. O. 2000). Parts of an extensive layer with large quantities of burnt clay, pottery, flint and stone tools, amber beads, a decorated slate stone and animal bones from the final Funnel Beaker Culture were excavated in 1999. These bones have still not been analysed but they are the only unburned examples that have survived on the palisade enclosures in Scandinavia.

Fig 4.12. Axes and chisels from Rispebjerg. The two in the middle are fire cracked – probably deliberately. Photo: K. Rasmussen (from Nielsen, F. O. 2001 Fig. 9).

There are no megalithic graves in the immediate surroundings, but five megaliths are situated within a radius of 5km from Rispebjerg. Settlements of a permanent character with several longhouses dating from the MNAV have been excavated in the area between the palisade enclosures at Rispebjerg and Vasagård (Nielsen, F. O. & Nielsen, P. O. 1985, 1991, Nielsen, P. O. 1999a). The area to the south of Rispebjerg is especially rich in votive deposits belonging to the Funnel Beaker Culture, the Battleaxe Culture as well as the Late Neolithic (Nielsen, F. O. 1996). One of the largest Middle Neolithic axe hoards in southern Scandinavia, the Brogård hoard, was found beside (or in?) a spring in the meadowland along the river at the foot of the western slope of the Rispebjerg hill. The hoard actually represents two spatially separated but adjacent depositions and consists of 19 unpolished flint axes of type B and 6 flint chisels (Nielsen, P. O. 1979). Both undamaged as well as fragmentary axes can still be collected in this relatively large meadowland situated between two springs. They were the closest sources of fresh water for the users of the enclosure and therefore this piece of land is clearly an integral part of the enclosure complex.

Sigersted I

(Davidsen 1978)

Sigersted is situated in the central part of Zealand. The site is located on the western part of a flat sandy plateau surrounded by rivers on three sides. The Vebaek, the excavator of the site, initially interpreted the post rows as palisades in 1974, but later Davidsen (1978) changed this interpretation to a longhouse belonging to the final part of the Funnel Beaker Culture. According to Andersen the palisades were possibly parts of a defensive structure (Andersen 1997). Today several huts and houses of the Funnel Beaker Culture are known in southern Scandinavia. The situation is therefore fundamentally different since Davidsen interpreted the site and the post-rows at Sigersted I are not comparable with any of these houses. Nevertheless, the dating (MNAV), location and deposits of a flint axe, pottery and several hundred flakes from flint axe production in some of the postholes indicate that the palisades of Sigersted I should most probably be regarded as the relics of a palisade enclosure.

There are plenty of prehistoric remains in the surrounding area. Several Neolithic artefacts have been collected within a roughly100m wide zone around the excavation area, which is today completely destroyed by gravel-pits. Several Middle Neolithic pits and cultural layers have been recorded a few hundred metres to the south (Sigersted II). A causewayed enclosure (Sigersted III) is located on a raised terrace just 300m to the south-west. (Nielsen, P. O. 1985, 1998, 1999b). At least two destroyed long dolmens are recorded less than 1km eastwards. Also several post-Neolithic barrows have been present, but only a few remain. Human skeletons were found about a hundred metres to the north of the palisades. According to prior information a battleaxe from the final Funnel Beaker Culture was found with one of these skeletons, but a definite association cannot be verified (Nielsen, P. O. 1985).

Two parallel NW-SE oriented rows of posts were recorded during the 1974 excavations (Davidsen 1978). The excavator has argued that the full and original extent of the palisades had been uncovered but there are several arguments against this statement. From the photos taken during the excavation and also in the report by Vebæk it is obvious that the easternmost part of the palisade system was cut by a gravel pit (Archive report, National museum). The topsoil was not stripped in a satisfactory way according to present standard and the area chosen for excavation was too small since the size of this area corresponds to the extent of the palisade system. Because the excavation area was too small and the exact geographical position of the trench is unknown it is not possible to draw any conclusions about the form and extent of the palisades. But the Tuel River flows about 150m westwards and if we assume that there is a close spatial connection between the enclosure and the water (as with the other palisade enclosures) it is likely that the palisade system extended to the river.

A total of 89 postholes and one pit (pit 3) were excavated. Another five pits (pits A-E) were excavated to the east of the palisades by an amateur archaeologist the same year. The undulating eastern palisade had a documented length of 25.5m and consisted of rather close-set postholes. The postholes in the western palisade were mostly set in pairs with a distance between them of 1-1.5m The distance between the to palisades was 5-6m. The postholes were 0.18-0.5m wide and 0.11-0.45m deep. No profile documentation was undertaken, so whether or not post-pipes were present is not known. Further postholes were located south of the palisades and five of these formed an arc.

According to the inspection prior to the excavation, burnt flint and lumps of red burnt clay were recorded on the tops of the postholes and the fills of some features were described as almost black (Archive report, National museum). Burnt clay was documented in 7 of the postholes, only a few pieces of burnt flint were found and the occurrence of charcoal is not reported at the excavation. If the stratigraphy resembles that of Dösjebro this discrepancy between the inspection and the excavation can be explained. Only the upper part of the postholes in Dösjebro contained burnt material. So, therefore the large pieces of burnt clay and flint recorded in the top of the postholes at Sigersted could very well be the very bottom of the burnt part of the posthole. Such a thin layer could easily be destroyed when the excavation area was stripped. The modest depth of the postholes also indicates that a great deal of the upper filling has gone.

Several finds from the postholes in the palisade system must be regarded as deliberate deposits. Some of these are identified and presented by Davidsen (Davidsen 1978). A reworked small thick-butted flint axe, interpreted as a votive deposit, was found in the northern palisade where also major parts of one and the same pottery vessel occurred in two neighbouring postholes. The pot is typical for the final phase of the Funnel Beaker Culture (MNA) and could hardly have found its way into the postholes by accident and must therefore be regarded as a deliberate deposition (Davidsen 1978, Karsten 1994).

There are also other finds, which most likely should be interpreted in the same way, but Davidsen has not given them a similar degree of attention. Flint flakes occurred in the majority of the postholes but normally less than 10 in each feature. However, according to the finds list presented by Davidsen, several hundred flakes were found in a few of the postholes (Davidsen 1978). Six of these features are situated in western part of the southern palisade and one in the arc. They contained between 112-379 flakes but only a few other artefacts mostly fragments from polished axes. The finds from four of these features have been discarded (Davidsen 1978). During a re-examination of the material from the remaining three postholes (1, 2 and 13) housed in the National Museum in Copenhagen it became evident that a large number are flakes from the final steps in the manufacturing of flint axes (Pihl forthcoming).

The standard of documentation for the excavation does not permit any statements about stratigraphy or the position of the finds in the postholes, which might ease our interpretation of the site. However, the occurrence of such a great number of flakes in specific and quite small features makes an interpretation of the flakes as re-deposited material unlikely. This seems obvious particularly when regarding the modest sized posthole 1, which contained nearly four hundred flakes – the flakes must have been deliberately packed around the wooden upright. If the axe flakes originate from activities prior to the construction of the palisade they might be expected to occur in the pit fills. The fact that the pits did not contain flakes from axe production indicates that the concentrations of flakes are the result of deliberate depositions and they constitute a close parallel to the enclosure in Dösjebro. Even if it can't be verified it seems reasonable to suggest that these deposits at Sigersted reflect an axe production area in the immediate vicinity.

The rather small and shallow pits were between 0.4-0.8m wide and 0.2-0.35m deep. One (pit 3) was rich in finds: undecorated pottery sherds, fragments of burnt clay, 91 flakes, a few cores, blades, retouched flakes and a single fragment from a grinding stone and as many as 30 flake scrapers. There were fewer finds in the other pits, but all contained fragments of thick-butted axes or chisels but only a few scrapers. It is notable that no unworked flakes occurred at all. The composition of the finds indicates that the features did not function as rubbish pits but were subjected to deliberate structured depositions. Fragments of Valby pottery date the pits, like the palisades, to the final phase (MNAV) of the Funnel Beaker Culture.

Helgeshøj

(Giersing 2000, lecture in Malmö March 2000)

The palisaded site at Helgeshøj is situated on a plateau close to a small river in the eastern part of Zealand, *c.*8 km from the coast. Due to recent exploitation, Københavns Bymuseum have excavated parts of the site on two occasions. It is reasonable that the palisades in the two excavation areas are parts of one and the same enclosure. The full extent of the palisade system is not known, but it is possible that an area of *c.*4ha around a low hill may have been enclosed. The passage grave, Helgeshøj, is situated immediately to the west of the enclosure.

The palisade system consisted of a ditch with close-set posts and a parallel fence with more sparsely set postholes. A small rectangular post-built structure was integrated with the ditch. Just a few finds that cannot be dated more precisely than within the Neolithic appeared in the palisade system. Activities from several phases are present at the site. The finds from the final phase of the Funnel Beaker Culture dominate. They are of spectacular character and have been regarded as contemporary with the palisades (Giersing 2000). Five axe blanks, some of them fire cracked, were deposited in one of the pits together with Valby pottery and fragmentary type B axes. The finds also include waste from flint axe manufacturing. Due to the combination of finds the enclosure is dated to the transition between MNA and MNB (Giersing 2000). The occurrence of a palisade without an associated ditch system in combination with deposits of axes and waste from the manufacturing of flint axes are characteristic features for the palisade enclosures from MNAV and MNB. A similar date therefore seems very reasonable for the enclosure at Helgeshøj, even if the palisade itself has not been directly dated.

Bakkegård

(Staal 1999, Boye lecture in Malmö March 2000)

The site at Bakkegård is located just 1km from Helgeshøj. Parts of the site were excavated by Sollerød museum in 1998 due to the building of a road. A palisade system was documented for *c.*150m beside the foot of a low hill. The palisade consisted of close-set postholes *c.*0.3m deep. However in one segment the posts were set in a palisade trench. In the southern part two rows of postholes were identified. No datable finds were present, but the palisade is situated close to three megalithic graves which may indicate a Neolithic date for the palisade (Boye lecture in Malmö March 2000).

Östra Torn

(Ericsson, Månsson & Serlander 2000)

Rows of posts, which probably constitute part of badly preserved palisade system, were discovered in 1999 by the Swedish National Heritage Board at test excavations on a plateau in the outskirts of the town of Lund in south western Scania. Three "parallel" rows of postholes formed an arc *c.*40m long between two low hills close to a fossil creek. The extent of the structure was mainly restricted to a depression in the local topography where the postholes survived the intense modern land use, but the palisade system most likely originally extended north- and westwards on or around the low hill. The distance between the palisades varied between 1 and 2.5m. The postholes in the two outer rows were 0.3-0.7m apart, but the innermost row had more sparsely placed postholes. Just a few postholes were excavated and they contained a few flint flakes but no datable artefacts. Two radiocarbon dates from charcoal from two of the postholes gave values of between 2920-2460 BC, which correspond very well with the dates from the other palisade enclosures in southern Scandinavia.

St. Herrestad

(Andersson 1999)

The palisade, that was discovered during a rescue excavation by the National Heritage Board in St. Herrestad in southern Scania in 1995, must also be discussed here even if the dating and the extent of the structure has not been fully established. The site is situated on a 200m wide low hill, which juts out like a promontory into a fen about 3km from the coast. The palisade, which consisted of quite close-set postholes, *c.*0.35m deep, was traced for110m across the entire excavation trench. House looking post-built features extended from either side of the palisade. They have been interpreted as Late Neolithic houses (Andersson 1999) although their irregular construction is not characteristic of houses of this period, therefore both the dating and the layout of these structures can be questioned (Arthursson 2000). The dating of the palisade is problematic since neither primary artefacts nor charcoal from the posts were found. However, the topographical setting which is characteristic for Neolithic enclosures argues in favour of a Neolithic date (Andersson 1999).

Additional systems of posts were excavated nearby in1984 by the Archaeological Institute in Lund (1984 trench I-II). The slightly curved structure has been regarded as a house of the MNAIII (Larsson, M 1992), but both the dating and the character have been questioned (Tesch 1992). Only future excavations can demonstrate if the two structures constitute one and the same system of posts. If so then the palisade system has cut off or enclosed the entire promontory.

PALISADE ENCLOSURES. THE SECOND GENERATION OF ENCLOSED SITES IN NORTHERN EUROPE

Distribution and Dating

The first discovery of a palisade enclosure in southern Scandinavia was made in 1989 (Svensson 1991). Since then the number of comparable sites has increased and at present five sites can be defined as palisade enclosures, since both their dating and characters are well established – Dösjebro, Hyllie and Bunkeflo in Scania and Vasagård and Rispebjerg on Bornholm (FIG. X). Sigersted I and Helgeshøj on Zealand should most probably be added to this group. To these may possibly be added some new discoveries such as the palisades of Östra Torn and St. Herrestad in Scania and Bakkegård on Zealand, whose character and dating have not yet been fully established.

Both the relative and absolute (radiocarbon) dates clearly demonstrate that the palisade enclosures represent a second generation of enclosed sites in south Scandinavia. They differ distinctly from the Sarup type in terms of layout and dating. The principal feature in the Sarup type is extensive ditch systems. These may sometimes be combined with palisades and smaller timber structures. The enclosures of the second generation consist of single or multiple palisades, they lack contemporary ditches and are later, dating to about 2900 BC to 2500 BC. This corresponds to both the final phase of the Funnel Beaker Culture (MNAV) and the Battleaxe Culture (MNB).

The palisade enclosures so far discovered are situated in southern Sweden and eastern Denmark. It is notable that palisade enclosures are not found in areas in western Denmark, like the island of Fyn and the eastern part of Jutland, both of which have concentrations of causewayed enclosures. The present pattern of distribution may very well be explained by the state of current research rather than to a genuine prehistoric situation.

The fact that both the final phase of the Funnel Beaker Culture and the Battleaxe Culture made use of the same kind of enclosures is of great interest because the relationship between these two cultures is still a controversial and classical problem within Scandinavian archaeology. The complex cultural relationships during the Middle Neolithic lie beyond the scope of this paper and will only be mentioned briefly here. A fundamental problem concerns chronology. The Battleaxe Culture is principally later than the Funnel Beaker Culture. However, recent studies dealing with the situation in Scania have suggested an overlap of a few hundred years, around 2700 BC, between the final Phase of the Funnel Beaker culture and the introduction phase of the Battleaxe Culture (Larsson, L. 1989, 1992, Larsson, M. 1997).

One major problem here is the lack of radiocarbon dates from the early part of the Battleaxe Culture. The palisade in Dösjebro is the first finds-associated radiocarbon dated context from the early Battleaxe Culture in Sweden and the statistically similar dates ranging between 2880-2590 BC suggests at least a regional overlap between the late Funnel Beaker Culture (MNAV) and the early Battleaxe Culture. The dates from the two other Battleaxe Culture palisades range between 2880-2470 BC. Radiocarbon dates from the palisades of the Funnel Beaker culture are restricted to dates from a pit at Vasagård with finds from the same phase, MNAV, as the palisade system. These dates ranges between 2910-2460 BC and correspond to the dates from the palisades associated with Battleaxe Culture material. The radiocarbon dates are still too few to form a base for a detailed chronology for these sites, but the available data do not support a chronological difference between palisades of the Funnel Beaker Culture and the Battleaxe Culture. There are no closed find contexts in Scandinavia, except in a very few cases, which might prove the contemporaneity of the two cultural traditions at a local level. The number of palisade enclosures is still limited, but the available evidence suggests that there seems to be some local differences within south Scandinavia. For example, the palisade enclosures of Bornholm and Zealand are associated with the final phase of the Funnel Beaker Culture while the sites from the Battleaxe Culture are in Scania. As mentioned earlier, such local variations were already discernable during the currency of the causewayed enclosures.

Construction and Function

As already has been pointed out, the characteristic construction element of the enclosures of the second generation is that they consist of a single or several palisades. Furthermore we notice the absence of associated ditch systems - the principal feature of the Sarup type. Several components in the construction can be identified but I will not discuss this matter at length but instead give some examples of the method of construction of the palisade itself, the entrances and the circular structures.

The size of the enclosed area, where it can be estimated, varies from 2-6ha. At some sites this internal area was probably completely enclosed by palisades, while at others like Dösjebro it is also possible that the river course was incorporated into the perimeter of the site. Since only parts, and usually just minor parts, of the enclosures have been excavated, the full extent of the palisade systems is not fully known at any site. At Dösjebro and Rispebjerg there are even signs of further but divergent palisade systems. The number of palisades ranges from 1 to 14, however the stratigraphy between the 14 palisades at Rispebjerg demonstrates that there were at least 3 different phases, while the 5 palisades at Hyllie seem so related to each other that they may have constituted a contemporary structure.

The posts were close-set in palisade trenches or in individual postholes, but there also examples of more widely spaced posts. Finds of burnt clay indicate that the gaps had probably been filled with wattle and daub or by clay-covered planking. The depths of the postholes and trenches vary considerably even within the same site, from shallow features to up to 0.7m deep foundation pits. Most features have been considerably reduced by cultivation and these differences can at least partly be explained by variations in the preservation conditions. When allowances are made for this plough truncation, the original depth of the majority of the postholes and the trenches can be estimated at about 0.5-1m. The height of the timber above ground can be calculated in various ways and several factors have to be considered (Russel 1980, Sydkraft AB personal communication). It is, however, most probable that the majority of the palisade posts reached at least head height. The diameters of the recorded post-pipes show that round timbers with a diameter of between 0.1-0.5m were used. No systematic analysis of charcoal has been undertaken in order to determine the types of wood that had been selected, but the samples so far analysed from the palisade at Dösjebro demonstrate the presence of both oak and pine. Based on models from Sarup (Andersen 1988) and prehistoric longhouses (Björhem & Säfvestad 1987, 1993), calculations have been undertaken to estimate the necessary amount of labour to construct the palisade enclosures at Dösjebro and Hyllie. To sum up, the estimated work effort range from 2400 to 6000 workdays and suggest that the work could be carried out by 30 to 80 persons over three months. These figures correspond to or somewhat exceed the calculations for Sarup II but are far below the work efforts necessary for the construction of Sarup I (Andersen 1988, 1977). Nevertheless, the construction of the palisade enclosures was not a task for a single settlement but would most likely have been undertaken by the local community.

Entrances have been identified at some sites. They are important because the shape of the entrances can shed light upon the movement and communication between the inside and the outside. Most of the entrances are constructed as narrow openings or corridors through the palisade, often combined with larger postholes, perhaps marking some kinds of gateway. Hyllie and Rispebjerg are distinct examples of palisades with entrances constructed and located in such a way as to prevent direct access to the interior area by the shortest route. Flint axes and other probably deliberately deposited artefacts are often found at the entrances. This practice is evident at the sites from the Battleaxe Culture and indicates that the movement in and out of the enclosed area involved rituals and was probably restricted and regulated (Svensson 1991). The palisades in Scandinavia seem to have formed closed walls, restricting both physical and visual communication between the inside and the outside. Probably they expressed opposed relations between those who were inside and those who were outside.

The presence of burnt clay, charcoal and results of MS-analysis demonstrate the former presence of fire at some of the sites. The investigations at Dösjebro has shown that nearly all of the upper fills of the post-pipes contained soot or charcoal. These observations, together with the fact that the packing stones and the deposited artefacts were also fire cracked, indicate that the palisade enclosure was burnt down rather than that the posts had been charred before they were put into the ground. The palisade came to an end in a massive fire. It could have been caused by hostility, but it could also have been the result of a ritual performance - the dead and the transformation of the enclosure. At any rate, such a conflagration could hardly have been accidental.

Our knowledge about the interior area is limited. At Hyllie, where quite an extensive area was excavated, not a single contemporary structure or artefact was found. This situation seems to be similar at the other Battleaxe Culture sites in Scania. The cultural layers with domestic material at Dösjebro are principally found outside the enclosure yet they seem to be connected to the system of posts and dated to the late Funnel Beaker Culture as discussed above. However, in this respect the palisade enclosures at Bornholm are quite different, with extensive cultural layers and structures. For example, there are the several almost identical circular structures each with a diameter of between 8-10m. The function of these structures is debatable since they also occur on settlement sites (Nielsen, F. O. & Nielsen, P. O. 1991, Nielsen, P. O. 1999). However the axe deposit, and especially the oversized posts that were utilised in the construction of the circles at Rispebjerg, suggest a non-domestic use. The size of these posts even exceeds the roof supporting post in the large and well built houses of the Late Neolithic (Björhem & Säfvestad 1989). Comparable circular structures are not found elsewhere in Scandinavia and the closest parallels in form and date outside Bornholm are to be found among sacred or ceremonial buildings - the timber circles of the British Isles (Nielsen, F. O. 2000).

The presence of extensive cultural layers with finds of a domestic nature at Rispebjerg and Vasagård has been interpreted as evidence for regular settlements within the enclosures (Nielsen, P. O. 1999, Nielsen, F. O. 2000). The best indication for more permanent occupation might be proved if the presence of longhouses could be established. In this respect, several single rows of postholes have been proposed as foundation pits for the roof supporting posts of two aisled Neolithic longhouses (Nielsen, F. O. 2000). However the absence of wall postholes makes this interpretation uncertain, especially in the case of Rispebjerg, where the excavation areas were very small and where there are also other "unusual" structures and a complex history of occupation. So this domestic material could equally represent shorter but probably recurrent visits.

Large contemporary settlements with longhouses are known within a few kilometres from the enclosures at Bornholm (Nielsen F. O. & Nielsen P. O 1985, 1991). The situation in Scania is different with numerous older Funnel Beaker Culture settlements being known but no contemporary settlements have been identified either at or in the vicinity of the palisades. The few known settlements from the Battleaxe Culture are small and poor in finds and structural evidence and they reflect the well-known scantiness of corded ware settlements. Houses from the earlier part of the Battleaxe Culture in Sweden are completely lacking. This has been interpreted as the result of a more mobile way of life (Larsson 1989, 1992) however even Late Neolithic permanent settlements, with several generations of well-built longhouses, can be extremely bereft of finds (Arthursson 2000) in contrast to the numerous finds from Funnel Beaker Culture settlements. There seems to be a fundamental difference between the Funnel Beaker Culture and the Battleaxe Culture/Late Neolithic with respect to their attitudes to settlement waste. Therefore the *amount* of artefacts on Neolithic settlements need say very little, or indeed nothing at all, about whether the occupation was permanent or temporary.

Most of the palisaded sites display a close spatial relationship with monuments and remains of a sacred and ceremonial nature such as Sarup sites, megaliths and other graves or votive finds. Wetland deposits are also common, though this facet of prehistoric ritual is not always so obvious as, for example, at Hyllie. N. H. Andersen has demonstrated that the Sarup sites may have fulfilled the role of temporary burial places in the general funeral processes. He suggests that they may have been "villages for the souls of the dead" (Andersen 1997). The fact that some of the palisade enclosures are located on or very close to Sarup type enclosures and that the majority are situated near graves may imply that the palisade enclosures also played a role within the funeral rites, although empirical data such as human bones are missing. However, it must be pointed out that, with the exception of Rispebjerg, unburned bones are not preserved at these sites.

Just one of the sites is located close to the former coastline. The others are, with one exception, located by waterways some kilometres inland. Rispebjerg is situated on a raised and exposed promontory with steep slopes. The topography is excellently defensive and this is well illustrated by the Iron Age hill fort within the enclosure. The many tanged arrowheades found here may support the idea of conflict (Davidsen 1978, Nielsen, F. O. 2000), but the composition of the finds and the structural evidence clearly demonstrate that defence was not the only function of the enclosure at Rispebjerg. In general there are many arguments against interpreting the palisade enclosures as defensive sites. Their considerable size makes them hard to defend and some, for instance Hyllie and Dösjebro, have a very unfavourable defensive position since they are lying low on slopes or at the bottom of valleys at the foot of surrounding hills.

Recent investigations at Neolithic enclosures in northern Germany display a close correlation between their location and Early Medieval main roads. It is assumed that the historical lines of communication reflect much older routes, as they are dependent on ground features such as fords, passes, ridges and swamps (Raetzel-Fabian 2000). Links between communication routes and enclosures have also been claimed for the enclosures at Anlo in the Netherlands (Jager 1985) and Markildegård in Denmark (Sørensen 1995). It is of course hazardous and most often impossible to grasp the Neolithic communication routes in detail and except for Dösjebro this aspect is still not been generally explored with regard to the palisade enclosures. The large quantities of imported flint for the axe production at Dösjebro required some kind of transport facilities. We do not know how goods were transported, but today it is not possible to use the river for transport all the way to the enclosure. Empirical data about roads as well as finds of wagons from Denmark demonstrate their existence in the Middle Neolithic period (Jørgensen 1987, Schovsbo 1987), but the extent of the Neolithic road network should not be exaggerated and roads were probably just of local significance (Nielsen, S. 1999). The location of Dösjebro close to the confluence of two rivers, its proximity to a Medieval crossing point with a main road, ford and bridge, and the position of the linear cemetery which points to a river crossing place may all be taken to support the presence of Neolithic communication routes close to the palisade enclosure. This site may therefore have been situated on important lines of access and communication and its location may therefore have encouraged gatherings and exchange.

The data suggest that the deposition and consumption of axes as well as the manufacturing and probably also the distribution and exchange of axes were important activities at the palisade enclosures. The great but varied significance of the axe is stressed by the fact the axe has a prominent position in every archaeological context – on settlements, in graves, and at ritual sites. The axe has functional and economic as well as ritual and symbolic meanings. The flint axe is widely distributed in Scandinavia, even far outside areas rich in flint. This indicates an organised network where axes were circulated and exchanged.

Our knowledge about flint axe manufacturing is principally based on experiment (Madsen 1993). How the production was organised is still an unsolved problem since just a few manufacturing sites have been properly excavated and published (Vemming Hansen & Madsen 1983, Högberg 1999). The palisade enclosure at Dösjebro is the first enclosure in Scandinavia where specialised axe production has been identified and several flint axe workshops were excavated close to the enclosure. The abundant waste material, several hundred thousand pieces, reflects extensive production as well as the reshaping of flint axes and the workshops represent the largest assemblage of this category in Scandinavia. This is despite the fact that the site is situated outside the area of primary flint sources. Deposits of knapping waste in the postholes prove that the palisade and the axe production are contemporary. It may be that the production of powerful axes could have been associated with isolation and mysticism and was for that reason carried out at the enclosure. In any case the almost complete absence of waste from axe production on the Neolithic settlements in the neighbourhood is striking.

The absence of coarse primary flakes and grinding stones indicates that the first as well as the final steps in the production were undertaken somewhere else – probably a sign of a specialised mode of production. It seems reasonable that the axe blanks were produced at the flint sources. The nearest known source with nodules large enough for axes is situated in the beach ridge along the coast about 10km away. If this was the case in the Neolithic considerably quantities of flint, probably several tons, must have been transported to the palisade enclosure. The fact that several Middle Neolithic axe hoards consist of unpolished axes, like the large hoard at Brogård, Bornholm, (Nielsen 1979) implies that axes left the places of production and were distributed, sometimes over long distances, before they were polished.

The manufacturing and distribution of axes were probably important activities at other palisade enclosures. At Sigersted I, large amounts of flakes from axe manufacturing were deposited in the postholes of the palisade, resembling the deposits in Dösjebro. At Helgeshøj, rough outs, some of them cracked by fire, occurred in a pit (Giersing 2000). These deposits of axe debitage indicate the presence of a factory site in the vicinity. There are nolarge native flint nodules on the island of Bornholm. Consequently all such flint is imported and this may explain why no axe manufacturing sites are found on the island. The many grindstones and small polished axe fragments from Rispebjerg (Nielsen oral.) indicate that the axes were finished there and were also reshaped when necessary. That Rispebjerg had a prominent position within the wider network of exchange and acted as a significant consumer as well is demonstrated by the considerable number of axes and chisels used in rituals (Nielsen F. O. 2001). This role is further stressed by the large axe hoard deposited nearby.

The hundreds of axe rough outs that have been collected in the flint rich beach ridge close to the palisade enclosure at Bunkeflo, represent extensive axe production (Salomonsson 1971). The manufacturing site is closely associated with the palisade both in time and space and therefore it seems reasonable that they were also connected functionally. As at Dösjebro, the production seems to have been fulfilling more than local demands. Contrary to the axe knapping areas in Dösjebro this production was concentrated at a rich flint source and involved the production of blanks and rough outs. We do not know if the final steps were also undertaken at the shore, since no flakes have been collected, but recent excavations have revealed extensive axe knapping areas, so far undated, about 1km inland (Sarnäs 2000).

Several studies of monuments and other ritual sites from the British Isles and the Continent have emphasised the importance of these sites for the production and especially the circulation of axes (Burl 1976; Patton 1991; Edmonds 1995; Sherratt 1998; Cooney 1998,1999). In Scandinavia the connection between the production and distribution of flint axes and palisade enclosures has been established by the excavations at Dösjebro. Axe manufacturing is recorded at Büdelsdorf in Northern Germany (Hassmann 2000) but not on any of the Sarup sites in Denmark (Andersen 1997). So the palisade enclosures might have been associated with somewhat different activities than the Sarup type. However, the axe manufacturing areas at Dösjebro have been located outside the enclosure. Usually this outer space has not been excavated or has just been subjected to minor investigations (Andersen 1997). This may explain the rare occurrence of axe manufacturing at the Scandinavian enclosures. In addition the remains of axe manufacturing can easily be missed in situations where culture layers have not survived, since they constitute only finds and the knapping process does not necessarily generate features dug beneath the ground surface.

Artefacts are found in special contexts or have been deposited in a manner that indicate deliberate ritual deposition as at the Sarup type enclosures. Deposits of flint axes, often fire cracked, are a well-documented ritual practice in Scandinavia (Müller 1886, Karsten 1994, Larsson 1999). Flint axes are also found at all the palisade enclosures in postholes, palisade trenches or in small shallow pits. Both whole and undamaged flint axes and chisels were deposited in far the greatest numbers at Rispebjerg but there are also a lot of burnt fragments from intentionally destroyed axes (Nielsen, F. O. 1998). Furthermore, one of the largest axe hoards in south Scandinavia has been found at the foot of the Rispebjerg hill. Other deposits at the palisade enclosures include pottery, hoards of scrapers and heaps of flint axe debitage. Since deposits of axe debitage have only recently been recorded in Scandinavia, they are of special interest. They are frequent and well documented at Dösjebro but also occur at Sigersted I. The stratigraphical evidence suggests that the flakes were deposited, sometimes tightly packed, during the refilling of the postholes when the palisade posts were being stabilised. This also proves that the axe production and the palisade were contemporary. It is notable that all deliberate deposits with flint axe debitage have been found in the palisade and within the enclosed space while the manufacturing areas were outside.

Cooney has studied stone and flint working and has stressed the ritual aspects of axe production (Cooney 1998, 1999). Axe production sites in Britain and Ireland are often located at spectacular and probably sacred places in the landscape. The quarrying and the knapping are regarded as dangerous activities in both a physical and metaphysical sense and the work involved rituals such as the deliberate deposition of production waste. The enclosure at Goodland in Ireland is a striking example. Here, extensive deposits were made in ditches and pits and amongst other materials, these deposits contained axe debitage. These deposits have been interpreted as acts to ensure the fertility of the earth to maintain a continued supply of flint nodules (Case 1973).

The palisade enclosure in Dösjebro is situated away from the primary sources of flint. Therefore it also seems reasonable to regard the depositions there as a deliberate maintenance of memories of a significant work and important event of exchange. The deposits also functioned as active instruments to secure the supply of flint nodules - a guarantee for the reproduction of these events. Exchange has always been central to the reproduction and renewal of relationships and competition between groups. Giving gifts brought prestige and respect. It must have been essential to gain control over the production and the distribution of axes in order to create, reproduce and increase the communication network and alliances between different groups. During a period of cultural diversity and probably of competition, as the transition from MNA to MNB, such ambitions probably became more urgent.

To sum up the functions of these sites, both activities of a sacred or ritual nature as well as the manufacture and probably also the distribution of flint axes all seem to have been carried out on site. In addition, there is also material of a more domestic nature that has been identified at the palisade enclosures. Current knowledge indicates that one and the same site could have been used for different purposes. The multiple roles may have varied or have been emphasised in different ways at different sites. For example there was the production of axes in Dösjebro and the ritual destruction of axes at Rispebjerg. Besides being a Christian temple, a Medieval church could also have been used for defence or as a storehouse for grain. It's therefore reasonable that a sacred space or structure in the Neolithic could also have been used both for ceremonial or sacred activities as well as profane. Communal rituals usually took place at fixed and recurrent points of time and it is therefore possible that, at other times, the sites were used for more profane activities. This does not have to be at the expense of the cult ceremonies. I believe that, when it comes to palisade enclosures, the sacred and the profane were two integrated spheres and that the sites acted as central places to enable local communities to foster communication and contact with the physical, metaphysical and spiritual worlds. They were places for gatherings, places for rites of passage, to honour the dead and for contacts with the gods, places for exchange and competition with others.

The Wider Perspective

Considered in a wider perspective it seems that enclosures emerge in certain regions in connection with periods of expansion and change, only to later disappear or decline in number and importance (Whittle 1988, Raetzel-Fabian 1999). Southern Scandinavia provides a striking example where the erection of enclosures is limited to two separate chronological horizons. The first generation is represented by the causewayed enclosures dated to the transition between the Early Neolithic and the Middle Neolithic - a period of many other innovations like the raising of megalithic tombs, the introduction of the ard and the first metal objects (Andersen 1997, Madsen 1988).

The second generation is characterised by the palisade enclosures from the final phase of the Funnel Beaker Culture and the Battleaxe Culture. The introduction of the Battleaxe Culture in Scandinavia was, like the Corded Ware Culture in most regions of Europe, also a period of radical change in many aspects of Neolithic society - settlement structure, burial custom and material culture. The traditional view has linked the introduction of the Corded Ware Culture, in the beginning of the 3rd millennium BC, with a general period of decline and indeed the end of the tradition of enclosed sites in most areas of Continental Europe (Andersen 1997). From this period it is mainly in the British Isles that enclosed sites are known. For that reason it is not surprising that palisade enclosures, contemporary with the Scandinavian sites, are found there. While, as far as I know, just a few contemporary palisaded sites are known from other parts of Europe although several considerably older sites are well known.

Regional overviews of the situation in parts of the Continent including France, Germany and south eastern Europe are presented in this volume. I will therefore pay attention to a site from another region, Šventoji 1A in Lithuania (Rimantienė 1980, 1997). The site is interesting in several respects. It is surrounded by a palisade, contemporary with the Scandinavian sites and extremely well preserved. The site is interpreted as a gathering place for cult ceremonies (Rimantienė 1997). It is situated in a peat district by a former lagoon close to the Baltic coast (fig 4.13). Excavations took place in the late sixties. A palisade was recorded for a distance of c.150m, which partly fenced off an area "empty" except for a large oak post, probably to be interpreted as a cult object. Numerous fragments of pottery and artefacts of stone and wood were deposited, probably on the ancient ground surface, outside the narrow entrance. The site is dated to the regional early Corded Ware Culture, the Haffküstenkultur, and is radiocarbon dated to 2880-2490 BC (Rimantienė 1997). Connections between southern Scandinavia and the Baltic region during the Early Corded Ware horizon are suggested by the close similarities in pottery forms and settlement types such as at Bornholm and (*inter alia*) Šventoji (F. O. Nielsen & P. O. Nielsen 1990, F. O. Nielsen 1997).

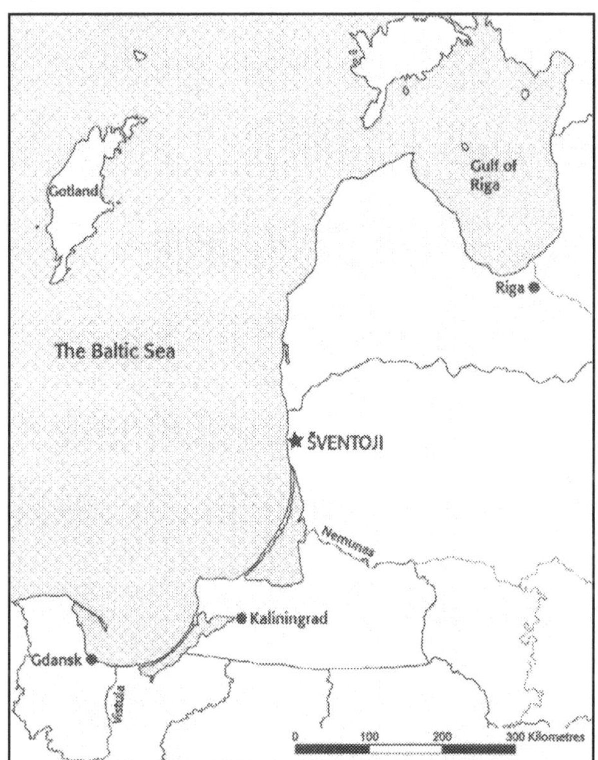

***Fig 4.13**. Location map of Šventoji.*

When the first identified palisade enclosure in Scandinavia was published 10 years ago, some similarities between this site in Hyllie and palisade enclosures on the British Isles were observed (Svensson 1991). As in Scandinavia the number of sites has increased since then and today the palisade enclosures in Britain and Ireland represent a category of their own (Whittle 1997, Gibson 1998a). They are all located in river valleys on plateaux or deep in the bottom of valleys, close to water like most of the Scandinavian sites. The perimeter consists of palisades only. However, there is a striking difference between the Scandinavian and the British palisades and that is the dimension of the timbers that have been used. In this respect the Scandinavian sites were dwarfs in comparison to the palisades in the British Isles which may have held oak posts 4-9 metres high (Gibson 1998a). Consequently a lot more labour must have been necessary for the construction of the British palisades (Whittle 1997, Gibson 1998a). In spite of their size (1-34ha) the entrances are few and narrow (Gibson 1998a). Some have enclosed timber circles and were integrated into ceremonial landscapes like the Avebury area (Whittle 1997, Gibson 1998b). Probably some of the palisades were burnt down (Whittle 1997, Hartwell 1998). The radiocarbon dates cover the time span between c. 3000-2000 BC (Gibson 1998a) and the early part of this sequence matches the dates for the Scandinavian sites in a striking way.

To conclude we have to ask what the roughly contemporary development of palisade enclosures, despite their geographical spread, in the northern and north western parts of Europe from about 3000 BC actually means. Do they reflect contacts between the regions where they were used? Do they perhaps even represent a common concept? Or were the palisades just frames varying in content and significance from region to region and from culture to culture? The palisade enclosures are quite a new phenomenon in the archaeology of Europe and at this stage of study it seems premature to grasp these problems. This publication is the first effort to achieve a basic survey of the material from different countries and regions in Europe.

Postscript

Since this paper was written in the spring of 2001 an extensive rescue excavation has been carried out at the palisade enclosure at Hyllie. Almost the entire enclosure has been uncovered, but unfortunately only limited areas of the exterior have been investigated. The actual extension corresponds very well to the estimated enclosed area shown in fig 4.4, even if the form turned out to be a little more kidney-shaped than expected. While writing this postscript the excavation is in full progress. The results so far support several of the interpretations presented in this paper. For example the complete failure of any of the palisades to intersect confirm that they are parts of a fairly contemporary structure. The preliminary results also suggest that the entire interior area seems to lack structures contemporary with the palisades and that at least parts of the palisades have been burnt down. The deliberate depositions of flakes from axe manufacturing found in several of the post-holes further stress the general importance of this practice at the palisade enclosures. These deposits also include fragments of hollow-ground flint axes, which confirm the dating of the palisades to the Battleaxe Culture. Information regarding the excavation at Hyllie was gratefully received from the excavation leader Kristian Brink of Malmö Heritage.

ACKNOWLEDGEMENTS
I would like to thank my colleagues Per Karsten and Henrik Pihl who made helpful comments on the text and checked my English, Henrik and Staffan Hyll for the illustrations and Finn Ole Nielsen and Esbjörn Jonsson for giving me information regarding the palisade enclosures on Bornholm and at Bunkeflo.

BIBLIOGRAPHY

Almquist, U. & Svensson, M. 1990. Palissaderna från Annetorpsleden. En märklig fyndplats från stridsyxekulturen. *Limhamniana* 1990.

Andersen, N. H. 1988. Sarup. *Befæstede kultpladser fra bondestenaldern.* Århus.

Andersen, N. H 1997. *The Sarup Enclosures. The Funnel Beaker Culture of the Sarup site including two causewayed camps compared to the contemporary settlements in the area and other European enclosures.* Sarup vol. 1. Jysk Arkæologisk Selskab. Moesgaard.

Andersen, N. H 1999a. *Saruppladsen. Sarup vol. 2.* Jysk Arkæologisk Selskab. Moesgaard.

Andersen, N. H 1999b. *Saruppladsen. Sarup vol. 3.* Jysk Arkæologisk Selskab. Moesgaard.

Andersson, M., Grønnegaard, T. & Svensson, M. 1999. Mellanneolitisk palissadinhägnad och folkvandringstida boplats. Skåne, Västra Karaby sn, Västra Karaby 28:5, Dagstorp 17:12, VKB SU 19. *Riksantikvarieämbetet, UV Syd Rapport* 1999:101. Lund.

Andersson, M. & Svensson, M. 1999. Palissadkomplexet i Dösjebro. In Burenhult, G. (ed). *Arkeologi i Norden* 1. Stockholm.

Andersson, T. 1999. Boplatslämningar från stenålder-äldre järnålder. Skåne, St. Herrestads sn, Herrestad 68:88 m. Fl. RAÄ 60. Arkeologisk slutundersökning 1995. *Riksantkivarieämbetet, UV Syd Rapport* 1999:8. Lund.

Arthursson, M. 2000. Stångby stationssamhälle. Boplats- bebyggelselämningar från senneolitikum till yngre järnålder. Skåne, Vallkärra sn, väg 930. *Arkeologisk förundersökning och undersökning. Riksantikvarieämbetet, UV Syd Rapport* 2000:79. Lund.

Björhem, N. & Säfvestad, U. 1987. *Stenåldershus. Rekonstruktion av ett 4000 år gammalt hus.* Rapport 2. Mamö Museer, Stadsantikvariska avdelningen. Malmö.

Björhem, N. & Säfvestad, U. 1989. Fosie IV. *Byggnadstradition och bosättningsmönster under senneolitikum.* Malmöfynd 5. Malmö Museer. Malmö.

Björhem, N. & Säfvestad, U. 1993. Fosie IV. *Bebyggelsen under brons- och järnålder.* Mamöfynd 6. Malmö Museer. Malmö.

Blomquist, R. 1951. *Lunds Historia 1.* Medeltiden. Lund.

Burl, A. 1976. *The Stone Circles of the British Isles.* London & Newhaven: Yale.

Case, H. 1973. A ritual site in north-east Ireland. In Daniel, G. & Kjærum, P. (eds). *Megalithic Graves and Ritual.* Jutland Archaeological Society. Moesgard.

Cooney, G. 1998. Breaking Stone, Making Places. In Gibson, A. & Simpson, D. (eds). *Prehistoric Ritual and Religion: Essays in Honour of Aubrey Burl.* Stroud: Sutton Publishing.

Cooney, G. 1999. *Landscapes of Neolithic Ireland.* London and New York: Routledge.

Davidsen, K. 1978. *The Final TRB Culture in Denmark. A Settlement Study.* Arkæologiske Studier, vol. V. København.

Edmonds, M. 1995. *Stone Tools and Society. Working Stone in Neolithic and Bronze Age Britain.* London: Batsford.

Engelmark, R. & Linderholm, J. 1997. Öresundsförbindelsen. Skjutbanorna, område 1C, palissaden. *Miljöarkeologisk rapport. Miljöarkeologiska Laboratoriet, Arkeologiska Instituitionen vid Umeå Universitet.* Umeå.

Eriksson, T. Månsson, S & Serlander, D. 2000. Brunnshög. Boplatslämningar från neolitikum, brons- och järnålder samt centralplats från mellanneolitikum. Skåne, Lunds stad, Östra Torn 27:2 m.fl. Arkeologisk förundersökning. *Riksantikvarieämbetet, UV Syd Rapport* 2000:88. Lund.

Giersing, T. 2000. Helgeshøjområdet. *Arkæologiske Udgravninger i Danmark 1999.* København.

Gibson, A. M. 1998a. Hindwell and the neolithic palisaded sites of Britain and Ireland. In Gibson, A. & Simpson, D. (eds). *Prehistoric Ritual and Religion: Essays in Honour of Aubrey Burl.* Stroud: Sutton Publishing.

Gibson, A.M. 1998b. *Stonehenge & Timber Circles.* Stroud: Tempus Publishing.

Hartwell, B. 1998. The Ballynahatty Complex. In Gibson, A. & Simpson, D. (eds). *Prehistoric Ritual and Religion: Essays in Honour of Aubrey Burl.* Stroud: Sutton Publishing.

Hassmann, H. 2000. *Die Steinartefakte der befestigten neolitischen Siedlung von Büdelsdorf, Kreis Rendsburg-Eckerförde.* Universitätsforschungen zur prähistorischen Archäologie. Band 62. Aus dem Institut für Ur- und Frühgeschischte der Universität Kiel. Bonn.

Heinemeier, J. et al. 1996. Danish AMS radiocarbon datings of archaeological samples, Aarhus 1995. *Arkæologiske Udgravninger i Danmark 1995.* København.

Hingst, H. 1971. Ein befestigdes Dorf aus der jungstenzeit in Büdelsdorf (Holstein). *Archäologisches*

Korrespondenzblatt I. Mainz.

Högberg, A. 1999. Child and Adult at a Knapping Area. A technological Flake Analysis of the Manufacture of a Neolithic Square Sectioned Axe and a Child's Flintknapping Activities on an Assemblage excavated as Part of the Öresund Fixed Linked Project. *Acta Archœologica* vol. 70. København.

Högberg, A. 2000. En alldeles speciell yxa. In Björhem, N. (ed). *Föresundsförbindelsen. På väg mot det förflutna*. Stadsantikvariska avdelningen, Kultur Malmö. Malmö.

Jager, S. 1985. A prehistoric route and ancient cart-tracks in the gemeente of Anlo (province of Drenthe). *Paleohistoria 27*. Groningen.

Jonsson, E. 1995. Delområde 1. Skjutbanorna. *Öresundsförbindelsen. Rapport över arkeologiska förundersökningar*. Stadsantikvariska avdelningen, Malmö Museer. Malmö.

Jørgensen, E. 1977. *Hagebrogård – Vroue – Koldkur. Neolitische Gräberfelder aus Nordwest-Jütland*. Arkœologiske Studier, vol. IV. København.

Jørgensen, M. S. 1987. *Fœrdsel over stenaldersfjorden. Om den œldste vej i Tibirke*. Fortidsminder og kulturhistorie. Antikvariske studier 9.

Karsten, P. 1994. *Att kasta yxan i sjön*. En studie över rituell tradition och förändring utifrån skånska neolitiska offerfynd. Acta Archaelogica Lundensia. Series in 8°. N° 23. Stockholm.

Karsten, P. & Svensson, M. Plats 8B:6/Väg 1178/1179 Syd – Centralplats från trattbägarkultur, boplats från järnålder samt våtmarksfynd från senneolitikum och järnålder. In Svensson, M. & Karsten, P. (eds). Arkeologisk förundersökning. Skåne, Malmöhus län, Järnvägen Västkustbanan. Avsnittet Landskrona – Kävlinge. *Riksantikvarieämbetet UV Syd Rapport* 1997:83. Lund.

Kaul, F. 1997.Tegnøvelser. *Skalk* 1997:1.

Kjellmark, K. 1903. *En stenåldersboplats i Järavallen vid Limhamn*. Stockholm.

Larsson, L. 1982. A Causewayed Enclosure and a Site with Valby Pottery at Stävie, Western Scania. *Meddelanden från Lunds universitets historiska museum 1981-1982*. Lund.

Larsson, L. 1989. Boplatser, bebyggelse och bygder. Stridsyxekultur i södra Skåne. In Larsson, L. (ed). *Stridsyxekultur i Sydskandinavien*. University of Lund, Institute of Archaeology, Report Series No 36. Lund.

Larsson, L. 1992. Settlement and Enviroment during the Middle and Late Neolithic. In Larsson, L., Callmer, J. & Stjernquist, B. (eds). *The Archaeology of the Cultural Landscape. Field Work and Research in a south Swedish rural region*. Acta Archaeologica Lundensia. Series in 4°. N° 19. Lund.

Larsson, L. 2000. Axes and Fire – Cotacts with the Gods. In Olaussson, D. & Vankilde, H. (eds). *Form, Function & Context. Material culture studies in Scandinavian Archaeology*. Acta Archaeologica Lundensia. Series in 8°. N° 31. Lund.

Larsson, L. 2001. De senaste kvartsseklets stenåldersarkeologi i Skåne. In Bergenstråhle, I, & Hellerström, S (eds). *Stenåldersforskning i focus. Inblickar och utblickar i sydskandinavisk stenåldersarkeologi*. Riksantikvarieämbetet arkeologiska undersökningar skrifter 39. University of Lund, Institute of Archaeology – Report series nr 77. Lund.

Larsson, M. 1992. The Early and Middle Neolithic Funnel Beaker Culture in the Ystad area (Southern Scania). Economic and social change, 3100-2300 BC. In Larsson, L., Callmer, J. & Stjernquist, B. (eds). *The Archaeology of the Cultural Landscape. Field Work and Research in a south Swedish rural region*. Acta Archaeologica Lundensia. Series in 4°. N° 19. Lund.

Larsson, M. 1997. Gropkeramikerna - fanns de? Sydsverige. In Larsson, M. & Olsson, E. (eds). *Regionalt och interregionalt. Stenåldersundersökningar i Syd- och Mellansverige.* Riksantikvarieämbetet Arkeologiska undersökningar 23. Stockholm.

Lindhé, E., Sarnäs, P. & Steineke, M. 2000. *Citytunneln och spåren i landskapet. Projektprogram och undersökningsplaner för arkeologiska förundersökningar för Citytunnelns spårsträckningar samt slutundersökning av Hoteltomten och Bunkeflo bytomt.* Stadsantikvariska avdelningen, Kultur Malmö. Malmö.

Madsen, B. 1993. Flint - udvinding, forarbejdning og distribution. In Hvass, S. & Storgaard, B. (eds). *Da klinger i muld...25 års arkæologi i Danmark.* Århus.

Madsen, T. 1988. Causewayed Enclosures in South Scandinavia. In Burgess, C., Topping, P., Mordant, C. & Maddison, M. (eds). *Enclosures and Defences in the Neolithic of Western Europe.* B.A.R. International Series 403 (ii). Oxford.

Malmer, M. P. 1962. *Jungneolitische Studien.* Acta Archaeologica Lundensia. Series in 8°. N° 2. Lund.

Müller, S. 1886. Votivfund fra Sten og Broncealderen. *Aarbøger 1886.* København.

Müller, S. 1904. Vei og Bygd i Sten- og Bronzealdern. *Aarbøger 1904.* København.

Månsson, S. & Pihl, H. 1999. Gravar, yxtillverkning och hus från mellanneolitikum. Skåne, Dagstorps sn, Särslöv 3:6 m.fl., VKB SU 17. *Riksantikvarieämbetet, UV Syd Rapport* 1999:98. Lund.

Nielsen, F. O. & Nielsen, P. O. 1985. Middle and Late Neolithic Houses at Limensgård, Bornholm. A Preliminary Report. *Journal of Danish Archaeology,* vol. 4. Odense.

Nielsen, F. O. & Nielsen, P. O. 1989. Vasegård. *Arkæologiske Udgravninger i Danmark 1988.* København.

Nielsen, F. O. & Nielsen, P. O. 1990. The Funnel Beaker Culture on Bornholm. In Jankawska, D. (ed). *Die Trichterbecherkultur. Neue Forschungen und Hypotesen,* Teil 1. Posnan.

Nielsen, F. O. & Nielsen, P. O. 1991. The Middle Neolithic Settlement at Grødbygård, Bornholm. . In Jennbert, K. & Larsson, L. & Petré R. & Wyszomirska-Webart, B. (eds.). *Regions and Reflections. In Honour of Märta Strömberg.* Acta Archaeologica Lundensia. Series in 8°. N° 20. Lund.

Nielsen, F. O. & Nielsen, P. O. 1994. Vasagård. *Arkæologiske Udgravninger i Danmark 1993.* København.

Nielsen, F. O. 1996a. *Forhistoriske intresser.* Bornholms Amt. Tekniske Forvaltning. Rønne.

Nielsen, F. O. 1996b. Borggård. *Arkæologiske Udgravninger i Danmark 1995.* København.

Nielsen, F. O. 1997a. The Neolithic Settlement on Bornholm. In Król, D (ed). *The Built Enviroment of Coast Areas during the Stone Age. The Baltic Sea-Coast landscapes Seminar Session No. 1.* Gdansk.

Nielsen, F. O. 1997b. Brogård. *Arkæologiske Udgravninger i Danmark 1996.* København.

Nielsen, F. O. 1998a. Nyt om Ringborgen på Rispebjerg. *Bornholms Museum, Bornholms Kunstmuseum 1996-1997.* Rønne.

Nielsen, F. O. 1998b. Brogård. *Arkæologiske Udgravninger i Danmark 1997.* København.

Nielsen, F. O. 2000. Bornholms museums antikvariske arbejde. *Bornholms Museum, Bornholms Kunstmuseum 1998-1999.* Rønne.

Nielsen, F. O. 2001. Evaluering af et regionalt stenaldersprojekt. In Bergenstråhle, I, & Hellerström, S (eds). *Stenåldersforskning i focus. Inblickar och utblickar i sydskandinavisk stenåldersarkeologi.* Riksantikvarieämbetet arkeologiska undersökningar skrifter 39. University of Lund, Institute of Archaeology – Report series nr 77. Lund.

Nielsen, P. O. 1979. De tyknakkede flintøksers kronologi. *Aarbøger 1977.* København.

Nielsen, P. O. 1985. De første bønder. Nye fund fra den tidligste Tragtbægerkultur ved Sigersted. *Aarbøger 1984.* København.

Nielsen, P. O. 1988. Sigersted III. *Arkæologiske Udgravninger i Danmark 1997.* København.

Nielsen, P. O. 1999a. Limensgård and Grødbygård. Settlements with house remains from the Early, Middle and Late Neolithic on Bornholn. In Fabech, C & Ringtved, J. (eds). *Settlement and Landscape. Proccedings of a conference in Århus, Denmark, May 4-7 1998.* Jutland Archaeological Society. Moesgård.

Nielsen, P. O. 1999b. Sigersted III. *Arkæologiske Udgravninger i Danmark 1998.* København.

Nielsen, S. 1999. *The Domestic Mode of Producrion – and Beyond. An archaeological inquiry into urban trends in Denmark, Iceland and Predynastic Egypt.* Nordiske Fortidsminder, Serie B, Vol. 18. København.

Patton, M. A.1991. Axes, Men and Woman: Symbolic Dimensions of Neolithic Exchange in Armorica (north-west France). In Garwood, P. et al (eds). *Sacred and Profane. Proceedings of a Conference on Archaeology, Ritual and Religion. Oxford, 1989.* Oxford university Committee for archaeology Monograph No. 32. Oxford.

Raetzel-Fabian, D. 1999. Der umhegte Raum – Funktionale Aspekte jungneolitischer Monumental-Erdwerke. *Jahresschrift für mitteldeutsche Vorgeschichte 81.* Berlin.

Raetzel-Fabian, D. 2000. Monumentality and Communication: Neolithic Enclosures and Long Distance Tracks in Neolithic Central Europe. (Added December 12, 2000. Updated January 12, 2001.) http://www.comp-archaeology.org/FabianSAA2000.htm

Rimantiené, R. 1980. *Šventoji. Pamariu kultūros gyvenvietés.* Vilnius.

Rimantiené, R. 1997. Die A-Horizon-Elemente in der Haffküstenkultur in Litauen. *Early Corded Ware Culture. The A – Horizon – fiction or fact? International symposium in Jutland 2nd – 7th May 1994.* Arkæologiske Rapporter nr. 2, 1997. Esbjerg Museum.

Russel, H. S. 1980. *Indian New England before the Mayflower.* Hanover, New Hampshire.

Salomonsson, B. 1971. Malmötraktens förhistoria. In Bjurling, O. (ed). *Malmö stads historia.* Malmö.

Sandén, U. 1995. Bevare oss väl. En studie av megalitgravarnas bevaringsgrad på Söderslätt. *Seminar paper. University of Lund, Institute of Archaeology.* Lund.

Sarnäs, P. 2000. Fyra ton flinta. In Björhem, N. (ed). *Föresundsförbindelsen. På väg mot det förflutna.* Stadsantikvariska avdelningen, Kultur Malmö. Malmö.

Schovsbo, P. O. 1987. *Oldtidens vogne i Norden. Arkæologiske undersøgelser af mose- og jordfundne vogndele af træ fra neolitikum til ældre middelalder.* Fredrikshavn.

Sherratt, A. 1998. Points of Exchange: the Later Neolithic Monuments of the Morbihan. In Gibson, A. & Simpson, D. (eds). *Prehistoric Ritual and Religion: Essays in Honour of Aubrey Burl.* Stroud: Sutton

Publishing.

Skaarup, J. 1985. *Yngre stenalder på øerne syd for Fyn*. Meddelelser fra Langelands museum. Rudkøbing.

Staal, B. 1999. Bakkegård. *Arkæologiske Udgravninger i Danmark 1998*. København.

Stenholm, L. 1986. *Ränderna går aldrig ur – en bebyggelsehistorisk studie av Blekinges dansktid*. Lund Studies in Medieval Archaeology 2. Lund.

Straunsbjerg Thorsen, M. 1999. Brogård. *Arkæologiske Udgravninger i Danmark 1998*. København.

Straunsbjerg Thorsen, M. 2000. Brogård. *Arkæologiske Udgravninger i Danmark 1999*. København.

Svensson, M., Pihl, H. & Andersson, M. 2001. Palissadkomplexet i Dösjebro. Seminariegrävning vårterminen 2000. *Riksantikvarieämbetet, UV Syd Rapport* 2001:8. Lund.

Svensson, M. 1986. Trattbägarboplatsen "Hindby mosse" – aspekter på dess struktur och funktion. *Elbogen* 16:3. Malmö.

Svensson, M. 1991. A Palisade Enclosure in South-West Scania – a Site from the Battle-Axe Culture. In Jennbert, K. & Larsson, L. & Petré R. & Wyszomirska-Webart, B. (eds.). *Regions and Reflections. In Honour of Märta Strömberg*. Acta Archaeologica Lundensia. Series in 8°. N° 20. Lund.

Svensson, M. 1998a. Det neolitiska rummet. In Karsten, P. & Svensson, M. Projektprogram. I Stenåldersdalen. Det mesolitiska och neolitiska rummet. Projektprogram inför arkeologiska slutundersökningar av Järnvägen, delen Helsingborg-Kävlinge. Avsnittet Landskrona-Kävlinge. *Riksantikvarieämbetet, UV Syd Arbetshandling* 1998. Lund.

Svensson, M. 1998b. Västkustbanan. Det neolitiska rummet – de tidig- och mellanneolitiska fynden från förundersökningarna i Saxå – Välabäcksdalen. *Bulletin för arkeologisk forskning i Sydsverige* nr 1, 1998. Lund.

Söderberg, S. 1884. Hällkista från Bronsåldern. *Kongl. vitterhets och Antiqvitets Akademins Månadsblad 154 –156*, 1884. Stockholm.

Sørensen, P. Ø. 1995. Markildegård. En tidigneolitisk samlingsplats. *Kulurhistoriske studier*. Sydsjællands Museum. Vordingborg.

Tesch, S. 1992. House, farm and village in the Köpinge area from Early Neolithic to the Early Middle Ages. In Larsson, L., Callmer, J. & Stjernquist, B. (eds). *The Archaeology of the Cultural Landscape. Field Work and Research in a south Swedish rural region*. Acta Archaeologica Lundensia. Series in 4°. N° 19. Lund.

Thörn, R. 1998. Det rituella landskapet. Från Svedab- till Vägverksdel av Öresundsförbindelsen. *Öresundsförbindelsen och arkeologi II. Projektprogram och undersökningsplaner för arkeologiska slutundersökningar*. Stadsantikvariska avdelningen, Malmö Museer. Malmö.

Vang Petersen, P. 1993. *Flint fra Danmarks oldtid*. København.

Vemming Hansen, P. & Madsen, B. 1983. Flint Axe Manufacture in the Neolithic. An Experimental Investigation of a Flint Axe Manufacture Site at Hastrup Vænget, East Zealand. *Journal of Danish Archaeology*, vol. 2. Odense.

Whittle, A. 1988. Context, Activities, Events – Aspects of Neolithic and Copper age Enclosures in Central and Western Europe. In Burgess, C., Topping, P., Mordant, C. & Maddison, M. (eds). *Enclosures and Defences in the Neolithic of Western Europe*. B.A.R. International Series 403 (i). Oxford.

Whittle, A. 1997. *Sacred Mound Holy Rings. Silbury Hill and the West Kennet palisade enclosures: a later Neolithic complex in north Wiltshire*, Monograph 74. Oxford: Oxbow Books.

Winge, G. 1976. *Gravfältet vid Kastanjegården.* Malmöfynd 3. Malmö Museer.

Winther, J. 1935. *Troldebjerg. En bymœssig bebyggelse fra Danmarks yngre stenalder.* Rudkøbing.

CHAPTER 5

PALISADED ENCLOSURES IN THE GERMAN NEOLITHIC

Michael Meyer

INTRODUCTION

Ditched enclosures are common in the older, middle, younger and late Neolithic in Germany[1]. They enter the archaeological record at the beginning of the Linearbandkeramik (LBK). During the LBK large, often oval, enclosures occur as do small oval, rectangular or rounded enclosures. The former often have settlement traces inside, whereas at a number of the latter internal buildings are definitely lacking (Lüning 1988; Höckmann 1990; Kaufmann 1997). Both categories of enclosure seem to continue into the middle Neolithic, the smaller ones becoming a very clearly definable type called *Kreisgrabenanlage* (circular ditched enclosure) (Petrasch 1990, 488 ff.; Matuschik 1999, 1065; sceptical: Trnka 1991, 315). In the Michelsberg culture of the later Neolithic the circular enclosures vanish, and these sites seem to revert to the traditional large enclosures of the early and middle Neolithic (Matuschik 1999, 1065; see also Jeunesse 1996). However, they exhibit a large variety of form, position in the landscape and size including new, extremely large sites enclosing up to 90ha (Raetzel-Fabian 1999, Abb. 5). In the Altheim culture smaller enclosures reoccur and they continue to be constructed in the later Neolithic. The larger enclosures of this period only occur in the central German mountain area (Matuschik 1991; Meyer 1995; Raetzel-Fabian 1999).

These enclosures have been a subject of research since the beginning of the 20th century (Petrasch 1998, 187f.), with an increasing intensity from the 1970's onwards. This revived interest was generated by the large-scale excavations that took place at the open-cast coalmines of the Rhinelands and, from the 1980's, through the onset of systematic aerial photography. In eastern Germany both aerial photography and large-scale rescue excavations greatly increased after 1990 and this led to the discovery of an impressive number of new enclosures. It also produced completely new sites such as pit alignments, which seem to date almost exclusively to the late Bronze Age and the early Iron Age (Stäuble 1999, 169 ff.).

Types Of Enclosure

Ditched Palisades

Many of these enclosures, of all periods, consist of one or more ditches and one or more palisades, usually within the line of the ditch(es). The palisades are generally interpreted as a part of an earth rampart, either as a front or back revetment depending on their distance from the ditch (Matuschik 1991, 34). An impressive example of this is the Chasséen-enclosure from Compiègne, where the postholes have an outward slant in the direction of the ditch which can be interpeted as resulting from the pressure of an earth rampart (Toupet 1988). In some cases the 'palisade' is seen as a supporting wooden construction within the rampart (Dohrn-Ihmig 1983, 21 Abb. 14). At the Michelsberg enclosure of Bonn-Venusberg the rampart is still preserved, and a small excavation produced the remains of a wooden construction inside it. Unfortunately the excavation is only published in interim form and the rampart construction is not described in detail (Gechter 1987; Eckert 1990, 403). At Heilbronn-Klingenberg, also belonging to the Michelsberg culture, remains of a burned palisade were found. This wall was constructed of horizontal planks 30cm wide which were supported by vertical round posts. This structure was found in a secondary position in the ditch and is interpreted as the front revetment of the earth rampart which may or may not have had a low ramp in front of it (Biel 1998, 98; Matuschik 1991, 32 ff.).

Besides these cases where a combination of ditch, palisade and rampart could be interpreted, it has also been possible to devise a chronological sequence for the erection of the different ditches and palisades at some sites. Famous examples are the LBK-enclosures of Köln-Lindenthal (Bernhardt 1990) and the younger Neolithic enclosure of Urmitz (Boelicke 1976/77). As there are hardly any cases with direct stratigraphic evidence for phasing, such as the cutting of one ditch by another (*e.g.* see. Höhn 1997), the main arguments for the different phases must be found in other data. Such strands of evidence comprise the dating of the finds from the features, the varying distances between individual ditch systems and/or palisades that seem to suggest a different layout and, finally, interruptions (gates) in one perimeter that are not present in the others.

None of these arguments are unequivocal. The finds from palisade ditches might come from an earlier phase and be in a secondary position, or they may have found their way into the postholes after the extraction of the posts. In hardly any case has the exact position of the finds been published in detail. As a result, it is sometimes impossible to determine whether they come from the whole fill or only the upper fills of the posthole or the ditch (see the discussion about Urmitz: Boelicke 1977, 103 ff.; Andersen 1998, 182 f.). The varying distance between palisade and ditch might have been for functional reasons. It may have been due to the position of the rampart, for example, though this does not seem very likely, especially if the distances vary considerably. The most problematic argument is the differing position of the gates in ditch and palisade. Matuschik (1991, 35) has pointed out that not every causeway is really an entrance into the enclosure and this is certainly true. On the other hand a regular difference in the positions of these causeways can be interpreted as an intentional gate construction. To avoid misinterpretations, the differences should be irregular and should not concern only one gate but the whole outlay of the enclosure. Unfortunately this can rarely be checked because the enclosures have often been only partly excavated and/or the palisade was only preserved in short lengths. The point is less problematic with the *Kreisgrabenanlagen*, as here the regular outlay proves that each gate really did lead into the enclosure[2].

It is therefore clear that there are certain problems when trying to phase palisades and ditches. This is certainly also true for some of the enclosures discussed below and has to be kept in mind as a perennial problem due to the state of research at many enclosures. Nevertheless it can be shown, or at least shown to be likely, for quite a number of the complex enclosures that a palisade must have been the only feature existing on the site at a particular time.

Palisades without ditches

The second group of palisades comprises those sites without any other ditches. Unlike the ditched enclosures, these are much more difficult to detect either by aerial photography or geophysical survey, especially if the palisade is of individual posthole construction. As palisades were not dug as deep into the ground as were the ditches, they are therefore much more susceptible to destruction by erosion, although this, of course, is also true for the ditched palisades. Finally, a palisaded enclosure without other features will tend to produce no surface finds, so that the discovery of such a site is often fortuitous. Despite these limitations to the data, it is still possible to give an overview of the German Neolithic palisades (see also: Höckmann 1990, 70 Abb. 11; Petrasch 1998, Karte 11)[3]. In the following text I shall only consider the features from dry land conditions.

DEFINITIONS

As a starting point it is necessary to discuss some points of definition. A palisade is understood here as:

- a row of postholes set at more or less equal distances
- a narrow trench within which are traces of postholes
- a narrow trench without such traces
- a narrow trench with postholes on one side of it and set at regular distances.

All these features must be traceable for at least a length of several meters, and longer lengths display a degree of curvature. It is clear that a satisfactory distinction between 'palisade' and 'fence' is not possible with these definitions. Since information regarding the thickness of the posts is rarely available (thin posts might suggest a fence) palisades and fences are differentiated here only according to their length and shape (see Gibson 1998, fig. 6.6; 6.7) and to their position in the settlement. Any of the four features given above and that are clearly associated with a house and enclose a rather small area of not more than about 2000m^2 is regarded as a fence. A larger and more extensive structure is regarded as a palisade. This usage of these terms is pragmatic. A palisade is not necessarily seen as a fortification and it is also accepted that fences can also cover a large area.

THE GERMAN PALISADE ENCLOSURES

Fenced Enclosures

It is almost impossible to give a complete catalogue of Neolithic fenced sites in Germany, as for this an examination of every publication of a Neolithic settlement would be necessary. For this reason the map (fig. 5.1) shows only the sites of more recently excavated early and middle Neolithic fenced sites and is certainly incomplete. As the Neolithic in northern Germany begins at the end of what is the middle Neolithic in other parts, there can be no evidence from this region and the lack of evidence

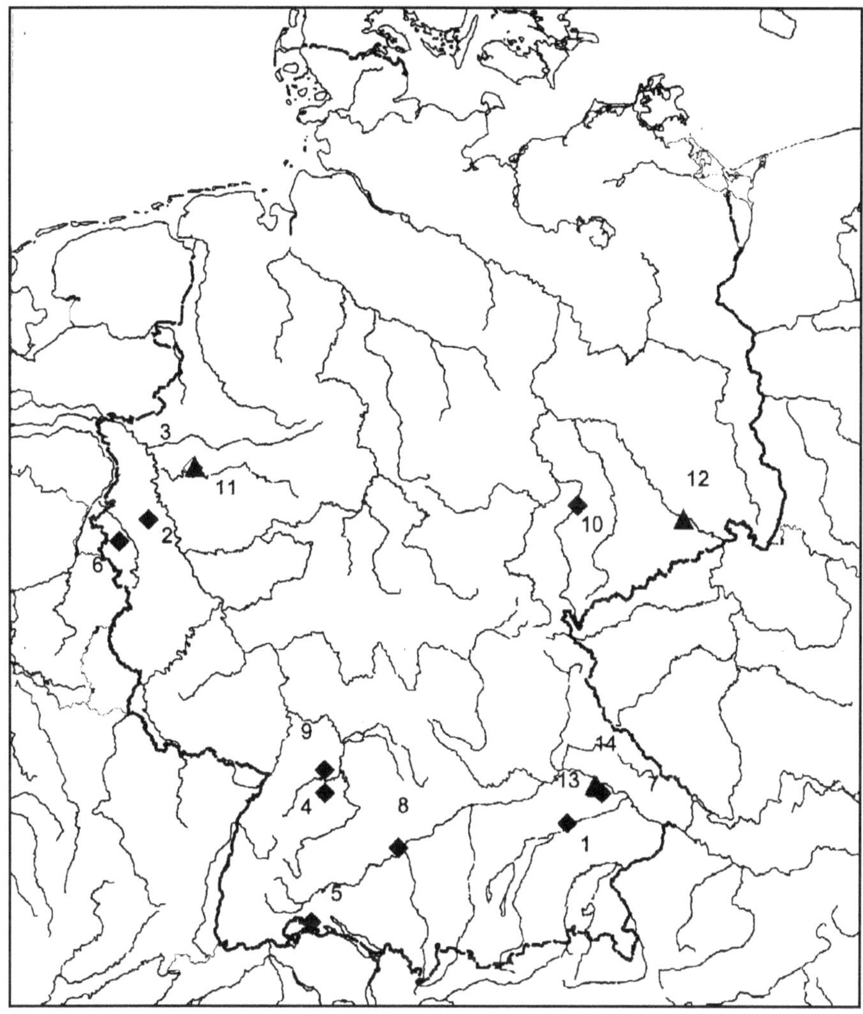

***Fig 5.1**: Fences in settlements of the older (◆) and middle Neolithic (▲) in Germany mentioned in the text. Open symbols uncertain. See Appendix 1, Table 1.*

from the central part of Germany is certainly fortuitous. It is interesting to see that fenced sites starting from the appearance of longhouses in the northwest occur quite regularly in LBK as well as in MN contexts (fig. 5.2,1). Generally, however, the whole extent of the fence can not be reconstructed and the complete fence from Bochum-Hiltrop (fig. 5.2,2) still remains unique. Nevertheless, among all these fenced sites it can clearly be seen that they each belong to one specific house and so define an area of special activity outside and around the house. The archeological data give no clear evidence about what kind of activity this might have been. To the writer's knowledge, no phosphate analysis has yet been undertaken on such an area and as the original ground surface is generally missing in these settlements (but see Altdorf: Meixner 1998), the distribution of surface finds provides only limited information. The construction of the fences varies from palisade trenches to post holes set at a distance of *c.*2m. However unclear the particular function of these fenced enclosures may be, it is very interesting to note that there is, as yet, no case known where the house is completely surrounded by the fence (but see Žlkovce: Pavúk 1991, 350 ff.). The house itself is part of the fence. This makes it clear that the fences inside settlements have nothing to do with the fortification of particular houses or farmsteads. It is much more probable that they represent a yard for cattle and/or some other inner structuring of the settlement, and this can be clearly exemplified at Vaihingen/Enz where a fence system inside the settlement also includes the palisade behind the ditch (Krause 1998, Beil. 2).

Circular Palisaded Enclosures (*Kreispalisadenanlagen*)

Among the ditched enclosures the middle Neolithic circular sites defined by one or more circuits of ditches (*Kreisgrabenanlagen*) could at one time be defined very clearly. This was not only on account of their circular form, but also their size, the profiles of their ditches and the fact that they do not appear to enclose any contemporary features (Petrasch 1990, 418 f.; with varying priorities Trnka 1991, 11 f.; Podborský 1988, 304). Recently, however, the situation has become more complicated as there is clear evidence for similar but much younger enclosures such as that from Schkölen-Räpitz (fig. 5.3,3). This site produced late Bronze Age ceramics even from the lower fills of the ditches[4]. This site makes it clear that circular ditches can not be dated morphologically by aerial photographs or by geophysical prospection alone.

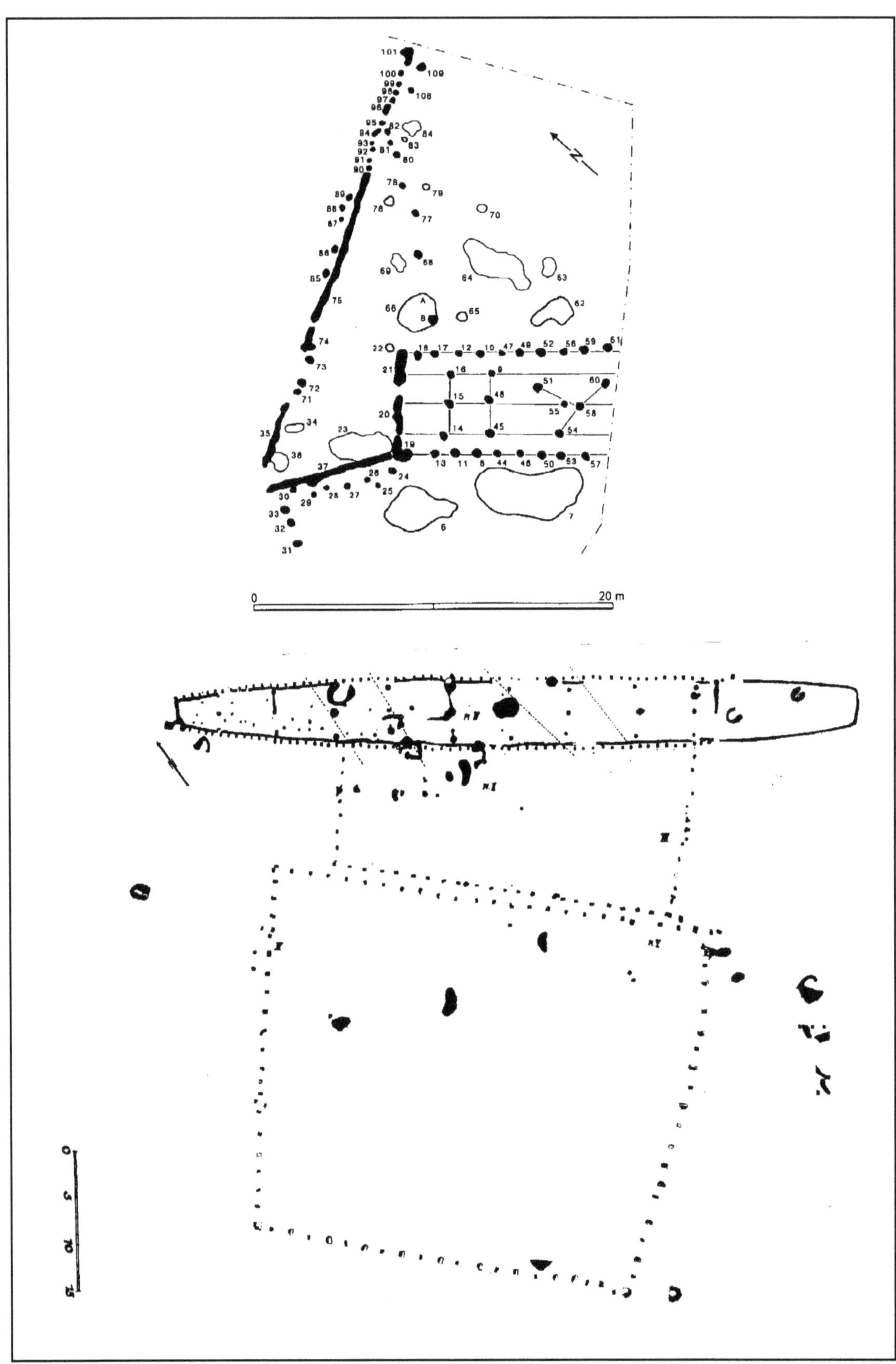

Fig 5.2: *Examples of Neolithic fences. 1 – Gerlingen, LBK (Appendix1,Table 1,4); 2 – Bochum-Hiltrop, Hillerberg, Rössen (Appendix1,Table 1,10; the northwestern part of the building is reconstructed). Different scales.*

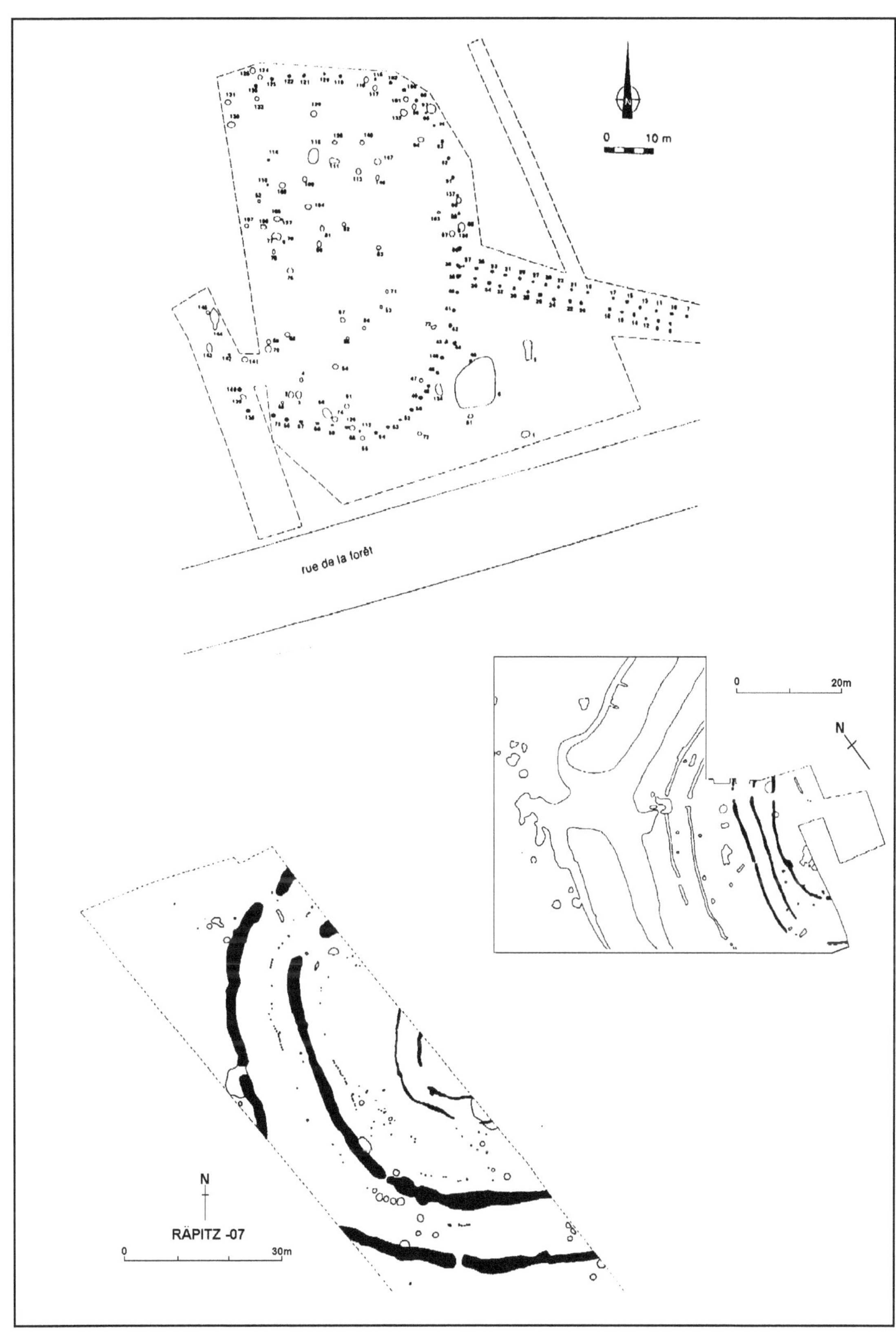

***Fig 5.3**: Examples of circular palisades in Germany and France. 1 - Wittenheim (Haut-Rhin), Rössen III (Appendix1,Table 2,6); 2 - Künzing-Unternberg, MN (Appendix1,Table 2,3); 3 - Schkölen-Räpitz, Kr. Leipziger Land, Late Bronze Age (Steinmann 1999, Abb. 12).*

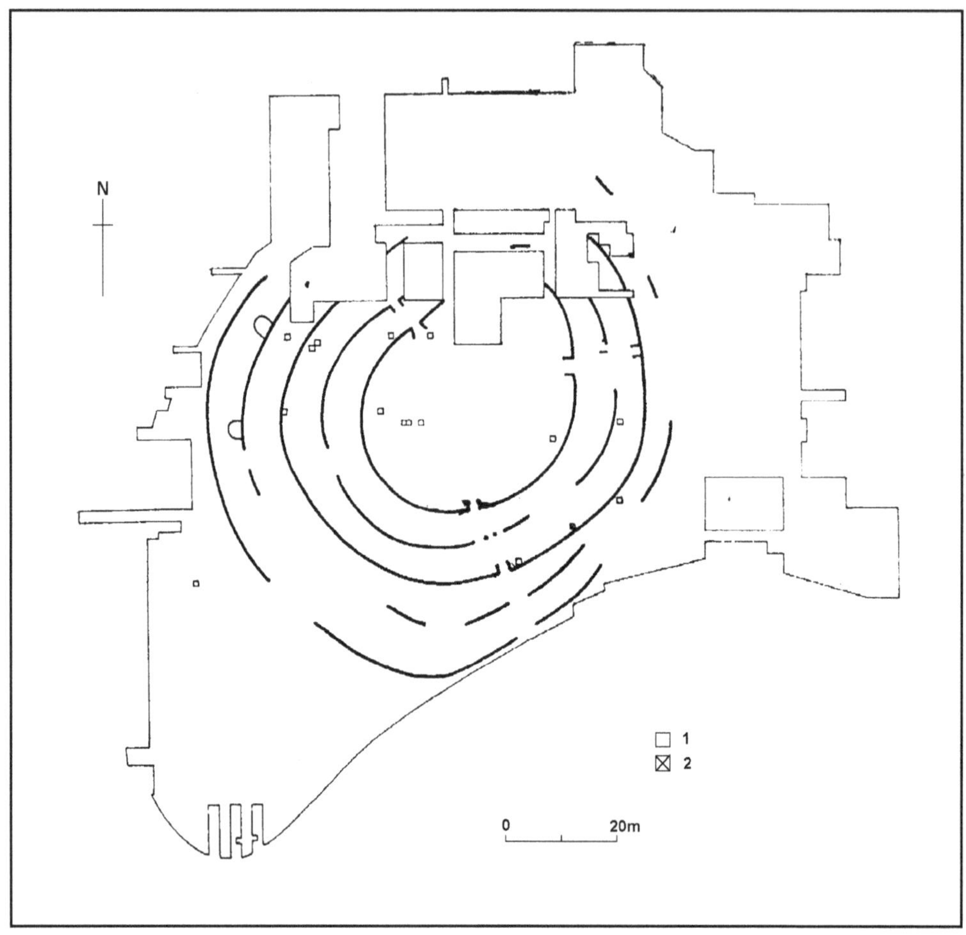

Fig 5.4: *Kreispalisadenanlage (circular palisaded enclosure) from Quenstedt, Schalkenburg (Appendix1,Table 2,4).*

A group of circular palisaded enclosures can seen to date to a later stage of the development of the middle Neolithic *Kreisgrabenanlagen* (fig 5.5). These are the so called *Kreispalisadenanlagen* (Petrasch 1990, 486 ff.). Petrasch (1990, 524) has listed three enclosures of this type which each have differing features. In Künzing-Unternberg (fig. 5.3,2; Appendix 1, Table 2,3) three partly excavated palisades inside the *Kreisgrabenanlage* form an independent enclosure which is presumed to be younger and to date to a later phase of the middle Neolithic. It can probably be reconstructed to have roughly the same shape as the enclosure from Quenstedt (fig. 5.4; Appendix 1,Table 2,4; with an emphasis on the differences Trnka 1991, 315). In recent years two circular enclosures from Saxony have been excavated in which the varying positions of the gates suggest that the palisade rings existed independently of the ditches (Appendix1,Table 2,1.2)[5]. The fragment of a probably ellipsoid palisade from Riekofen (Appendix1,Table 2,5) also belongs to the early phase of the later Neolithic and these three enclosures also fit this type[6]. A third enclosure listed by Petrasch was excavated in Žlkovce (Pavúk 1991, 350 ff.). This was roughly in the center of a Lengyel II settlement, itself surrounded by a palisade, and there was a more or less circular enclosure which was renewed six times and which is likely to have enclosed a single building in all periods of its existence. It is clear that these palisades have a completely different character with a direct domestic function, and obviously expressing the important role of the one central house in the settlement. This has nothing to do with the criteria for *Kreisgrabenanlagen* which emphasise an inner area without settlement traces and it would at least change the character of their presumed function as a central meeting place with a mainly social or religious character (Petrasch 1990, 518). For this reason I suggest that the term *Kreispalisadenanlage* should not be used for rounded settlement palisades (or fences) like Žlkovce.

Recently, in the Haut-Rhin area of eastern France, another circular palisade has been excavated which dates to the final phase of the Rössen culture (fig. 5.3,1; Appendix1,Table 2,6). It is of a slightly irregular shape and is unusual in having an extraordinari long entrance formed by two rows of posts

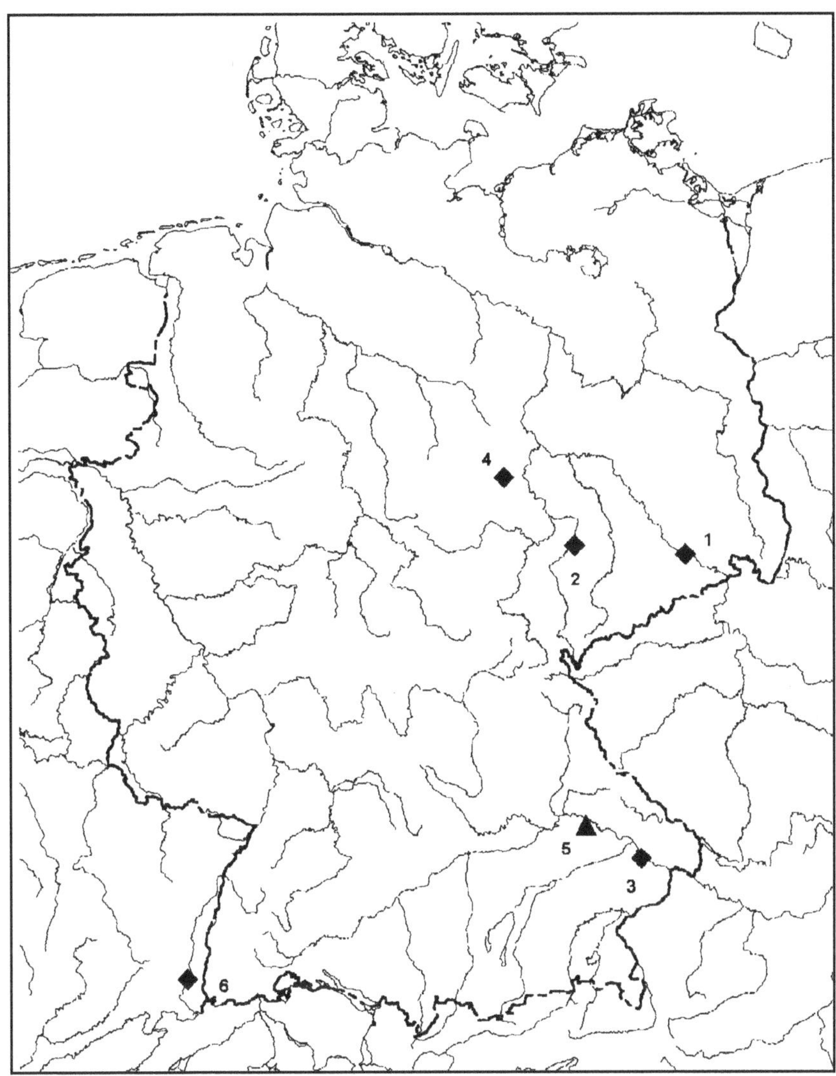

***Fig 5.5**: Kreispalisadenanlagen (circular palisaded enclosures) and similar features of the middle Neolithic (◆) and the younger Neolithic (▲) in Germany and France. See Appendix 1,Table 2. No. 4 and 6: only palisade; No. 1, 2 and 3: the palisades are presumed not to be contemporary with the ditches because of a difference in plan, 1 and 2 are uncertain; No. 5: the ditch is stratigraphically later than the palisade.*

traceable over a distance of 48m. Although there are parallels for gateways among the *Kreisgrabenanlagen* (Lefranc/Jeunesse 1998; see also below Appendix1,Table 2,1) the Wittenheim enclosure is unique. This is not only because of its construction, but also because the *Kreisgrabenanlagen* have until now been restricted to the central Danube, Bohemia and Moravia and eastern Germany (Petrasch 1990, Abb. 2 (without the east German enclosures discovered since 1990, *e.g.* see Meyer 1999)). Circular ditches, not defined as *Kreisgrabenanlagen,* also occur in the Rhineland (Petrasch 1990, 524). This is also reflected in the distribution of the *Kreispalisadenanlagen* (Abb. 5). The dating of the Wittenheim enclosure fits well into Petraschs' concept of the *Kreispalisaden-anlagen* representing the earliest stage of development of the *Kreisgraben-anlagen.* The enclosure from Riekofen which belongs to the early phase of the younger Neolithic suggests that this type of enclosure is not only restricted to the late phase of the middle Neolithic (see also Kállay 1990).

Palisaded Enclosures, Early and Middle Neolithic

Whereas these circular palisades form a more or less homogenous group (this homogeneity also extends to their size (fig. 5.6,1)) the other Neolithic palisades cannot be so easily grouped. Estimations of size are possible for only 3 of the palisaded enclosures of the LBK in Germany (fig. 5.7). These three examples seem to point towards two different size-groups. The first is the enclosure from Meindling (fig. 5.8,1) which is rather small, approximately 60m in diameter, whereas the palisade from Köln-Lindenthal (fig. 5.8,2) with its perimeter of 190 x 155m is clearly much larger. Despite this, the palisades from Sittard in the Netherlands (Modderman 1958/59), the larger palisade measuring at least 155 x 110m and the smaller one with a perimeter of 90 x 75m show that at present no significant classes of size are recognisable. A ditched enclosure at Plaidt may be similar to that at Darion in Belgium (Jadin/Cahen 1992), where for lengths of 50m the perimeter is marked only by a palisade instead of the ditch (*contra* Ihmig 1971, 25 ff.). The reason for this supposition is that the excavator of Plaidt has described the same phenomenon (Lehner 1912, 279). The distribution of the LBK palisades probably reflects the current state of research with its main centre in the Rhineland, just as did the older distributions of ditched enclosures (Lüning 1988, 155).

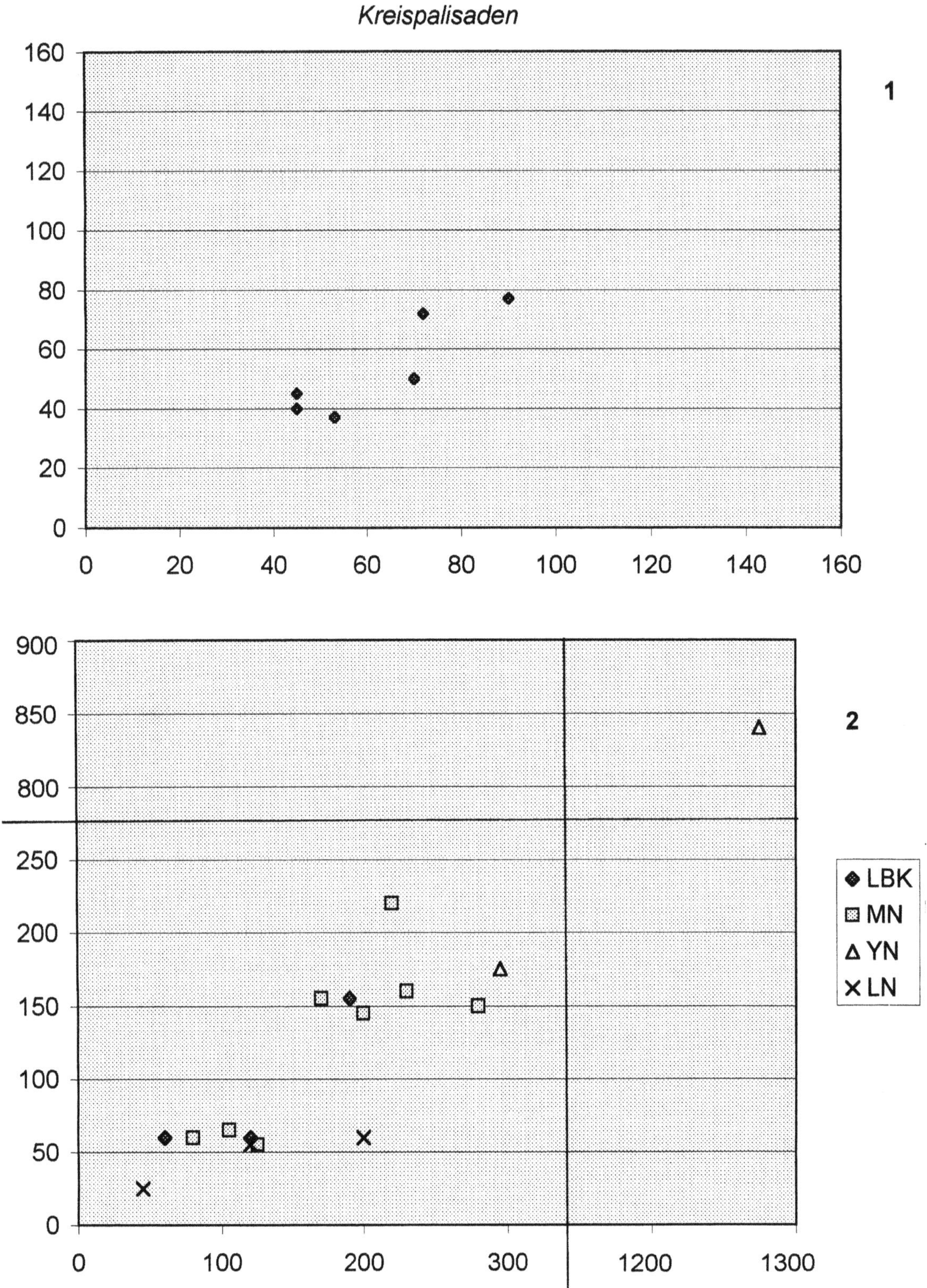

***Fig 5.6**: Length and width of Neolithic palisaded enclosures (in meters). 1 - Kreispalisadenanlagen (circular plisaded enclosures) of the late middle and early later Neolithic from Germany and France (see Appendix 1,Table 2); 2 - Non-circular palisade enclosures of the German Neolithic (see Appendix 1,Table 3-5). In some cases the measurements are estimated (for the data see lists 2-5).*

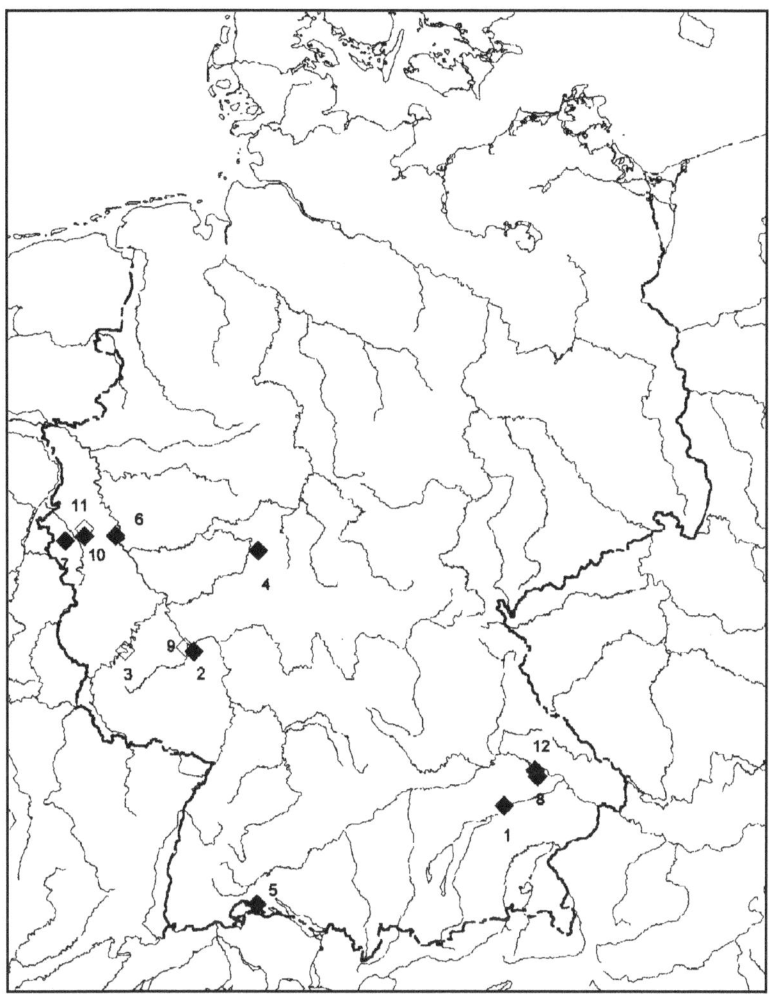

***Fig 5.7**: Palisaded enclosures of the LBK in Germany. Open symbols uncertain. See Appendix 1, Table 3.*

most all of the LBK palisades were erected on settlements (fig. 5.9) and might have surrounded the settlement, or at least greater parts of it, at a certain point in time as seems to have been the case at Sittard (Modderman 1985, 83 ff.). At Köln-Lindenthal, Bernhard (1986, Abb. 160) has suggested that the palisade enclosed no contemporary houses. This might support Lüning's (2000, 159 with fig. 55) suggestion that the larger palisade at Langweiler 2 which measured *c.*60x120m, was built outside the settlement and served the function of enclosing a small valley, probably for cattle breeding or farming[7]. A division like that suggested for the middle Neolithic *Kreisgrabenanlagen* (*i.e.* the larger ditched enclosures were associated with settlement traces and smaller ones were not) can not at present be detected among the LBK palisades.

In the middle Neolithic the distinction between *Kreispalisadenanlagen* and other palisades is obvious (fig. 5.6,1.2) and is also reflected in the differing distributions (fig. 5.5 and 10). The latter are much more widespread in the settled part of middle Neolithic Germany and are not so closely linked to the Stichbandkeramik and the SOB (*Südostbayerisches Mittelneolithikum*, see Nadler/Zeeb 1994). Among the non-circular sites, there is a small group of smaller oval enclosures (fig. 5.6,2; 11,1). These are, however, unlikely to represent a special type since at the enclosures of Hambach and Langweiler 12 there is no unequivocal evidence for an independent palisade phase. Furthermore, the small enclosure form Bad Friedrichshall is part of a larger one. Almost all of the middle Neolithic enclosures are constructed at (possibly) contemporary settlements (fig. 5.9). In Inden different fences are seen as being contemporary with the different phases of the settlement (fig. 5.11,2). In south-eastern Bavaria the palisade from Meisternthal even surrounds a *Kreisgrabenanlage* (fig. 5.11,3) and this can be paralleled at several ditched enclosures. Both features are also known, for example. from Czech and Slovac sites such as Žlkovce (Pavúk 1991) and Bylany (Pavlúk/Rulf/Zapotocká 1986, 377).

In comparing the LBK and the MN palisades, it becomes clear that, at today's state of research, hardly any differences can be identified. If one accepts the suggested function of the LBK palisades from Köln-Lindenthal and Langweiler 2, it might seem that there is a tendency towards an increase in settlement functions for the ditched enclosures of the MN. This, as postulated by Petrasch (1998, 197), might also be true for the palisades, though the evidence is rather weak. More important are the similarities. The enclosures cover roughly the same areas (fig. 5.6,1), they rarely form the earlier or later phases of a more complex system of ditch(es) and palisad(es) and they are, in almost all cases, connected with settlement features (fig. 5.9).

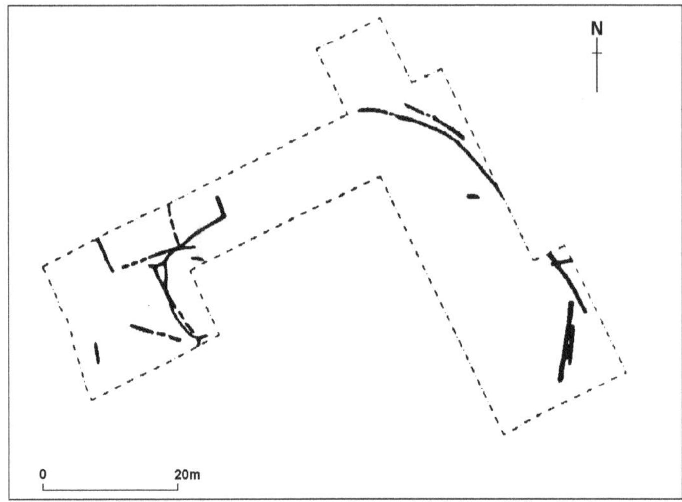

***Fig 5.8**: Examples of LBK palisades in Germany: 1 - Meindling (Appendix 1, Table 3,8); 2 - Köln-Lindenthal: phases according to Bernhard 1986 (not to scale). The palisade was erected in phase 12 and it is assumed that it did not enclose any contemporary houses*

Palisaded Enclosures, Younger and Late Neolithic

A change of these parameters takes place at the transition from the middle to the later Neolithic. The few palisaded enclosures of this time, for which the size is known, are larger (fig. 5.6,2) and almost all of them represent the initial phase of a later ditched enclosure (fig. 5.9). Their distribution also varies, as they occur only in central and western Germany (fig. 6.12). They tend towards the larger size as can be more clearly seen at the ditched enclosures (Raetzel-Fabian 1999). The frequent combination of a palisade with a later ditched enclosure is certainly largely due to the fact that, in contrast to easily detectable ditched enclosures, open, 'unfortified' settlements have not been intensively researched.

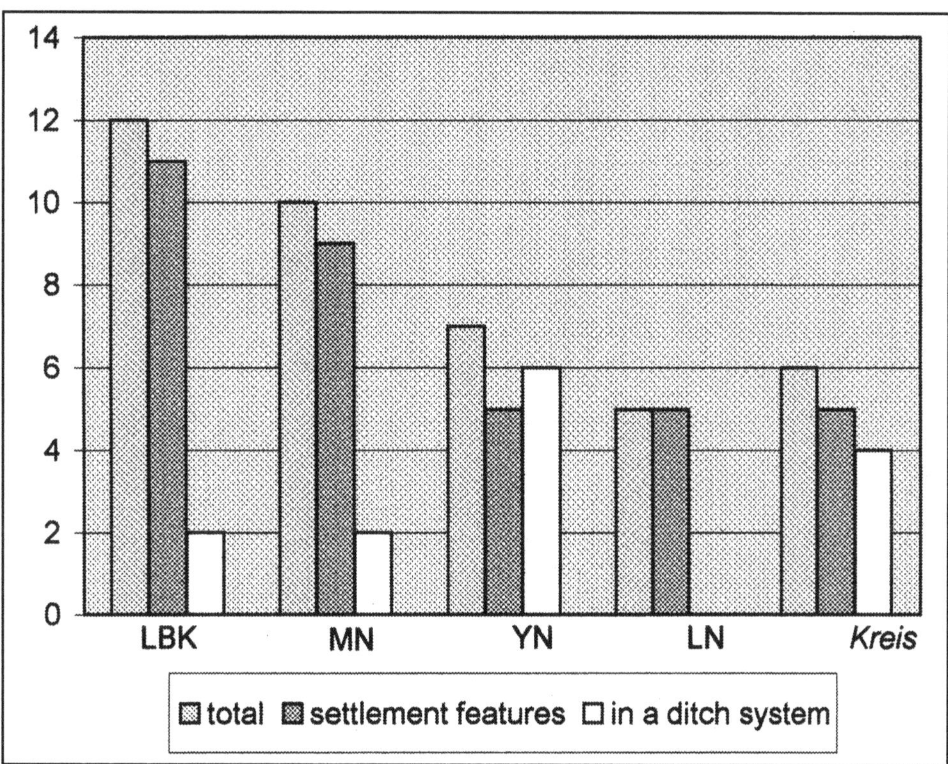

***Fig 5.9**: Diagram showing the number of palisades with associated settlements and with an earlier or later ditch system in the different periods. As far as it can be said the settlement traces inside the Kreispalisadenanlagen are not contemporary. Kreis = Kreispalisadenanlagen.*

Where research has taken place, they have often yielded only a very few settlement pits (Lüning 1998, 283 f.). Another reason that comparatively few settlement sites are known might be the undecorated nature of most of the ceramics, especially of the Michelsberg culture, which are difficult to identify among collections of surface finds. As a result we know very little about the structure of the settlements and the nature of the houses (exceptions f. e. Marolle 1998; Höhn 1991).

It is obvious that up until now the chances of finding a Michelsberg palisaded enclosure are slight unless the site is combined with a ditched enclosure. Furthermore, if a single palisade is discovered by chance there are obviously problems with the dating of the site as is the case at the only German example from Eschweiler-Würselen (Appendix1,Table 5,1). For these reasons, whether there were Michelsberg palisaded enclosures without later ditches is a question that cannot as yet be answered, but nevertheless it is striking to note that there are some documented cases where palisades form the initial phase of an enclosure (Appendix1,Table 5,3-8). A Michelsberg example of a complex enclosure with two initial palisade phases from outside Germany is the enclosure at Thiesies (Belgium). Here the two palisades enclose a much larger area than do the later ditches (Vermeersch/Walter 1978). The exact contemporaneity of the 5 palisades with the ditch at Mairy has also been discussed (Marolle 1998). Of the 4 phases of the enclosure from Noyen-sur-Seine I the initial and the final phase comprise only the palisade without the causewayed ditches of phases 2 and 3 (Mordant & Mordant 1988, fig. 13.5). Roughly from the time of the Michelsberg culture, very few examples of unditched palisades can be quoted from outside Germany. Notable examples are Jonquièrs "Le Mont d'Huette" (Chasséen) where, as at the Goldberg (Appendix1,Table 5.2), the flatter side of a hilltop was fortified with a palisade (Blanchet/Martinez 1988, 158 f.) and Tiszalúc-Sarkad (Hunyadi-halom) where a settlement was surrounded by a palisade (Patay 1990).

It is striking that the palisaded enclosures of the Michelsberg culture only occur in the north and west of the culture's distribution, but the lack of evidence in south-west Germany (for a general distribution including the ditched enclosures see Matuschik 1991, Abb. 3; 4) is possibly fortuitous. Nevertheless the distribution shows a gap towards the palisades in the wetland settlements of south-west Germany and the alpine region where, during the later Neolithic, fences or palisades around settlements

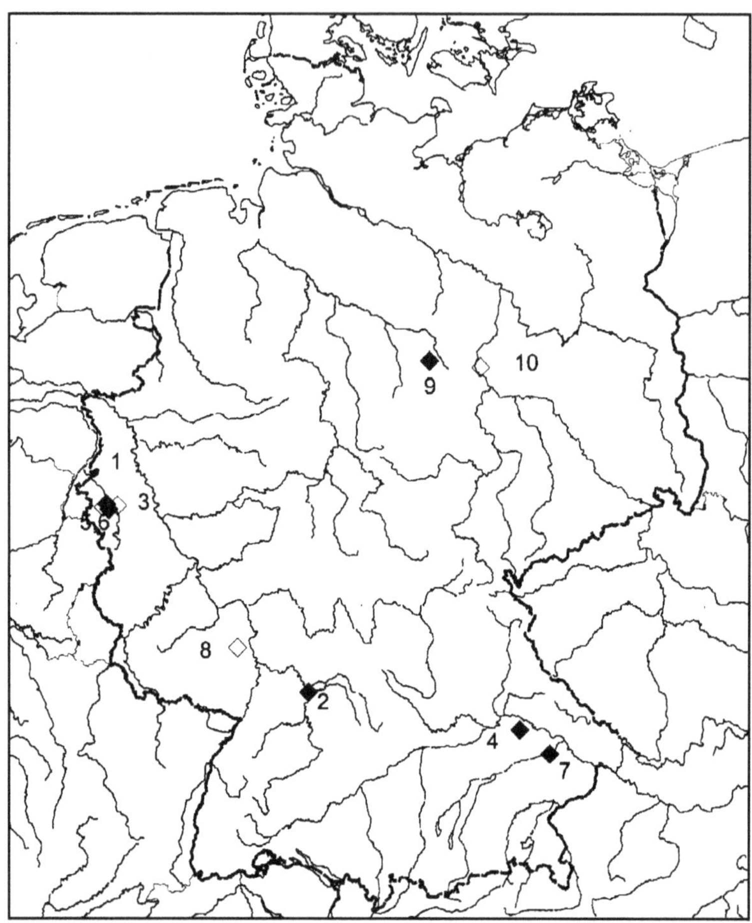

Fig 5.10: Palisade enclosures of the middle Neolithic in Germany. Open symbols uncertain. See Appendix 1,Table 4.

become more and more common (Schlichterle 1990, 211 and fig. 3; distribution: Petrasch 1998, map 11). The character of these enclosures is a matter of discussion. Whereas Petrasch (1998, 194) regards them as the boundaries of enclosed villages, Billamboz (1990, 197 with fig. 8) sees the palisades from Hornstaad-Hörnle IB not as marking the extent of the settlement area but as a reflection of the building development within the village. Hasenfratz and Gross-Klee (1995) state that the palisades are clearly not fortifications but instead can be seen as a result of successive enlargements of the settlements and, as the visible sign of a village or community, they may have had a legal function. Other functions that figure in the discussions are wind shelters, enclosures for the stockading of animals and methods of protecting stock and people from wild animals. It is interesting to see that in the Altheim culture the ditched enclosures of the dryland settlements compare well to the palisades from the wetland settlements of Pestenacker and Unfriedshausen (Matuschik 1999, 1063).

For the late and final Neolithic only very few palisaded enclosures are known and they are smaller than most of the middle and the later Neolithic ones (fig. 5.6,2). The distribution is restricted to central Germany (fig. 5.12) but this reflects the state of research. Few enclosures are known from the north German Funnel Beaker Culture (Haßmann 2000, fig. 1) and in western and south-western Germany (with the exception of the wetland area) the late Neolithic is something of a dark age (Raetzel-Fabian 1990). In the Bernburg and the Wartberg cultures these palisades are associated with hilltop settlements and can be regarded as fortifications. In two cases they comprise a combination of both ditched and palisaded elements (Appendix1,Table 5,11.12).

Timber Circles

Although the fundamental similarities are remarkable (Gibson 1998, 79), none of these Neolithic palisades can be directly compared with the rich British evidence, not least for chronological reasons in the early, middle and the first half of the later Neolithic. A closer link to British and Irish monuments is provided by the timber circle from Pevestorf, Kr. Lüchow-Dannenberg in Northern Germany (fig 5.12, star; fig. 5.14; Meyer 1993, 110 ff.). It was excavated in a sand dune above a cemetery of the late and early final Neolithic and beneath a system of ploughmarks which was in turn overlain by a cemetery of the Late Bronze Age (period IV). In the same stratigraphical position, a house and two graves were excavated. The house was dated by the deposition of a *Riesenbecher* in the very center of the building which places it in the *Spätneolithikum* in north German terminology. The graves belonged to the Únětice culture and are datable to around or probably before 2000 BC[8]. For stratigraphical reasons it is presumed that the circle also belongs to this time and there were no finds earlier than Únětice or later than period IV.

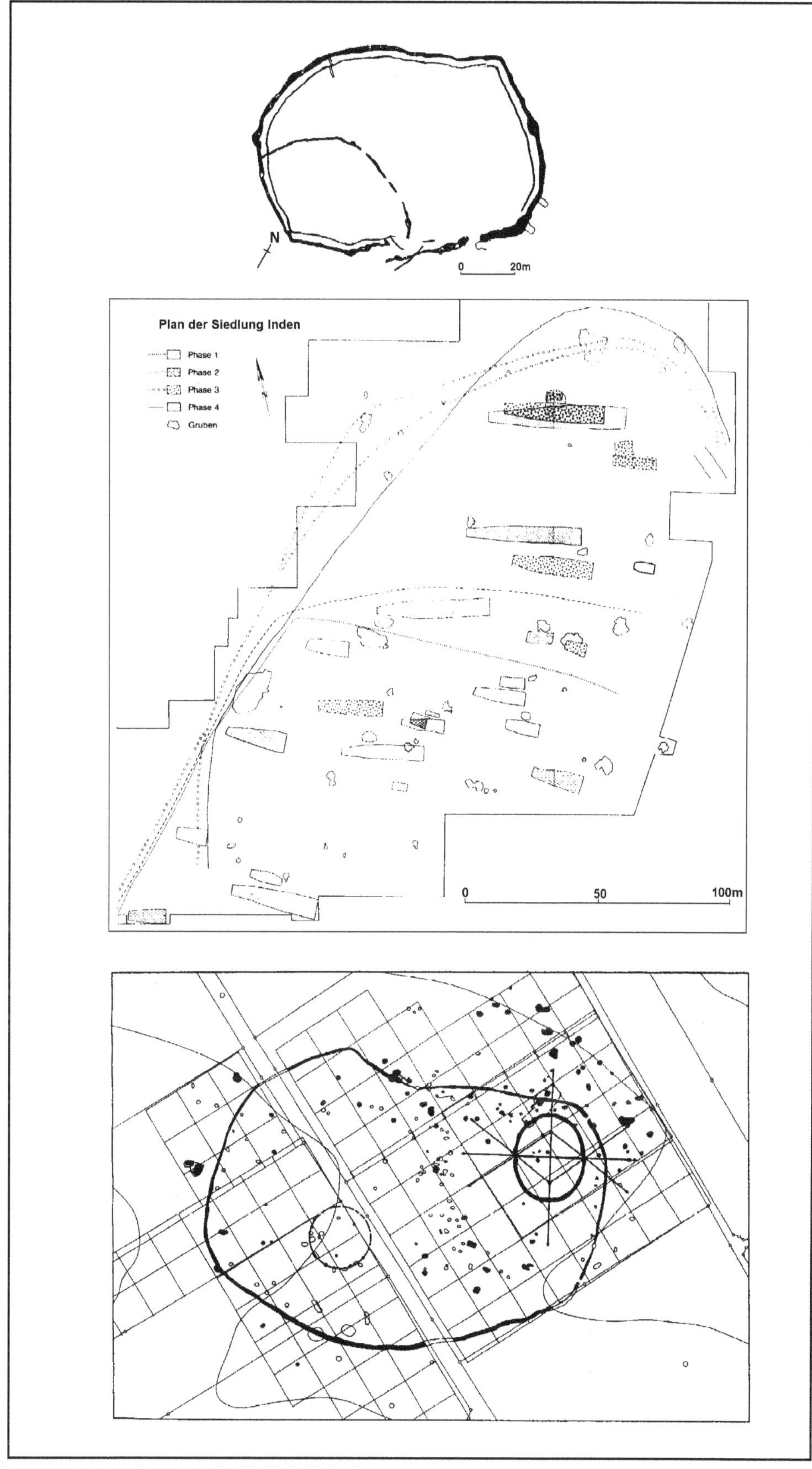

Fig 5.11: *Examples for MN palisades in Germany: 1 - Hambach 260: the excavator presumes that the palisade existed alone in the first phase; 2 - Inden; 3 - Meisternthal: the palisade encloses settlement features and an ellipsoid ditched enclosure.3 grids = 20m.*

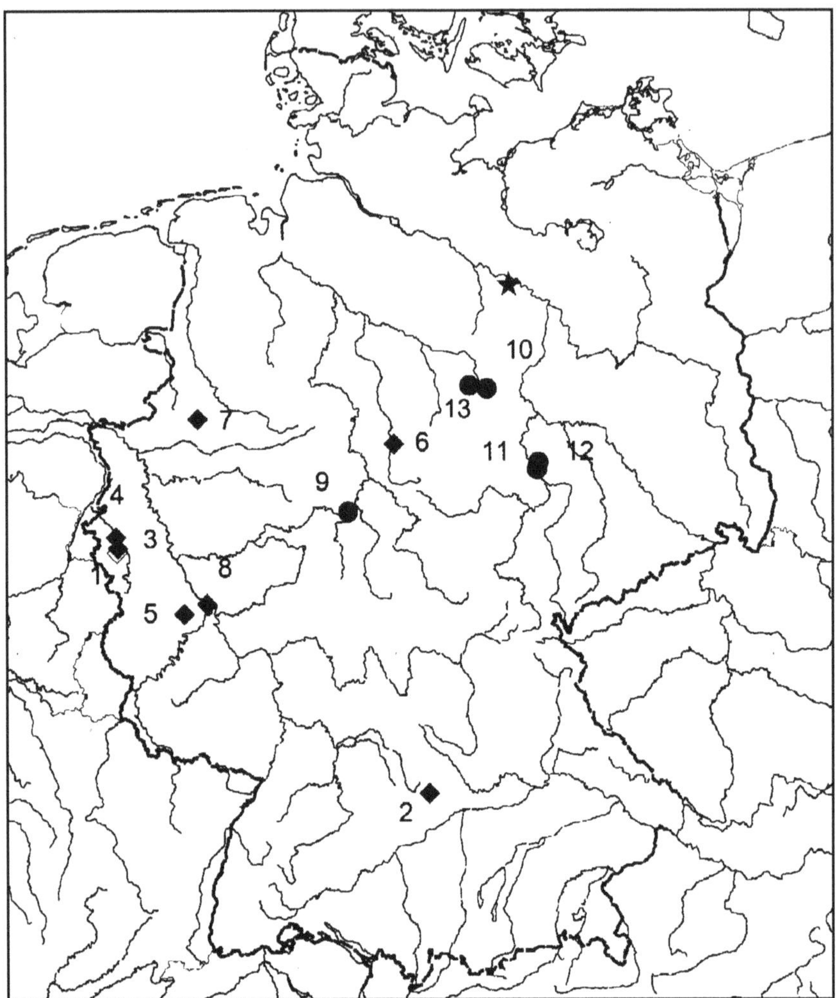

***Fig 5.12**: Palisaded enclosures of the younger Neolithic (◆) and the late- and final Neolithic (●) in Germany. Open symbols uncertain. See Appendix 1,Table 5. ★: final Neolithic/early Bronze Age timber circle from Pevestorf, Kr. Lüchow-Dannenberg.*

The circle measures *c.*13m in diameter and has an entrance marked by four stronger posts in the south. The two graves of the Únětice culture lie to the west of the entrance. None of the features inside of the circle are clearly associated with it and Laux's (1997, 757) assumption that the circle was erected around the cremation grave KbK 7 is not convincing[9]. The exceptional stratigraphical evidence at this site makes it clear that the circle did not originally surround a burial mound as can be paralleled elsewhere in the final Neolithic and the Bronze Age. This is because the mound would have had to have been destroyed completely before the ploughing which took place prior to period IV (*c.*1000BC). The closest parallels to this circle are the timber circles of Great Britain and Ireland that occur at about the same time. These may also be about the same size and some of them even have similarly marked entrances. The diagram given by Gibson (1994, fig. 40) shows that the single circular ones with a diameter between 10 and 20 m mainly belong to the period 2500 - 2000 BC or (in lesser quantity) 2000 - 1000 BC, and this fits well the proposed dates for the Pevestorf circle.

How can this be explained? Direct contact over such a long distance seems unlikely, especially as the cultural context of the graves, assuming that they are connected with the circle, suggests contacts with the south-east. Until recently, hardly any comparable continental parallels could be cited. The excavations at Zwolle, however, demonstrate what might be discovered on settlement sites, but this free-standing site is also unique in the Netherlands (de Jong 1998). The function of the Pevestorf circle also remains unclear. There were no finds that might hint at a special explanation, and the uneven shape of the circle and the plan of the entrance do not encourage astronomic or calendar interpretations. It defined a round area, which could be seen from the outside through the gaps between the posts (assuming that there was no form of walling between the posts). One could have entered through any of the gaps, yet the intended entrance was clearly marked. The circle probably did have something to do with the two burials, but we do not know whether the burials attracted the circle or the circle attracted the burials. The burials themselves give no further hints. It is striking that as many as 5 skulls had been laid on the base of grave K8, however there are many parallels for this practice that can be cited from cemeteries of the Únětice culture (Meyer 1993, 109). The ceremonies of 4000 years ago still remain unclear.

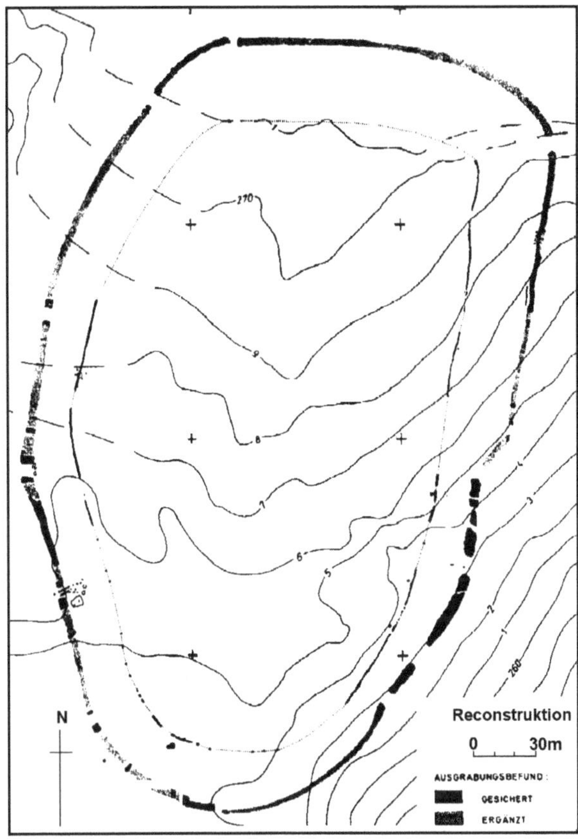

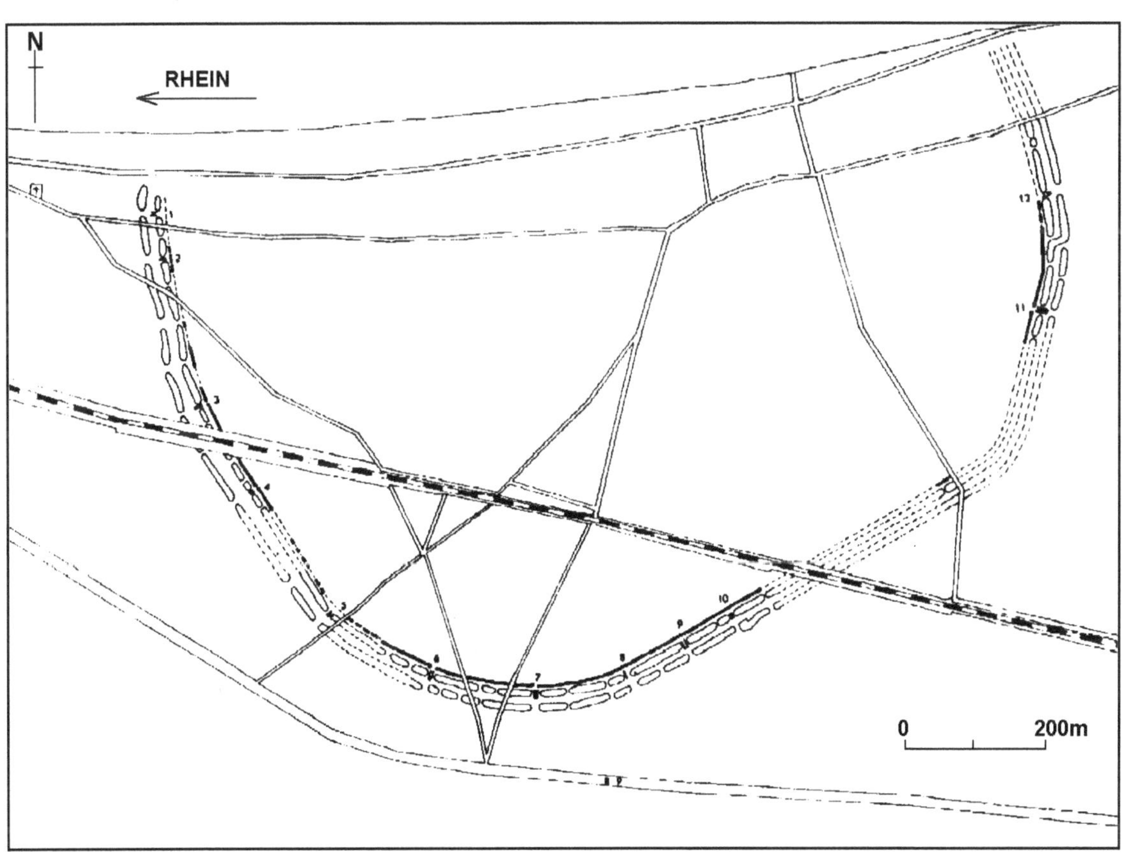

***Fig 5.13**: Enclosures of the later Neolithic with the palisade enclosure presumed to be an initial phase. 1 - Mayen (Appendix 1,Table 5,4); 2 - Urmitz (Appendix 1,Table 5,7), transition middle to later Neolithic (Bischheim). Different scales.*

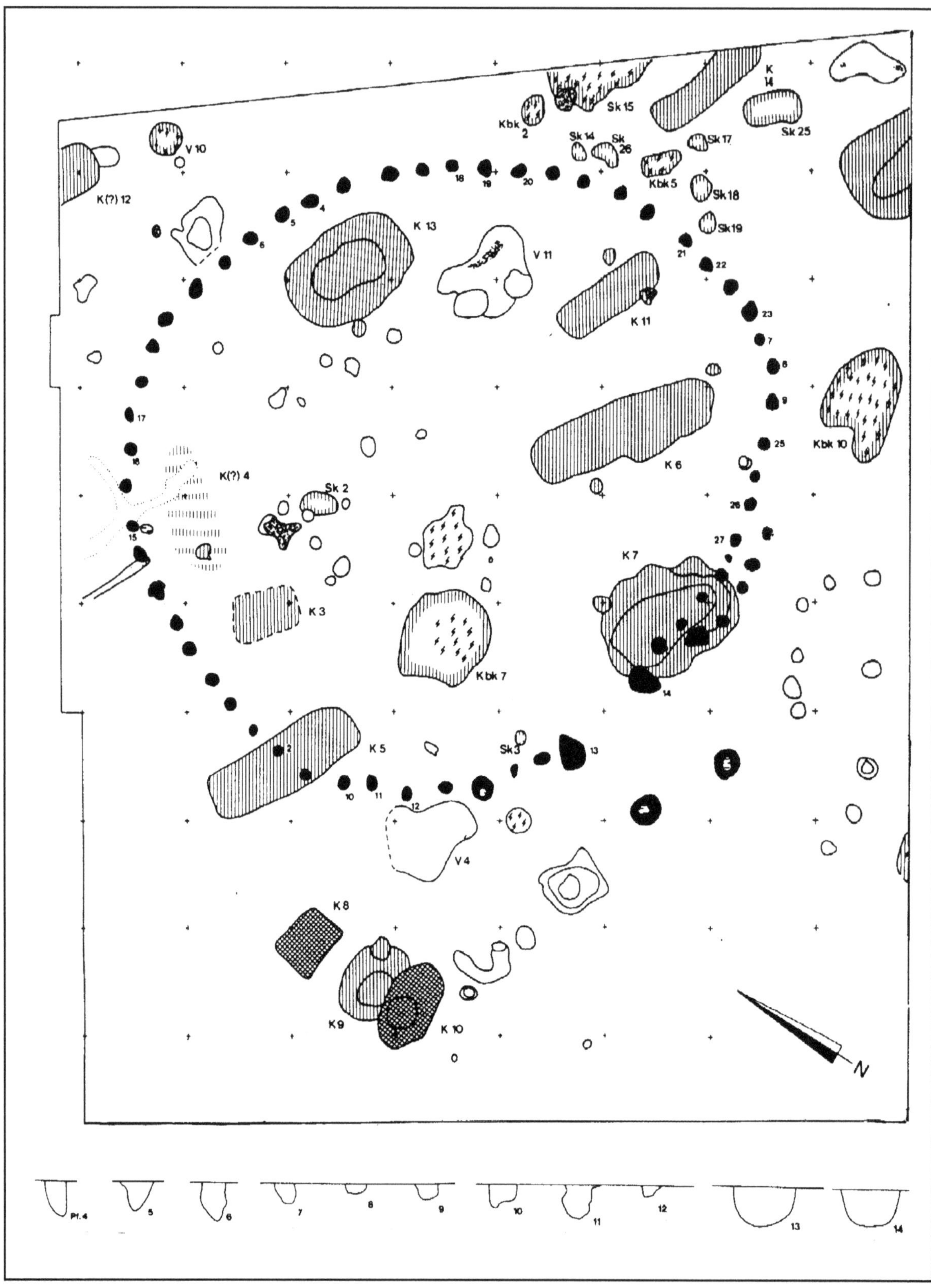

***Fig 5.14**: Timber circle of the final Neolithic/early Bronze Age from Pevestorf, Kr. Lüchow-Dannenberg with recorded sections of the posts (Meyer 1993, plan 1 and pl. 96). Black: posts of the circle; cross filling: Graves of the Únětice culture (K 8, K 10); filled with lines: inhumation of the globular amphorae culture. KbK - cremation graves of the gobular amphorae/Schönfeld culture; SK - concentration of sherds belonging to this cemetery; unfilled features are undated. Scale: 1:100, post-sections 1:50.*

CONCLUSION

In summing up, it has to be emphasised that the palisaded enclosures of the German Neolithic display the same steps of development as the ditched enclosures. As far as we can see there are no palisade forms which do not also occur as a ditched enclosure. On the other hand certain developments within the ditched enclosures are not followed by the palisades. The group of smaller ditched enclosures of the LBK, and from which the *Kreisgrabenanlagen* are derived, do not exist simply as palisades. The *Kreispalisadenanlagen* are restricted to a later part of the middle Neolithic than are the *Kreisgrabenanlagen* and continue into the beginning of the later Neolithic. This means that, according to current knowledge, the circular palisades have to be regarded as being independent of the development of the ditched enclosures. On the other hand, of the twelve later and final Neolithic palisades the fact that only some of the forms of the ditched enclosures are associated with palisades seems to be fortuitous and a result of to the low number of palisaded sites involved.

The general similarities between ditched enclosures and palisades are not only evident in their layout but also in their position in the landscape and their connection with settlements. Ditches can enclose settlements both in the LBK and the MN, and settlement traces within the enclosure ditches are also encountered in the later and final Neolithic. The *Kreisgrabenanlagen* mainly lack contemporary internal settlement features, and similarly in the *Kreispalisadenanlagen* the internal settlement features do not seem to be contemporary with the perimeter.

A chronological development from individual post holes (from the beginning of the 4th millenium BC onwards) to closely spaced postpits and then to palisade trenches as has been postulated for Britain (Gibson 1998, 73) can not be demonstrated at the German palisades. As far as the publications show, sketchy though some publications are, both trenches and individual post pits are known from the LBK and the MN, whereas generally palisade trenches were dug in the later (exception: Northeim-Kiessee, Appendix1,Table 5,5) and final Neolithic.

Why were some Neolithic enclosures constructed using palisades and others with ditches? One explanation given by Petrasch concerns the shift from the circular ditch and palisade system in Künzing-Unternberg to a circular palisaded enclosure. He sees this change as a reflection of a lack of manpower to renew the old enclosure. The settlement communities in the vicinity that had helped in the construction of the *Kreisgrabenanlage* had now shaken off their dependency and no longer wanted to take part in the rebuilding. The fact that a circular palisade was built shows a certain conservatism as the prime intention of the remaining builders was clearly the erection of something as similar as possible to the old *Kreisgrabenanlage* (Petrasch 1998, 192). It is also very possible that a change in the social system lead to a 'low-level-solution'. If this was the case, then it might be expected that a ditched enclosure without a palisade might have been built. This is because the time-estimations for the construction of the enclosure suggest that the 2 palisades would have been much more labour-intensive than the excavation of the ditches (Petrasch 1990, 499 f.).

It is interesting that the ditches of the *Kreisgrabenanlagen* were generally dug with an extreme V-shaped section so that an approaching person could not see the bottom of the ditch which therefore seemed bottomless (Petrasch 1990, 449). This aspect was obviously so important that the ditches were re-excavated several times. This can be seen especially well at Künzing-Unternberg (Petrasch 1998, 195). What the middle Neolithic people looking into these 'bottomless' ditches imagined to be down there, unseen, deep in the earth is beyond our ken. The renunciation of these ditches and a change to palisades certainly had a symbolic meaning. Whatever this meaning may have been, the main feature of the enclosed circular space did not change. Most authors presume that it was used as a meeting place for whatever purposes and not as a fortified area (but see recently Němejcová-Pavúková 1995, 215).

Whereas among the *Kreisgrabenanlagen* there is a probable shift from ditched to palisaded enclosures (but see the later exception Riekofen: Appendix1,Table 2,5), on the larger ditched palisaded enclosures, especially those of the later Neolithic, the palisades were obviously built before the ditches. Taking the example of the Beusterburg in Lower Saxony, Raetzel-Fabian suggests a primary palisade parallel with which earthworks were constructed and other activities took place. The result of this lead to the causewayed enclosure with ramparts (Raetzel-Fabian 1998, 102)[10]. This hypothesis, that the palisades acted as marking-out lines for the earth works which in turn resulted in the ditched enclosure is not very probable in the cases summarised in Appendix1,Table 5. This is because of the essential differences in the overall ground-plans and the model given by Raetzel-

Fabian which sees the primary erection of the palisade is difficult to prove and no certain case is known to the present writer.

This is a pity as it would be important to know whether the builders of the palisade had already planned the ditch and therefore whether there was an existing overall plan of the complete enclosure when its first phase, the palisade, was built. This does not seem very likely, at least in the cases where the layouts differ, and furthermore there also seem to be palisades which lack a later ditch system. This has consequences for the interpretations of the ditched enclosures and the activities connected with the filling and recutting of the ditch. In the cases where an independent palisade already existed the builders of the ditched enclosure were not free in their choice of place. It was not the various aspects of the landscape and relief that influenced the builders, but the position of the palisade. This means that in these cases the usage of the ditches and the topographical situation need not be necessarily connected.

It is striking that at the German palisaded enclosures with later ditch systems, no human bones have been found in the ditches even although this is very common among Michelsberg ditched enclosures. The existence of bones in Belgian and French enclosures with primary palisades (Nickel 1997, 133 ff.) makes it likely that the absence in Germany is due to the state of research. Whether the processes of ditch filling that led to discoveries such as the concentrations of sherds and other finds at the ditch terminals of Mayen (Eckert 1992, 89 ff.) were also performed at palisaded enclosures cannot yet be determined as the original ground surfaces are nearly always missing.

Reasons for the preference for building palisades rather than digging ditches can not as yet be satisfactorily given. With the exception of Mayen all other palisaded enclosures of the German Neolithic[11] could have been settlement enclosures, even if this can not be proved beyond doubt in every case. To the contrary, the question of function can not be answered that easily for the ditched enclosures. As a result, the question has to be turned round and we must ask why did they dig a ditch (and erect a palisade and rampart) instead of just constructing a palisade? Futhermore, it can be shown that the alternative type of site, a simple palisade, was known and used in almost every phase of the German Neolithic.

Footnotes

1 The terms older Neolithic (*Altneolithikum*), middle Neolithic (*Mittelneolithikum*) younger Neolithic (*Jungneolithikum*) and late Neolithic (*Spätneolithikum*) are used here according to Lüning 1996. In Northern Germany a different system is in use (see Lüning 1996, Abb. 1), and in Central Germany also the system f. e. published by Behrens (1973, Abb. 72) is still used.

2 Also here a regular shifting of the palisade rings is possible, as maybe Petrasch's (1990, 561 Abb. 24) interpretation of the *Kreisgrabenanlage* from Vochov (Pavlě 1982, Abb. 1) shows.

3 Independent palisades within ditched enclosures of different phases are given as 'Erdwerk with Palisade' by Petrasch. Unfortunately no lists for the distribution maps were printed. The manuscripts for this handbook were submitted at the end of the 1980's.

4 The late bronze age metal finds however - which should be more or less contemporary with the ceramics - only come from the upper fillings. The final publication of the ceramics and the C14-dates are awaited. - The Räpitz enclosure has a palisade between the ditches which is rare in the middle Neolithic examples.

5 Enclosures where a missing gate in the palisade is only suggested by geographical prospection like Ramsdorf (Becker 1990, Abb. 8) and Osterhofen-Schmiedorf (Becker 1998, fig. 5) are not included here. Whether the circular enclosure from Kyhna with four concentric ditches really does consist only of palisade trenches (Ausgr.- u. Forschber. Sächs. Bodendenkmalpfl. 37, 1995, 220) is not yet clear as it is only known from aerial photographs.

6 The enclosure from Buĕany (Pavúk 1991, 349 f.) does not seem to have an independent palisade-phase (*contra* Lefranc/Jeunesse 1998, 68), as the palisade and the ditches including the very particular construction of the gates share the same scheme of construction.

7 It should be kept in mind that two houses were excavated inside the suggested palisade and that the central part of the interior remains unexcavated.

8 The pre-classic Aunjetitz cup from one of the graves can no longer be used to provide a precise date since recent C14-dates show that the perceived different 'chronological' phases are, in fact, contemporary (Müller 1999, 24).

9 Laux (1997, 754 ff.) has suggested that the cremation graves of the globular amphora culture and the (early) Schönfeld culture from Pevestorf should be dated to the Single Grave Culture and would form an independent cemetery of which the Únĕtice graves would be the youngest. This is surprising as there are no secure finds of the Single Grave Culture on the site. The ceramics found in the cremation graves belong to the globular amphorae/ Bernburg/Schönfeld culture, and the complete amphora from cremation grave 1 shows that they can not all be reworked (Meyer 1993, Taf. 104,1; without taking the published photograph of the complete amphora into consideration Laux (1997, 756) assumed that it had been in sherds). Besides this no cremation grave cuts an inhumation burial - due to the excellent excavation technique with many documented recuttings in the inhumation burials such features would certainly have been identified.

10 On the other hand, the excavator saw palisade, ditch and rampart as contemporary (Tackenberg 1951, 25), therefor the enclosure is not listed in Appendix1,Table 5. Because of the smallness of the excavated areas it is unclear whether the palisade encloses the whole area (ibd., 3).

11 With the exception of the *Kreispalisadenanlagen*. - In Langweiler 12 (where no settlement features were found inside the enclosure) it is not clear whether the palisade really existed alone, and in Köln-Lindenthal and Langweiler 2 it remains questionable as to whether there really were no houses inside the palisade during its lifetime. Even the suggested function of the reconstructed palisade in Langweiler 2 as an enclosure for cattle breeding or farming may be regarded as directly connected with the settlement.

APPENDIX 1

LIST OF PALISADES

Table 1: Fences Inside LBK & MN Settlements			
No	**Name**	**Description**	**Reference**
1	Altdorf, Kr. Landshut	MLBK-settlement with 'fence-like post rows'. This exceptional settlement was largely destroyed by erosion but is not yet published. Large-scale excavation	Meixner 1998, 28
2	Bedburg-Garsdorf, Kr. Bergheim-Erft	Two post rows which lead from the western corner of house 2 to the northwest and to the southwest, probably a fence-system of house 2. MLBK-JLBK, partially excavated.	Piepers 1974, 146; 149 Abb. 2, 170 f
3	Bochum-Altenbochum, Stadt Bochum	Three sides of a rectangular fence north of house II (or northwest of house I?), two lines with rows of three posts inside, presumed by the excavator to have supported a roof. This presumption is not unequivocal and it might as well be possible, that parts of the 'fence' are in fact parts of another house (?). LBK. Partially excavated.	Brandt 1967, 64 & Taf. 9.
4	Gerlingen, Kr. Ludwigsburg	two smaller fenced enclosures, starting at the western corner of house 14 and 19, to which they belong. ELBK. Large scale excavation, fences partly at the edge of the excavated area.	Neth 1999, 76 f.
5	Hilzingen-Forsterbahn	(see: palisades): fences, ELBK-JLBK.	
6	Langweiler 8, Kr. Düren	The excavators describe 15 parts of fences and some small narrow ditches, which all lie in the northern (*i.e.* older) part of the settlement. In no case can the form of the enclosure be reconstructed, but in three cases the fences seem to belong to a house (1, 10, 13) and start at their northwest-corner. ELBK-JLBK. Large-scale excavation. Langweiler 2: at least some of the parts of the fences described above did probably belong to short fences.	Boelicke & v. Brandt 1988, 299; Boelicke 1988, 435 ff.
7	Meindling, Kr. Straubing-Bogen	(see: palisades): small fence systems. Possibly ÄLBK.	
8	Ulm-Eggingen, Stadt Ulm	One row of postholes which goes in a regular bow from the northeastern corner of house 6 to the southeast, and one system of a narrow ditch that belongs to house 12. MLBK. Large scale excavation.	Kind 1989
9	Vaihingen/Enz, Kr. Ludwigsburg	Settlement surrounded by a ditched enclosure with palisades; the palisades are included in a fence system that defines the settlement. Complete excavation planned.	Krause 1998.
10	Zwenkau-Harth, Kr. Leipziger Land	Fence, partly with two rows of postholes, starting at the wall of a house and moving around it, probably disturbed by a later house. JLBK. Partly excavated.	Höckmann 1990, 24.

No	Name	Description	Reference
11	Bochum-Hiltrop, Stadt Bochum	Quadrangular arrangement of postholes of 38 x 13m and18m. To the eastern side of an extraordinarily long house, east of this a second trapezoid area of 38 x 48 and 42m, spacing of the posts 2m. Rössen, partially excavated.	Brandt 1967, 65 and pl. 13; Germania 1954, 260 ff.
12	Dresden-Nickern, Stadt Dresden	Farmsteads, in some cases their fences were also excavated. StBK, large scale excavation.	Kurz 1994, 25.
13	Rinkam, Kr. Straubing-Bogen	StBK-house with fence. Partially excavated, not yet published.	Engelhardt 1995, 34.
14	Straubing-Lerchenhaid, Stadt Straubing	Fence, starting at the northwestern corner of a StBK-house, not extensively seen during excavation. Large scale excavation.	Brink-Kloke 1992, Abb. 1.8

Table 2: *Kreispalisadenanlagen* (Circular Palisaded Enclosures) MN & JN			
No	**Name**	**Description**	**Reference**
1	Dresden-Nickern, Stadt Dresden	*Kreisgrabenanlage*, the palisade is not interrupted behind both excavated causeways of the ditch. StBK, Large scale excavation.	Kurz 1994
2	Eythra, Kr. Leipzig	Completely excavated *Kreisgrabenanlage*, the palisade was preserved only at two causeways. At one causeway (south-east) the palisade shows no interruption. StBK.	Stäuble 1999
3	Künzing-Unternberg, Kr. Deggendorf	Double circular ditch with 5 inner palisade rings. As the centre of the three inner rings and their gates differ from those of the ditches and as the distance towards the two outer palisades is unusually great an independent *Kreispalisadenanlage* is presumed. It is regarded as later as it disturbs two pits in contrast to the ditches and the outer palisade where no such situation can be discerned. Also the oldest finds which correspond to the oldest 14C dates come from the ditch floor of the *Kreisgrabenanlage*. Partially excavated. MN.	Petrasch/Kromer 1989, 235; Petrasch 1990, 486 f.; Petrasch 1998, 192.
4	Quenstedt, Kr. Mansfelder Land, Schalkenburg	5 concentric palisades, the outer two not complete. Large scale excavation. Probably JStBK, one sherd from the third palisade proably Baalberge. One 14C date 5660 ± 65 BP(KN 2864) =. 4544-4404 cal. BC (1 sigma) rsp. 4682-4353 cal. BC (2 sigma).	Behrens & Schröter 1980; Behrens 1981; Schröter 1989.
5	Riekofen, Kr. Regensburg-Land	Probably elipsoid palisade inside a larger oval ditched enclosure, disturbed by a later *Kreisgrabenanlage*. Because of the latter the original form of the palisade can not be reconstructed beyond doubt. Late Münchhöfen and Polling (= EJN). Partially excavated.	Becker & Tillmann 1995, 39
6	Wittenheim (Haut-Rhin)	Circular palisade with long entrance. Rössen III. Large scale excavation	Lefranc & Jeunesse 1998

TABLE 3: LBK Palisades			
No	**Name**	**Description**	**Reference**
1	Altdorf, Kr. Landshut	30 m long, slightly curved palisade ditch with one interruption. MLBK and JLBK, but also some StBK. Contemporary settlement pits inside and out. Small area excavated.	Höckmann 1990, Nr. 5
2	Aspisheim, Kr. Mainz-Bingen	Palisade ditch, LBK.	Höckmann 1990, Nr. 33
3	Bernkastel-Kues, Kr. Bernkastel-Wittlich	In the area of a MLBK and JLBK settlement. One palisade ditch with traces of postholes, straight for the whole excavated length of 68m, in one place a second ditch branching off, which could not be excavated any further. Depth up to 1.80m. Probably intrusive medieval sherds in the uppermost filling of the ditch. In the lower filling LBK sherds. Dating of the palisade uncertain. Partly excavated.	Kilian 1956/58, 46; Gollub 1967, 27; 32 Abb. 8; Schmidgen-Hager 1993, 205
4	Großseelheim, Kr. Marburg-Biedenkopf	At the border of the area of an ELBK-MLBK-settlement and close to the slope towards the lowland. Four to five narrow and partly parallel ditches, which often show traces of posts in their sections. „A reconstruction as parts of fences or palisade ditches has to be considered“ (Höhn 1992/93, 12 ff.). Partly excavated.	Höhn 1992/93, 12 ff.
5	Hilzingen-Forsterbahn, Kr. Konstanz	Three more or less strongly curved fences close to each other (length. 15m max) and one more fence probably belonging to one house (not clearly to be seen on the plan). It is quite certain that long parts of the fences were destroyed by erosion. The settlement dates from ÄLBK to JLBK	Dieckmann & Fritsch 1990, 32
6	Köln-Lindenthal, Stadt Köln	Oval palisade of about 190 x 155m, which belongs to the LBK settlement and is dated probably to the beginning of JLBK (Köln-Lindenthal phase 12). That would mean that it is older than the different ditches. Partly destroyed by erosion. Completely excavated.	Bernhard 1990, 347 ff.
7	Langweiler 2, Kr. Düren	Parts of 'fences and palisades', inside and outside the ELBK and JLBK settlement. The posts were *c.*1m away from each other. The longest part of the fence was 11m. „It is striking, however, that overall the stretches of fencing appear to delineate a roughly rectilinear grid covering 200m or more“ (Whittle 1988, 97 mit Abb. 3.29). Lüning (2000, 159) sees palisades and fence-systems which cover rectangular or polygonal areas with a length of, as far as can be seen, 60-120m. These lead out of the settlement and include a hollow that leads to the river. Large scale excavation.	Kuper 1973, 50.

No	Name	Description	Reference
8	Meindling, Kr. Straubing-Bogen	Oval palisaded enclosure of about 60m in diameter on an LBK settlement, but also smaller fence/palisade systems. Possibly ÄLBK. Half of it excavated.	Höckmann 1990, Nr. 9.
9	Münster-Sarmsheim, Kr. Mainz-Bingen	U-sectioned, steep-sided ditch 0.75-080m wide at the base. Slanting profile in the upper part, width at the top 1.80-2.00m. Contrary to the post-walls inside the ditches as described by Ihmig (1971) it can be assumed here that because of the width of the base and the steep lower profile the ditch was originally a palisade ditch the edges of which later collapsed and therefore produced a v-shaped profile. Settlement features inside. LBK. Partially excavated.	Lehner 1917, 119 with Taf. VIII.
10	Niederzier-Steinstraß, Kr. Düren	In a settlement area with a length of 20m (from edge to edge of the excavated area) slightly curved palisade ditch with posts also in front of it, obviously at regular distances from each other. JLBK.	Höckmann 1990, Nr. 41.
11	Rödingen, Kr. Jülich	Unpublished excavations in a LBK settlement showed a palisade of 12m length. According to Lüning 1988, 158 Anm. 4 uncertain.	Rhein. Ausgr. 19, 1979, 349
12	Staubing-Lerchenhaid, Stadt Straubing	One longer row of postholes, slightly curved. Obviously not a house wall, as the opposite wall is missing. Settlement features inside and outside. LBK or StBK.	Brink-Kloke 1992, 11 mit Abb. 1

TABLE 4: MN Palisades

No	Name	Description	Reference
1	Aldenhoven, Kr. Düren	According to the excavator two palisade ditches, although the ditches are unusually broad. Inside there are houses. Each palisade with one interruption; as the settlement is only partly excavated it is possible that the palisades enclosed a large area. Rössen.	Jürgens 1979, 397 ff. and Abb. 2.
2	Bad Friedrichshall, Kr. Heilbronn	MN settlement which was enclosed by two palisade ditches (distance: 1.5m) of oval form, 170 x 155m. On the inside, at a distance of 12m, a weaker palisade with similarly orientated gates. The inner palisade is split up in the southwest and encloses a smaller area of 55 x 125m, inside of which is an extraordinary number of boat-shaped houses. Hinkelstein to 'fully developed' Rössen. Large scale excavation.	Biel 1991.
3	Hambach 260, Kr. Düren	Oval ditched enclosure and palisade (105 x 65m), houses inside and outside. In the publication there are differing statements about the contemporaneity of the ditch and the palisade: either it was built earlier and was not contemporary (Dohrn-Ihmig 1983, 19) or it was built earlier but was mainly contemporary with the ditch (ibd., 21). It remains unclear, if a second, slightly curved and partly excavated ditch represents a ditch or a palisade trench. Großgartach/Planig-Friedberg.	Dohrn-Ihmig 1983.
4	Haimbuch, Kr. Regensburg	Short part of a palisade ditch within an MN cemetery.	Bayer. Vorgeschbl. 54, 1989, 42; 64.
5	Inden 1, Kr. Düren	5 different fences, of which some show double posts which allow a reconstruction as a post and stake wall. The settlement was enclosed by a fence during all its phases. Min. 280 x 150m. Late Rössen.	Kuper/Lüning 1975, 95 with Beil. 2.
6	Langweiler 12, Kr. Düren	Oval palisade and ditch system (palisade: 80 x 60m), in the publication the different positions of the interruptions (5m) is seen to suggest a different age for the palisade and ditch (Dohrn-Ihmig 1983). Completely excavated, no settlement traces inside.	Dohrn-Ihmig 1983.
7	Meisternthal, Stadt Landau, Kr. Dingolfing-Landau	Oval palisade of 230 x 160m with a northeastern gate. Encloses a MN 'ellipse' and a small circular ditch. Small scale excavation. Earlier than Oberlauterbach.	Becker & Kreiner 1993.

No	Name	Description	Reference
8	Monsheim, Kr. Alzey-Worms	Curved palisade ditch, preserved for a distance of *c*.280m. The dating is unclear. According to Schumacher (1921, Abb. 11) settlement pits from the inside belong mainly to the 'Rössener Stufe', very little also to the 'Michelsberger Stufe' and, on both sides of the palisade, to the 'Spiralkeramik' (=LBK). The size of the excavation is unclear.	Schumacher 1921, 34 ff. Abb. 11.
9	Schöningen, Kr. Helmstedt	Slightly curved palisade ditch, very flat, 60m still preserved. Internal houses. Rössen. Large scale excavation.	Jahresschr. Mitteldt. Vorgesch. 73, 1990, 364; Thieme & Maier 1995, 130 mit S. 125, Abb 118.
10	Wahlitz, Kr. Jerichower Land, Taubenberg	Enclosure, partly as a ditch (with a Rössen sherd), partly as a palisade (disturbed by a final Neolithic grave). According to the excavated area it may have a diameter of about 220m, but this is hard to tell. Inside (irregular) Rössen houses.	Schmidt 1970, 90 f. und Beil. 5.

TABLE 5: JN AND LN/EN Palisades			
No	**Name**	**Description**	**Reference**
1	Eschweiler-Würselen, Kr. Aachen	Excavated area of 230 x 17 m, slightly curved palisade ditch, no traces of a ditched enclosure. Unfortunately no datable finds from the palisade, but according to the excavators its fill was identical to the fills of the surrounding pits of the Michelsberg culture.	Tichelmann & Trier 1995
2	Goldburghausen, Ostalbkreis, Goldberg	The Goldberg I settlement on the hilltop (*c.*200 x 145m) is enclosed by a palisade on the easily approachable western side. Large scale excavation.	Schröter 1975, 103 f. and Beil. 4.
3	Inden 9, Kr. Düren	Small-scale excavation of a ditched enclosure. Internal palisade ditch (with slight traces of a second). The distance between palisade and ditch differs for a short distance of between 1.6-6m. At the only positive causeway through the ditch the palisade has no gate. As the distance between ditch and palisade is in places extremely small, the palisade must be older than the ditch, particularly if there was an internal rampart. Michelsberg II, in the upper fill also Michelsberg II and IV.	Höhn 1997a.
4	Koslar 10, Kr. Düren	Two palisades in different techniques (split timber and round posts), both partially destroyed by a later ditch. Internal settlement traces and 'fragments from Michelsberg houses' (Eckert 1990a, 405). In both palisades the postholes were filled with finds and charcoal, so that it can be assumed that the posts and planks were removed before the ditch was dug. The flints from the palisades are similar to the settlement material but differ from the ditch material so it is likely that settlement material found its way into the postholes after the removal of the posts. Small scale excavation. Michelsberg I/II.	Höhn 1997.
5	Mayen, Kr. Mayen-Koblenz	Oval palisade of *c.*290 x 175m inside a ditch enclosure, 12–35m distance to the ditch. The differing distance between the palisade and the ditch, the lack of conformity between the entrances of the palisade and the ditch, and the finding of older artefacts in the palisade (Michelsberg I/II), make it certain that the palisade was erected first and existed alone. Large scale excavation.	Eckert 1990.

No	Name	Description	Reference
6	Northeim, Stadt Northeim, Kiessee	Ditched enclosure with three ditches (Michelsberg II and III), probably two phases. Internal palisade at a distance of 18m though only a small area excavated. The excavator envisages a small building on the outer side of the palisade. A break in the ditch has no corresponding break in the palisade. 'Because of its isolated position in the inside of the enclosure is possible that the palisade existed before the digging of the ditches.	Viemeier 1998.
7	Nottuln, Kr. Coesfeld	Palisade ditch with secure traces of single posts at a distance of 45m from a ditch, excavated only in a narrow section. The size of the enclosure is unclear. The palisade can only be dated to the Michelsberg culture in general terms, the ditch is Michelsberg III.	Eckert 1986; Eckert 1990a.
8	Urmitz, Kr. Mayen-Koblenz	Semi-circular enclosure directly adjacent to the present channel of the river Rhine, 1275 x 840m with an inner palisade ditch and two outer ditches. Palisade closed at several breaks in the ditches and therefor it is probable that it is not contemporary with the ditches. According to the excavators, the palisade trench was filled with undisturbed material from the erection of the inner wall. In the publication, the Bischheim sherds from one of the palisade posts are considered to be a foundation deposit. The Michelsberg II sherds from another post date the refilling of the palisade trench and the digging of the inner ditch. These phases are under discussion (see Anderson 1998, 182 f.), but nevertheless the different positions of the gates show that palisade and ditches are unlikely to be contemporary. Large scale excavation.	Boelicke 1977.
LN and EN Palisades			
9	Bürgel b. Gudensberg, Schwalm-Eder-Kreis	Probably oval palisade ditch enclosing an area of *c.*45 x 25m below the top of the hill. Partially excavated. As settlement traces were found inside, but also outside the enclosure, it might well be a fence inside a larger settlement.	Raetzel-Fabian 1988, 100 with Abb. 146.
10	Eilsleben, Bördekreis	rectangular palisade ditches with several interruptions. One enclosed area of 30 x 15m is more or less understood, some more of maybe the same size are partially excavated. Only one contemporary pit. Bernburg.	Kaufmann 1979, 127f.
11	Halle, Kr. Halle (Saale) Stadt, Dölauer Heide	Palisade, in some parts two parallel palisades, enclosing a Bernburg hilltop settlement of probably 120 x 55m, combined with a ditch in only in two short parts. One 'bastion' on the northwestern side. Large scale excavation.	Behrens/Schröter 1980, bes. 30 ff. mit Beil. IV.

No	Name	Description	Reference
12	Morl, Saalkreis	Bernburg hilltop settlement, *c.*200 x 60m, very steep slope on two sides, southwestern corner with a palisade, northeastern side with a narrow ditch. Partially excavated.	Müller 1990, 271.
13	Schöningen, Kr. Helmstedt	Palisade trench of the Schönfeld culture, slightly curved and with one interruption, which could be traced for a length of *c.*50m. Contemporary settlement traces were only found inside. Large scale excavation.	Thieme & Maier 1995, 152 ff.

BIBLIOGRAPHY

Becker, H., 1990. Mittelneolithische Kreisgrabenanlagen in Niederbayern und ihre Interpretation auf Grund von Luftbildern und Bodenmagnetik. *Vortr. Niederbayer. Archäologentag* 8, 1990, 139 ff.

Becker, H.,1998. Hochauflösende Verfahren zur magnetischen Prospektion in der Archäologie. In: H. von der Osten-Woldenburg (Hrsg.), Unsichtbares sichtbar machen. *Geophysikalische Prospektionsmethoden in der Archäologie. Materialh. Arch. Baden-Württemberg* 41 (Stuttgart 1998) 99 ff.

Becker, H. & Kreiner, L., 1993. Prospektion und Sondagegrabung der mittelneolithischen „Ellipse„ bei Meisternthal. *Arch. Jahr. Bayern* 1993, 34 ff.

Becker, H. & Tillmann, A., 1995. Eine Kreisgrabenanlage des frühen Jungneolithikums aus Riekofen. *Arch. Jahr Bayern* 1995, 37 ff.

Behrens, H. 1973. Die Jungsteinzeit im Mittelelbe-Saale-Gebiet. Veröff. *Landesmus. Halle* 27 (Berlin 1973).

Behrens, H. & Schröter, E. 1980. *Siedlungen und Gräber der Trichterbecherkultur und Schnurkeramik bei Halle (Saale)* (Berlin 1980).

Behrens, H. 1981. The first "Woodhenge" in Middle Europe. *Antiquity* 55, 1981, 172ff.

Bernhardt, G. 1986. Die linearbandkeramische Siedlung von Köln-Lindenthal. Eine Neubearbeitung. *Kölner Jahrb. Vor- u. Frühgesch.* 18/19, 1986, 7 ff.

Bernhardt, G. 1990. Die linienbandkeramischen Befestigungsanlagen von Köln-Lindenthal. Siedlungsökonomische Gesichtspunkte ihrer Lage und Entstehung. *Jahresschr. Mitteldt. Vorgesch.* 73, 1990, 345 ff.

Biel, J. 1988. Michelsberger Erdwerke im Raum Heilbronn. In: J. Biel/H. Schlichterle/M. Strobel/A. Zeeb (Hrsg.), Die Michelsberger Kultur und ihre Randgebiete – Probleme der Entstehung, Chronologie und des Siedlungswesens. *Materialh. Arch. Baden-Württemberg* 43 (Stuttgart 1998) 97 ff.

Billamboz, A. 1990. Das Holz der Pfahlbausiedlungen Südwestdeutschlands. *Ber. RGK* 71, 1990, 187 ff.

Blanchet, J-C. & Martinez, R. 1988. Les camps néolithiques Chasséens dans le Nord-Ouest du bassin Parisien. In: C. Burgess, P. Topping, C. Mordant & M. Maddison, (eds) *Enclosures and Defences in the Neolithic of Western Europe.* BAR S 403, (Oxford 1988) 149 ff.

Boelicke, U. 1976/77. Das neolithische Erdwerk Urmitz. *Acta Praehist. et Arch.* 7/8, 1976/77, 73 ff.

Boelicke, U. 1988. Sonstige Befunde. In: U. Boelicke, D. v. Brandt, J. Lüning, P. Stehli & A. Zimmermann, *Der bandkeramische Siedlungsplatz Langweiler 8, Gemeinde Aldenhoven, Kreis Düren* (Bonn 1988) 428 ff.

Boelicke, U. & v. Brandt, D. 1988. Zäune und andere Pfostensetzungen. In: U. Boelicke, D. v. Brandt, J. Lüning, P. Stehli & A. Zimmermann, *Der bandkeramische Siedlungsplatz Langweiler 8, Gemeinde Aldenhoven, Kreis Düren* (Bonn 1988) 296 ff.

Brandt, K. 1967. Neolithische Siedlungsplätze im Stadtgebiet von Bochum. *Quellenschr. Westdt. Vor- u. Frühgesch.* 8 (Bonn 1967)

Dieckmann, B. & Fritsch, B. 1990. Linearbandkeramische Siedlungsbefunde im Hegau. *Arch. Korrbl.* 20, 1990, 25 ff.

Dohrn-Ihmig, M. 1983. Neolithsiche Siedlungen der Rössener Kultur in der Niederrheinischen Bucht. *Mat. Allgemeinen u. Vergleichenden Arch.* 21 (München 1983).

Eckert, J. 1986. Ein mittel- und jungneolithischer Siedlungsplatz bei Nottuln, Kreis Coesfeld. Bericht über die Ausgrabungen 1983-1984. *Ausgr. u. Funde Westfalen-Lippe* 4, 1986, 39 ff.

Eckert, J. 1990. Das Michelsberger Erdwerk Mayen. *Ber. Arch. Mittelrhein u. Mosel* 3, 1992, 9 ff.

Eckert, J. 1990a. Überlegungen zu Bauweise und Funktion Michelsberger Erdwerke im Rheinland. *Jschr. Mitteldt. Vorgesch.* 73, 1990, 399 ff.

Engelhardt, B. 1994. Die Altheimer Feuchtbodensiedlung Ergolding-Fischergasse bei Landshut und ihr Hinterland. Die Entwicklung eines Kleinraumes von der Linienbandkeramik bis zum mittleren Spätneolithikum. *Vortr. Niederbayer. Archäologentag* 12, 1994, 41 ff.

Engelhardt, B. 1995. Ein neolithisches Erdwerk bei Rinkam. *Arch. Jahr Bayern* 1995, 34 ff.

Gechter, M. 1987. Das Michelsberger Erdwerk auf dem Bonner Venusberg. *Arch. Rheinland* 1987, 26.

Gibson, A. 1994. Excavations at the Sarn-y-bryn-caled cursus complex, Welshpool, Powys, and the timber circles of Grat Britain and Ireland. *Proc. Prehist. Soc.* 60, 1994, 143 ff.

Gibson, A. 1998. Hindwell and the Neolithic palisaded sites of Britain and Ireland. In: A. Gibson & D. Simpson (eds.), *Prehistoric ritual and religion* Festschr. A. Burl] (Stroud 1998) 68 ff.

Gollub, S 1967. Die bandkeramische Siedlung in Bernkastel-Kues. *Trierer Zeitschr.* 30, 1967, 20 ff.

Gross-Klee, E & Hasenfratz, A. 1995. Siedlungswesen und Hausbau. In: W. E. Stöckli, U. Niffeler, E. Gross-Klee (Hrsg.), *Die Schweiz vom Paläolithikum bis zum frühen Mittelalter II. Neolithikum* (Basel 1995) 195 ff.

Haßmann, H. 2000. Die Steinartefakte der befestigten neolithischen Siedlung von Büdelsdorf, Kreis Rendsburg-Eckenförde. *Univforsch. Prähist. Arch.* 62 (Bonn 2000).

Höckmann, O. 1990. Frühneolithische Einhegungen in Europa. *Jahresschr. Mitteldt. Vorgesch.* 73, 1990, 57 ff.

Höhn, B. 1991. Siedlungen der Michelsberger Kultur in der Wetterau. In: V. Rupp (Hrsg.) Archäologie der Wetterau. *Aspekte der Forschung* (Friedberg 1991) 137 ff.

Höhn, B. 1992/93. Vorbericht über die Ausgrabungen in der bandkeramischen Siedlung von Großseelheim, Stadt Kirchhain, Kr. Marburg-Biedenkopf. *Ber. Komm. Arch. Landesforsch. Hessen* 2, 1992/93, 7 ff.

Höhn, B. 1997. Das Steinmaterial der Michelsberger Siedlung Koslar 10, Gem. Jülich, Kr. Düren. In: J. Lüning (Hrsg.), Studien zur neolithischen Besiedlung der Aldnhovener Platte und ihrer Umgebung, Rhein. *Ausgr.* 43 (Köln 1997) 399 ff.

Höhn, B. 1997a. Das Michelsberger Erdwerk Inden 9, Gem. Jülich, Kr. Düren. In: : J. Lüning (Hrsg.), Studien zur neolithischen Besiedlung der Aldenhovener Platte und ihrer Umgebung, Rhein. *Ausgr.* 43 (Köln 1997) 473 ff.

Ihmig, M. 1971. Ein bandkeramischer Graben mit Einbau bei Langweiler, Kr. Jülich, und die zeitliche Stellung bandkeramischer Gräben im westlichen Verbreitungsgebiet. *Arch. Korrbl.* 1, 1971, 23 ff.

Jadin, I. & Cahen, D. 1992. Darion: Zwei benachbarte Dörfer. *Spurensicherung. Archäologische Denkmalpflege in der Euregio Maas-Rhein* (Mainz 1992) 509 ff.

Jeunesse, C. 1996. Les enceintes à fossés interrompus du Néolithique danubien ancien et moyen et leurs relations ave le Néolithique récent. *Arch. Korrbl.* 26, 1996, 251 ff.

Jong, J. de 1998. Timber circles at Zwolle, Netherlands. In: A. Gibson & D. Simpson (eds.), *Prehistoric ritual and religion* Festschr. A. Burl] (Stroud 1998) 80 ff.

Jürgens, A. 1979. Die Rössener Siedlung von Aldenhoven, Kreis Düren. *Rheinische Ausgr.* 19, 1979, 385 ff.

Kállay, A. Sz. 1990. Die kupferzeitliche Ringanlage von Füzesabony. Jahresschr. *Mitteldt.Vorgesch.* 73, 1990, 125 ff.

Kaufmann, D. 1979. Ergebnisse der Ausgrabung 1977 in der befestigten linienbandkeramischen Siedlung bei Eilsleben, Kr. Wanzleben. *Zeitschr. Arch.* 13, 1979, 123ff.

Kaufmann, D. 1997. Zur Funktion linienbandkeramischer Erdwerke. Vortäge 15 Niederbayer. *Archäologentag* (Deggendorf 1997) 41 ff.

Kilian, L. 1956/58. Die bandkeramische Siedlung von Bernkastel-Kues. Ergebnisse der Ausgrabung 1952. *Trierer Zeitschr.* 24-26, 1956/58, 11 ff.

Kind, C-J. 1989. Ulm-Eggingen. *Forsch. U. Ber. Vor- u. Frühgesch. Baden-Württemberg* 34 (Stuttgart 1989)

Krause, R. 1998. Die bandkeramischen Siedlungsgrabungen bei Vaihingen an der Enz, Kreis Ludwigsburg (Baden-Württemberg). *Ber. RGK* 79, 1998, 5 ff.

Kuper, R. 1973. Bauspuren. In: J. P. Farrugia, R. Kuper, J. Lüning & P. Stehli, Der bandkeramische Siedlungsplatz Langweiler 2. *Rhein. Ausgr.* 13, 1973, 22 ff.

Kuper, R. & Lüning, J. 1975. Untersuchungen zur neolithischen Besiedlung der Aldenhovener Platte. *Ausgrabungen in Deutschland 1.* Monogr. RGZM 1,1 (Mainz 1975) 85ff.

Kurz, S. 1994. Archäologische Untersuchungen im Gewerbegebiet Dresden-Nickern 1 – eine Bestandsübersicht. arch. *Aktuell* 2, 1994, 23 ff.

Laux, F. 1997. Review of Meyer 1993. *Germania* 75. 1997, 752 ff.

Lefranc, P. & Jeunesse, C. 1998. Wittenheim (Haut-Rhin, France). Un enclose palissadé de type „Kreispalisadenanlage„ dans le Roessen III du sud de la Plaine du Rhin supérieur? *Anthrop. et Préhist.* 109, 1998, 63 ff.

Lehner, H. 1912. Prähistorische Ansiedlung bei Plaidt an der Nette. *Bonner Jhb.* 122, 1912, 271 ff.

Lehner, H. 1917. Vorgeschichtliche Ansiedlungen bei Sarmsheim an der Nahe. *Bonner Jhb.* 124, 1927, 104 ff.

Lüning, J. 1988. Zur Verbreitung und Datierung bandkeramischer Erdwerke. *Arch. Korrbl.* 18, 1988, 155 ff.

Lüning, J. 1998. Betrachtungen über die Michelsberger Kultur. In J. Biel, H. Schlichterle, M. Strobel & A. Zeeb (Hrsg.), Die Michelsberger Kultur und ihre Randgebiete – Probleme der Entstehung,

Chronologie und des Siedlungswesens. Materialh. *Arch. Baden-Württemberg* 43 (Stuttgart 1998) 277 ff.

Marolle, C. 1998. Le site Michelsberg des "Hautes Chanvières" avec bâtiments et einceinte à Mairy, Ardennes - France. In J. Biel, H. Schlichterle, M. Strobel & A. Zeeb (Hrsg.), Die Michelsberger Kultur und ihre Randgebiete – Probleme der Entstehung, Chronologie und des Siedlungswesens. Materialh. *Arch. Baden-Württemberg* 43 (Stuttgart 1998) 21 ff.

Matuschik, I. 1991. Grabenwerke des Spätneolithikums in Süddeutschland. *Fundber. Baden-Württemberg* 16, 1991, 27 ff.

Matuschik, I. 1999. Rez. zu N. H. Anderson, The Sarup Enclosures (Moesgaard 1997). *Fundber Baden-Württemberg* 23, 1999, 1051 ff.

Meixner, G. 1998. Paläoböden und Siedlungsbefunde der Linearbandkeramik von Altdorf, Lkr. Landshut. Vorträge 16. *Niederbayerischen Archäologentages* 1998, 13 ff.

Meyer, M. 1993. Pevestorf 19. Ein mehrperiodiger Fundplatz im Landkreis Lüchow-Dannenberg. *Veröff. urgesch. Slg. Landesmus. Hannover* 41 (Oldenburg 1993).

Meyer, M. 1995. Bemerkungen zu den jungneolitischen Grabenwerken zwischen Rhein und Saale. *Germania* 73, 1995, 69 ff.

Meyer, M. 1999. Im doppelten Kreis. Sondagegrabung an einer neolithischen Kreisgrabenanlage in Bochow, Landkreis Teltow-Fläming. *Arch. Berlin u. Brandenburg* 1999, 42 ff.

Modderman, P.J.R. 1958/59. Die bandkeramische Siedlung von Sittard. *Palaeohist.* 6/7, 1958/59, 33 ff.

Modderman, P.J.R. 1985. Die Bandkeramik im Graetheidegebiet, Niederländisch Limburg. *Ber. RGK* 66, 1985, 25 ff.

Mordant, C. & Mordant, D. 1988. Les enceintes neolithiques de la haute-vallée de la Seine. In C. Burgess, P. Topping, C. Mordant & M. Maddison (eds) *Enclosures and Defences in the Neolithic of Western Europe*. BAR S 403 (Oxford 1988) 231 ff.

Müller, D.W. 1990. Befestigte Siedlungen der Bernburger Kultur – Typen und Verbreitung. *Jsch. Mitteldt. Vorgesch.* 73, 1990, 271 ff.

Müller, J. 1999. Zeiten ändern sich. *Arch. Dtl.* 15/2, 1999, 20 ff.

Nadler, M. & Zeeb, A. 1994. Südbayern zweischen Linearbandkeramik und Altheim: ein neuer Gliederungsvorschlag. In: Beier H.-J. (ed.), *Der Rössener Horizont in Mitteleuropa*. Beitr. Ur- u. Frühgesch. Mitteleuropas 6 (Wilkau-Hasslau 1994) 127 ff.

Němejcová-Pavúková, V. 1995. Svodín 1. Zwei Kreisgrabenanlagen der Lengyel-Kultur. *Stud. Arch. et Mediaevalia* 2 (Bratislava 1995).

Neth, A. 1999. Eine Siedlung der frühen Bandkeramik in Gerlingen, Kreis Ludwigsburg. *Forsch. u. Ber. Vor- u. Frühgesch.* Baden-Württemberg 79 (Stuttgart 1999).

Nickel, C. 1997. Menschliche Skelettreste aus Michelsberger Fundzusammenhängen. Zur Interpretation einer Fundgattung. *Ber. RGK* 78, 1997, 29 ff.

Patay, P. 1990. Die kupferzeitliche Siedlung von Tiszalúc-Sarkad. *Jahresschr. Mitteldt. Vorgesch.* 73, 1990, 131 ff.

Pavlě, I. 1982. Die neolithischen Kreisgrabenanlagen in Böhmen. *Arch. Rozhl.* 34, 1982, 176 ff.

Pavlě, I .,Rulf, J. & Zápotocká, M. 1986. Theses of the Neolithic site of Bylany. *Památcky Arch.* 77, 1986, 288 ff.

Pavúk, J. 1991. Lengyel-culture fortified settlements in Slovakia. *Antiquity* 65, 1991, 348 ff.

Pavúk, J. 1993. La Slovaquie occidentale. In: J. Kozĕowski (dir.), *Atlas du Néolithique européen. Vol. 1: L'Europe orientale* (Liège 1993) 361 ff.

Petrasch, J. & Kromer, B. 1989. Aussagemögllichkeiten von 14C-Daten zur Verfüllungsgeschichte prähistorischer Gräben am Beispiel der mittelneolithischen Kreisgrabenanlage von Künzing-Unternberg, Ldkr. Deggendorf. *Arch. Korrbl.* 19, 1989, 231ff.

Petrasch, J. 1990. Mittelneolithische Kreisgrabenanlagen in Mitteleuropa. *Ber. RGK* 71, 1990, 407ff.

Petrasch, J. 1998. Graben- und Palisadenanlagen (Erdwerke). In J. Preuß (Hrsg.), *Das Neolithikum in Mitteleuropa* (Weissbach 1998) 187 ff.

Podborský, V. 1988. Těšetice-Kyjovice IV. *Rondel osady lidu s moravskou malovanou keramikou* (Brno 1988).

Raetzel-Fabian, D. 1988. Die ersten Bauernkulturen. *Vor- u. Frühgesch. Hessischem Landesmus. Kassel* 2 (Kassel 1988).

Raetzel-Fabian, D. 1990. Diskontinuität im Neolithikum Südwestdeutschlands? In F. M. Andraschko & W.-R. Teegen (Hrsg.), *Gedenkschrift für Jürgen Driehaus* (Mainz 1990) 161ff.

Raetzel-Fabian, D. 1999. Der umhegte Raum – Funktionale Aspekte jungneolithsicher Monumental-Erdwerke. *Jschr. Mitteldt. Vorgesch.* 81, 1999, 81ff.

Schlichterle, H. 1990. Aspekte der siedlungsarchäologischen Erforschung von Neolithikum und Bronzezeit im südwestdeutschen Alpenvorland. *Ber. RGK 71*, 1990, 208ff.

Schmidt, B. 1970. Die Landschaft östlich von Magdeburg im Neolithikum. *Jschr. Mitteldt. Vorgesch.* 54, 1970, 83 ff.

Schmidgen-Hager, E. 1993. Bandkeramik im Moseltal. *Universitätsforsch. Prähist. Arch.* 18 (Bonn 1993).

Schröter, E. 1989. Die „Schalkenburg„ bei Quenstedt, Kreis Hettstedt, eine frühneolithische Rondellanlage. In F. Schlette & D. Kaufmann, *Religion und Kult in ur- und frühgeschichtlicher Zeit* (Berlin 1989) 193 ff.

Schröter, P. 1975. Zur Besiedlung des Goldberges im Nördlinger Ries. *Ausgr. Deutschland 1. Monogr. RGZM* 1,1 (Mainz 1975) 98 ff.

Schumacher, K. 1921. *Siedlungs- und Kulturgeschichte der Rheinlande von der Urzeit bis in das Mittelalter Bd.* 1 (Mainz 1921).

Stäuble, H. 1999. Von der Linie zur Fläche. Archäologische Großprojekte im Südraum Leipzigs. Vorträge 17. *Niederbayerischen Archäologentages* 1999, 149 ff.

Steinmann, C. 1999. Immer im Kreis - Eine Ringanlage als rituelles Zentrum. *Archäologie an der JAGAL - 10.000 Jahre auf 300 Kilometern* (Wünsdorf/ Dresden/ Halle (Saale) 1999) 32ff.

Strobel, M. 2000. *Die Schussenrieder Siedlung Taubried I* (Bad Buchau, Kr. Bibrach) (Stuttgart 2000).

Tackenberg, K. 1951. Die Beusterburg. Ein jungsteinzeitliches Erdwerk in Niedersachsen. *Veröff. urgesch. Slg. Landesmus. Hannover* 13 (Hildesheim 1951)

Thieme, H. & Maier, R. 1975. *Archäologische Ausgrabungen im Braunkohlentagebau Schöningen, Landkreis Helmstedt* (Hannover 1975)

Tichelmann, G. & Trier, M. 1995. Urgeschichtliche Siedlungsplätze auf einer Trasse zwischen Weisweiler und Aachen. *Arch. Rheinland* 1995, 33 ff.

Toupet, C. 1988. The Chasséen enclosure at Compiègne, Oise. In C. Burgess, P. Topping, C. Mordant, & M. Maddison (eds), *Enclosures and Defences in the Neolithic of Western Europe*. BAR S 403 (Oxford 1988) 173 ff.

Trnka, G. 1991. Studien zu mittelneolithischen Kreisgrabenanlagen. *Mitt. Prähist. Komm. Österreischischen Akad Wiss.* 26 (Wien 1991).

Uenze, H.P. 1985. Das Grabenwerk der endneolithsichen Chamer Gruppe bei Piesenkofen, Gde. Obertraubling, Lkr. Regensburg/Opf. (Piesenkofen I). *Bayer. Vorgeschbl.* 50, 1985, 105ff.

Vermeersch, P.M. & Walter, R. 1978. Die Palisadengräben des Michelsberger Fundplatzes in Thieusies (Belgien). *Arch. Korrbl.* 8, 1978, 169ff.

Viehmeier, S. 1998. Northeim-Kiessee – Ein Michelsberger Erdwerk in Südniedersachsen. Eine Übersicht über die Befunde. In J. Biel, H. Schlichterle, M. Strobel & A. Zeeb (Hrsg.), Die Michelsberger Kultur und ihre Randgebiete – Probleme der Entstehung, Chronologie und des Siedlungswesens. *Materialh. Arch. Baden-Württemberg* 43 (Stuttgart 1998) 65 ff.

Whittle, A. 1988. *Problems in Neolithic archeology* (Cambridge 1988).

CHAPTER 6

ON PALISADES, HOUSES, VASES AND MINIATURES: THE FORMATIVE PROCESSES AND METAPHORS OF CHALCOLITHIC TELLS

Dragos Gheorghiu

INTRODUCTION

An eastern European Chalcolithic tell is a "cumulative place-value" (Chapman 1994 a, 138), that is to say a place which accumulates value through time. It is also an additional (Sherratt 1983, 192-3) as well as a subtractive result of many successive levels of habitation within a horizontal perimeter defined by wooden palisades and ditches. Despite the fact that the understanding of tells is of great importance to our comprehension of European prehistory, only a few archaeologists have discussed the subject in detail (Sherratt 1972: Tringham 1972: Tringham 1992: Tringham & Krstic 1990: Bailey 1990: Chapman 1991: Chapman 1994 b, Kostakis 1999, Marinescu-Bilcu 2000, Popovici *et al.* 2000).

The growth of tells is a complex process that deserves a specific cognitive method of study. In other words, we should not analyse the formative processes of the constitutive elements of the tell (i.e. the palisades, the "houses" (households, barns and stables), the ovens, the pots, the sacrificial and deposition pits and other social facets) separately but rather we should study them within the framework of their rhetorical relationships of making, functioning and dismantling. The aim of the present paper is to demonstrate that the metaprocess of formation in the tells deserves not a simple cognitive-processual approach (cf. Schlanger 1997), but rather a synoptical one that is simultaneously both synchronic and diachronic. This will enable the connections between the formative processes of addition and subtraction in the *chaines-operatoires* of the construction and deconstruction of the objects mentioned above to be revealed (Gheorghiu 2000a) (see Appendix 1).

The advantages of modelling the archaeological material in such a visual way, by highlighting parallels within the *chaines* (with the help of ethnological models that are available from the same area) can be readily recognised. It provides a rapid overview of the various operations involved, as well as easing the perception of the analogies between the *chaines'* stages and of their intersections or relationships. Moreover, the reader can check the interpretative processes of the author and at the same time produce his/her own interpretation (see Gheorghiu 2001).

However, even this kind of cognitive-processual approach in the exposure of the *chaines-operatoires*, even in a synoptical study such as this, is not sufficient to help the archaeologist to understand in detail the complexity of the phenomenon. Because of the analogies existing between technologies (a fact that reveals a common metaphorical base), the cognitive approach will extend to symbolism (see Renfrew 1997, 6) and rhetoric. In this perspective, additional information on invisible features in the archaeological record may be deduced from the cognitive study of iconography. In this instance, the clay miniatures provide information on the original form of the palisades (and of the appearance of the actual tells themselves), as well as the visual pattern recognition of the Chalcolithic populations in the metaphorical perception of space,. The ethnography used in this paper comes from the same region and it illustrates the permanence of a technological tradition resulting from the exploitation of local resources.

THE CULTURAL CONTEXT

East European Chalcolithic

The emergence of palisaded tells characterises the early and mature Chalcolithic cultures of eastern Bulgaria and south-eastern Romania. It occurs simultaneously with a differentiation in the settlements' complexity, a new strategy in the location of settlement, and a long-distance trade system in prestige goods. The Chalcolithic (5th–4th millennia BC) involved many cultural transformations in the social organisation and material culture of Neolithic societies in the eastern Balkan-south east Danubian plain (i.e., Marica II-IV (Karanovo V) - Boian III (Vidra phase) and Boian IV (Spantov phase or "transitional") (aprox. 4900–4500 BC) and Gumelnita-Karanovo VI (aprox. 4500–3900 BC)). These Chalcolithic populations practised a mixed subsistence economy, involving agriculture, that developed as a result of improvements in land cultivation and in methods of storage (Nania 1967, 19: Galbenu 1962, 303), animal domestication, fishing and hunting. Architecture was characterised by the emergence of surface architecture (built of clay and wood[1]) in small villages fortified by deep, wide ditches (Comsa 1974b, 126) and in tell settlements with wooden palisades. These latter sites can be seen to mark the beginning of permanent settlement on the same site and of long term inter-settlement relations (this process appears earlier in the southern regions of the Balkans, see Perles 1999, 53).

The fortified nucleated tells surrounded by ditches and simple or double wooden palisades and earth walls (Perniceva 1978, 164-165) were up to 15,000sq.m in area (Todorova 1978, 55). They were built according to a set plan (Todorova 1978, 48) and became predominant with the general spread of megaron-type (Todorova 1978, 51) surface architecture. An average tell level might contain between 10 and 15 houses, but there are cases where more buildings have been recognised. On many tells the first Gumelnita level of occupation overlaps with a Boian level, demonstrating that there is a degree of continuity between these cultures. It also suggests the presence of a 'powerful' ancestral space in which communities lived where their ancestors had once lived (Chapman 1994, 138: see also Kotsakis 1999, 74).

The presence of a small group of individuals who exercised authority within the society can be inferred from a number of strands of evidence. Firstly there is the labour control needed to build the tells' fortifications. Secondly, there are the differences between the dimensions and presumably functions of villages (Lichardus 1988, 91) and thirdly there are differences in funerary rituals including some rich burials with gold and copper artefacts. The Gumelnita – Karanovo VI elites developed long distance trade in prestige goods such as copper tools and gold artefacts. They probably also traded in salt, since the Lower Danube tells are situated near rivers that rise in the salt-rich Sub-Carpathian Mountains. They may also have established a trade network that linked the Balkans with the north Pontic area (Chernych 1992).

THE PALISADED TELL

The Location

In the Danubian alluvial plain, the Neolithic settlements were positioned on lower terraces, islands and river meadows and were not fortified. Only at the end of the epoch did the custom of surrounding them with ditches and probably also with wooden palisades become widespread.

Starting in the Chalcolithic, there is evidence for settlements being sited in new locations, mostly on high terraces and islands (Botzan 1996, 34-5). Such a strategic positioning not only served to protect the settlement from sporadic but devastating flooding (Bailey 1990, 29-30) but also provided unconstrained access to water, natural protection against human attacks and against predominant winds. It also provided a good visual position in the landscape. This latter observation served to advertise the community increasingly as the tell's growing contour became a dominant locale. Through the modelling of the natural dominant locales, and through the spatial organisation of the settlements, land use and circulation networks, a new landscape, specific for the new epoch was created.

Dwellings and Subordination

It is highly possible that around the ditch-enclosed palisaded tells there would have existed small open or even other palisaded settlements, related to, but also subordinate to, the main site. This may be deduced from the presence of small tells situated on the plain and sited close to the larger ones on the higher ground, such as at Tangaru, Uzunu (both unpublished), Burdusani-Popina or Valea Argovei-Vladiceasca (Marinescu-Bilcu 1997, 36-37) in the Lower Danubian plain. It is possible that there were two organisational styles in the settlements in the same area. For example at the early Chalcolithic site at Radovanu (fig 6.1), in the Lower Danube plain, the palisaded tell on the terrace was surrounded by an open site, an area of "workshops" at its base, and a necropolis (Comsa 1990, 70). This set-up could either be the result of a division of the population due to a demographic growth or equally from a seasonal organization. Besides being the permanent residence of a human group, the palisaded and ditched tells could also have functioned as refuges (or "*acropoloi*", Theocaris 1973) for the population of the hinterland during times of insecurity (cf. Rowlands 1972, 452).

***Fig 6.1**: The Radovanu tell, southern Romania.*

Perimeter and Ditches: the beginning of growth

The first task to be undertaken when building a Chalcolithic fortified settlement would perhaps have been the levelling of the ground surface, since the settlements were positioned on curved planes such as the tops of terraces or islands. Next might be that of outlining the perimeter of the settlement and its palisade. This might also involve marking out the ground plans of the buildings, as might have happened in Poljanica (fig 6.2). Such a sequence is documented in some of the descriptions of the ritual surrounding the founding of the cities of Antiquity (Plutarch, 11, Dionysos of Halicarnas 1885: Ovid, 1933, IV: all cited in Coulanges 1908) and these texts were used here for archaeological inspiration.

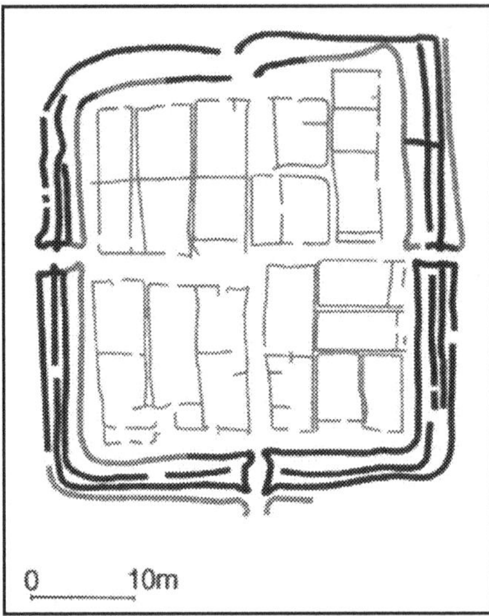

In the lower Danubian plain, ditch-defined tells dating to the Boian culture have been recorded at Spantov (see Morintz 1963, 265-282), to the Boian-Gumelnita culture at Radovanu (Comsa 1972, 44-45), and to the Gumelnita culture at Jilava (Comsa 1976, 105-127), Ostrov (Comsa 1955, 425), Vidra (Rosetti & Morintz 1961, 70—76), Magurele (Roman 1962, 259-262) and Teiu (Nania 1967).

***Fig 6.2**: Plan of the Poljanica tell, level I (after Todorova 1982), showing the plan of the palisade. The black lines represent a continuous wooden palisade made of posts bedded within a trench. The grey lines within the pattern of the palisade represent trenches without wooden posts, while those inside the perimeter of the palisade represent megaron or common houses.*

Wooden Palisades

Archaeological evidence for wooden palisades surrounding tells has only been recorded in north-eastern Bulgaria, where extensive excavations have taken place.

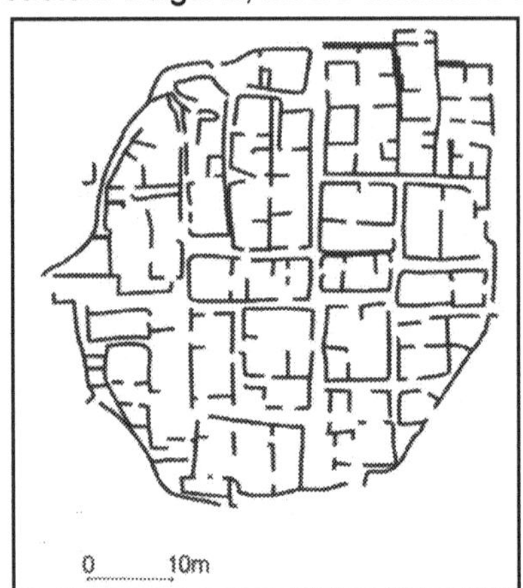

***Fig 6.3**: Plan of the Poljanica tell, level VIII (after Todorova 1982), showing the plan of the palisade.*

Palisades have many types of ground plan. They can form accurate geometrical shapes, as at Poljanica levels I-IV (fig 6.2), Ovcarovo level I (fig 6.4) and Radingrad levels I-V, or organic shapes that follow the natural contours (like Ovcarovo levels V–XII) (fig 6.5). However, it also seems that these ground plans may change over time. For example the palisades of the levels I-IV at Poljanica are squared compared to the organic form that follows the contour lines of levels V–VIII) (fig 6.3).

As mentioned above, the marking out of the perimeter of cities in Antiquity serves as an inspirational model in aiding the understanding of the possible processes relevant to the planning of the palisades (see Coulanges 1908). The processes envisaged here comprise the delineation of the perimeter, the marking of the entrances and the construction of a line of contiguous posts either set within a narrow trench or simply driven into the ground.

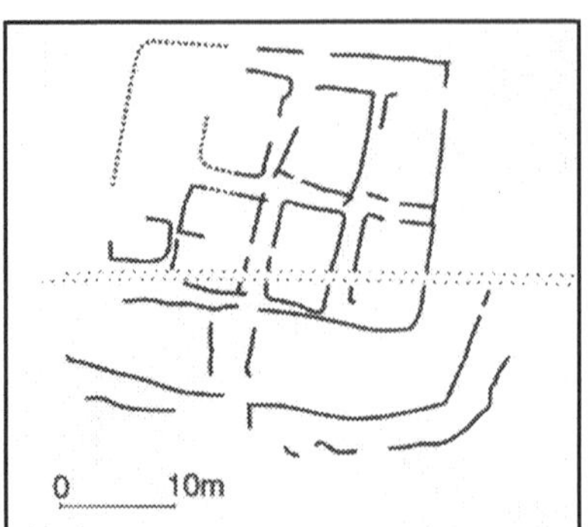

From the published Bulgarian material it seems that there were two kind of palisades: the type with posts of equal size, as at Goljamo Delcevo (see Todorova 1982, 183, figs. 114-115; 186, figs 120-121; 188, figs. 124-125; 189, fig . 126; 190, figs. 128-129), Ovcarovo (see Todorova 1982, 194, figs.135-137; 200, figs.147, 149; 202, figs.151,153; 204, figs. 154-157); Poljanica (see Todorova 1982, 218, fig . 71; 220, fig . 173), and the type with a mixture of thick and thin

***Fig 6.4**: Plan of the Ovcarovo tell, level I (after Todorova 1982), showing the plan of the palisade.*

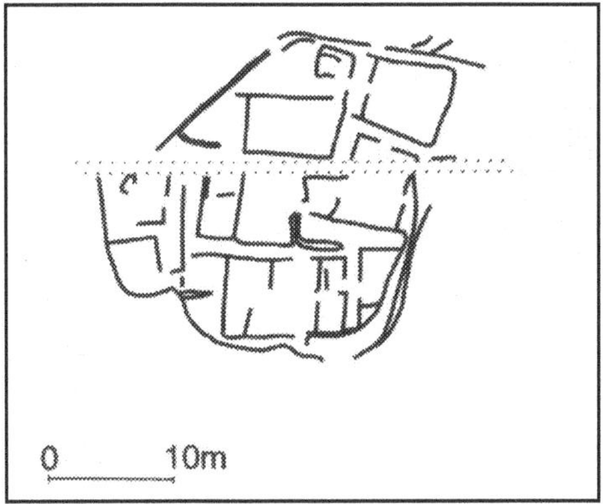

Fig 6.5: Plan of the Ovcarovo tell, level XII (after Todorova 1982), showing the plan of the palisade.

Fig 6.6: Barn from Uzunu village, southern Romania. The house was made with material taken from a Boian-Gumelnita tell.

posts as at Poljanica, levels II-IV (Todorova 1982, 206-212, figs. 159-165), Radingrad levels I-V (Todorova 1982, 222-226, figs. 175-183). This second type implies that there was a woven trellis between the vertical elements, similar to the method used for the walls of the houses. Such a technique of construction allows the shaping of loop-hole "windows" by spacing out the horizontal twigs of the trellis. This can be illustrated by ethnological examples from the Lower Danube area where barns, house walls and fences made of twigs and clay employ such devices (figs 6.6 and 6.7). Once the trellis has been woven (fig 6.8), it is possible that the facades of some palisades were covered with a layer of clay or daub, as in the case of the house walls (fig 6.9). There is evidence for the use of just such a finishing technique in phase A of the neighbouring Cucuteni culture. Ariusd is the only palisaded settlement to have traces of the wooden palisade still remaining (Laszlo 1911, cited in Laszlo 1993) and here some fragments of daub preserved the impressions of the wattle.

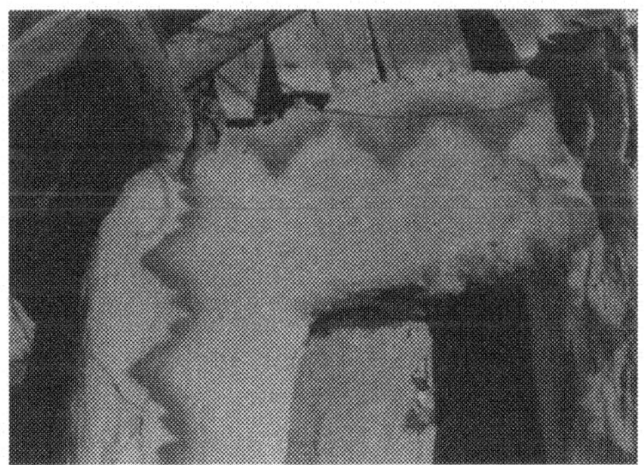

Fig 6.7: Detail of a window showing the many layers of repair with clay and painting.

Fig 6.8: Detail of a wall of a barn made of wattle, Uzunu village, southern Romania.

The enclosures might also be classified according to the number of palisades, from one to three rows. It seems that through time there was a process of reducing the number of barriers, as if the protective or prestige attributes of the palisades decreased as the settlement's size also decreased with the heightening of the tell. This is notable at sites such as Goljamo Delcevo (level I compared with levels II-XVII), Ovcarovo (levels I-III compared with levels IV-XII), Poljanica (levels I and III–IV compared with levels V-VIII), Radingrad (level I compared with levels II–V) (see Todorova 1982, 183–227).(figs. 6.2, 6.3, 6.4, 6.5). Sometimes the spaces between the

Fig 6.9: Detail showing the clay filling of the wattle work.

multiple palisades were filled with fragments of demolished dwellings added to strengthen the wooden walls (Todorova 1976, 49).

Entrances and Passages through the Palisades

Entrances and passages interrupt the two or three rows of perimeter screens. These passages were positioned according to geometrical rules and were related to the main streets of the earliest levels of occupation. One can infer that these passages later lost their architectural importance and, probably, their rituality, since the liminal zone between "outside" and "inside" practically disappeared as the enclosures reduced in area.

In the first stages of occupation, entrances seem to have had an important role. They were positioned on the cardinal points and were marked by imposing structures comprising posts thicker than those of the palisade. For example, four posts flanked the southern entrance at Poljanitsa, each more massive than the posts of the triple palisade (Todorova 1982, 206, fig. 159). Another cardinal orientation, possibly having a solar symbolism, with similarly marked entrances can be found at Neolithic timber circles in Britain and elsewhere (see Gibson 1998, 77).

That the internal structure of the palisades and tells had a solar orientation is a hypothesis that can be supported by two observations. Firstly, the four entrances of the palisade are positioned on the same axis and secondly, in the first phase of several tells, the horizontal alignment coincides with the equinoctial line (cf. Hawkins 1979, 288, fig 1). It is possible that the low winter sun would have lit the interior of the tell through the frame of the south entrance and through the windows in the trellis. In this respect, it may be possible to interpret the palisaded tells as "Kalendarbauten" (see discussion in Gibson 1998, 68). A miniature clay model from Cascioarele Island may support this hypothesis since the model's perforated walls may possibly represent the loop-windows of a palisade (this will be discussed later).

The Chalcolithic entrances are characterised by an ample width that in ritual terms indicates an extended liminal stage (see Leach 1976, fig 7) in the rite of passage. The same ritual reason seems to have lain behind the design of megaron houses of the Gumelnita-Karanovo VI culture.
Generally, the emphasis on the rite of passage in palisades was achieved architecturally by two wooden walls that closed the space between the rows of wooden posts of some palisades. This created a rectilinear corridor at each of the four entrances, corresponding to the four passages that divided the tell into equal parts as, for example, at Poljanica. This kind of entrance at the tell of Goljamo Delcevo levels VI-XII (Todorova 1982, 186-190, figs. 120-128) seems to have evolved through time. It follows the relief of the natural contour and extends outside the perimeter of the palisade, under a sheepfold, or a megaron-type house entrance.

In addition to the relationship between the geometrical shape of the palisade and the shape and position of the entrances there is another connection that deserves to be analysed. This is the analogy that exists between the general geometrical shape of the palisade and the shapes of the megaron houses and common houses built within the enclosure. In the tells' earliest occupation levels the geometrical arrangement of the palisade and of the houses is characterised by intelligible geometrical figures such as the square and the rectangle. In the final levels both shapes lose their geometry and an interdependence might be supposed between the processes of dissolution of the shape of the palisade and that of the houses. Within these processes it seems that a hidden relationship exists in some tells between the orientation of the palisades' entrances and the development through time of the process of growth.

Planning the Houses

Following the construction of the palisade, the process of building within the enclosure began. The first stage of construction seems to have been the orientation and planning of the houses (Todorova 1978, 48. For the generic term "house" see also Bailey 1990, 22-23). These were generally positioned in rows (Todorova 1982, 206 ff.: Marinescu-Bilcu 1997, 69) with their long axes orientated north-south (Todorova 1982, 183-231: Comsa 1990, 72, fig. 33).

This strict geometrical configuration (aligned on the north–south axis) could simply be interpreted as a device to enable a larger number of rectangular shapes to be squeezed into four groups (divided by the two main perpendicular passages). However some megaron houses were positioned on the east-west axis with their entrances facing the eastern entrance corridor. This seems to be the case at level I at Poljanica, where such a plot appears to defy logic in terms of maximising space, and the existing space would have better accommodated the houses if positioned on the north-south axis. The continuous change in plan during the tell's growth seems to have been the result of certain rules of change between the two main axes. At the Poljanica tell, for example, the replacement of the north-south buildings with east-west structures tried to preserve the original division of the houses into four lots (cf. Level I with level VII) but ultimately lead to the new orientation of these areas. Such a process of replacement within the perimeter of the palisade may have been, in my opinion, for two reasons. The first is a symbolical one, and the second is a functional one. In other words, by superimposing each settlement layer with a new layer of houses, it seems to have been presupposed that each new house should not coincide with the old one (*contra* Bailey 1990) and certainly they did not tend to use the old foundations. In

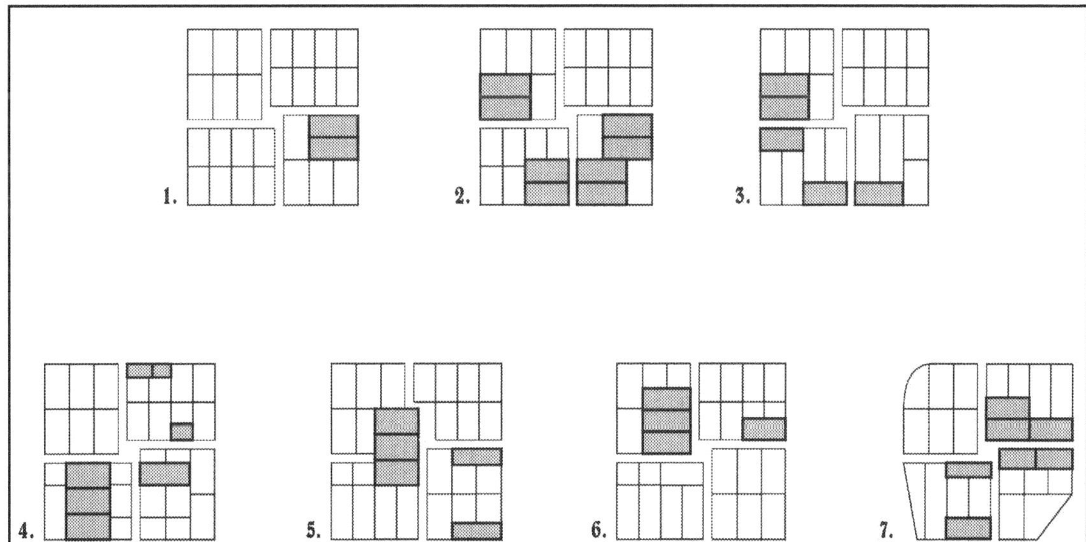

***Fig 6.10**: The rotation of houses on the east-west axis at Poljanica levels I - VIII.*

order to obtain a more solid foundation, the builders would have had to have changed the orientation of some of the new houses from time to time or to have enlarged their surfaces in order to avoid the old foundation trenches which still contained the remains of the old wooden posts. Within a system of continuous demographic growth within a relatively constant perimeter, this seems to have been the only adequate solution. Through a constant replanning, the repositioning of the houses through time seems to have followed a spiralling pattern turning around a small empty squared nucleus, crossed by the two main axes (fig 6.10).

In other cases, a re-orientation (Bailey 1990, 42) of the axes of all the houses in the final levels in some settlements, such as Radovanu level I (Comsa 1990, 76 ff.), or Tirgoviste level IV (Todorova 1982, 232, fig. 191), suggests a break in the building tradition. After the planning phase, the house foundation was dug as a continuous trench designed to receive the wall-posts (Marinescu-Bilcu *et al.* 1997, 68). It seems that the symbolical positioning of the hearths and ovens also took place at this time, since the oven platforms were built before the house floors were started (Comsa 1990, 86).

THE HOUSE

The Floor

In the case of some of the clay and wooden platform houses an additional process in the foundation of the houses can be detected. This was in the form of sacrifice and storage pits, the clay from which was probably used in the construction of the building. Generally children were buried under the floor as at Cascioarele Island, where five child skeletons were discovered (Dumitrescu 1986 a, 79) or at Bucsani (Marinescu-Bilcu 1996-1998, 111). However, fragments of adult skeletons have also been recorded as the selective burial of skulls also at Cascioarele Island demonstrates (Dumitrescu 1986 a, 78). Complete or fragmented, the human body was added to the settlement in a physical and symbolical process. Similarly, the filling of the wooden walls of the palisades with fragments from demolished houses may have been a symbolic action that possibly brought the bodies of the ancestors into the interface of the settlement.

The process of laying the house floors consisted of the preparation of a surface of clay mixed with straw over which were laid rows of parallel thin tree beams or planks (Comsa 1990, 85). These were also covered with a layer of clay mixed with straw (Comsa 1990, 85: Haita 1997, 87) and dung (Haita 1997, 88). The surface of the floor was then smoothed over and covered with mats of vegetable fibre (Haita 1997, 88).

The Walls

There is some evidence to suggest that the clay used to fill the wooden structure of the walls was formed into clod balls (Comsa 1990, 89). This seems to be similar to the construction of vases. The pieces of clay were then pressed on to the wooden structure. Not all the walls were timber framed[2] or filled with homogeneous clay. Sometimes the space between the wall posts and the trellis was filled with sediment mixed with domestic waste, straw (Comsa 1990, 90), ash, and potsherds (Marinescu-Bilcu 1996-1998, 111). This cumulative process is also found in the construction of palisades and ovens (Haita 1997, 87), as well as in potting (for example the recycling demonstrated by the use of grog as an opening material). There are other similarities between the construction of walls and vases. For example, the plastering of walls with daub (Haita 1997,88) and their painting (Berciu 1937, 6, fig. 5: Comsa 1990, 81) is analogous to the potting processes of smoothing, slipping and painting. One can conclude that in general the "walls" had a similar additive structure to pots.

The Pottery

An analogous *chaine-operatoire* to the palisade, the house or the oven is that of the construction of ceramic vases. After the different clays had been mixed with sand or chopped straws, ashes, grog or crushed fragments of walls or floors, and then modelled into clods, the construction of the base and coiled walls of the vases began. Some vases were covered by additional layers of graphite, coloured slip or applied rustication.

Selected sherds from ritually broken vases were deposited near the bodies of children or in pits, together with inorganic and organic substances. Some vases have house-shaped handles on the lids (Berciu 1956, 42, fig. 51: Todorova 1978, plate 9, fig. 3: Marinescu-Bilcu *et al.* 1997, plate 33) (fig 6.11). In these cases a relationship between ceramics and the architecture of the tell can certainly be inferred. Sometimes vase lids were decorated with spiral patterns and it seems important to note that some of these lid spirals occur with miniature representations of houses (see Berciu 1957, 46, figs. 58 and 59). The linear spiral-like design on some other lids follows the same pattern as that of the houses (see Todorova 1982, 105, fig. 58/12) (fig 6.12).

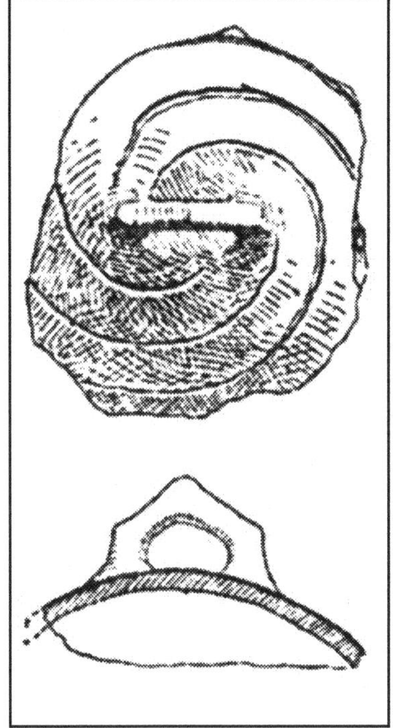

***Fig 6.11**: Lid from Pietrele tell, after Berciu 1956: 46, fig. 58*

***Fig 6.12**: Lid from Goljamo Delcevo tell, after Todorova 1982: 105, fig. 58/12).*

Subsequent Occupation Layers: the dissolution of the original shapes

The end of the construction process took place when an eaved roof was built (as shown by ceramic miniatures from Cascioarele, Gumelnita, Ovcarovo and Tirgoviste). The two intersecting gable beams resembled two horns, making the house look slightly bovine. From this moment on all the clay-built structures, as well as the tell's ground surface within the palisade, underwent layered cumulative growth. The architecture was augmented with layers of smoothing, coating, and painting, and the soil was covered intentionally with layers of clay mixed with inorganic and organic fragments, and unintentionally as a result of atmospheric processes or animal activity with fine layers of inorganic and organic material (Haita 2000, 53).

The Cessation of Growth and the Beginning of Decreasing

Considering that the wooden structures were quite flimsy, a characteristic of clay architecture, the houses and palisades needed periodical maintenance, including partial dismantling (Marinescu-Bilcu *et al.* 1997, 66). Sometimes certain houses changed their function, being transformed into stables (Popovici et al, 2000, 17) or waste depositories during the partial abandonment of the tell (Haita 1997, 88: Haita 2000, 53). The house with the oven (Popovici *et al.* 2000, 17) and the clay benches (habitation 48) at Hârsova, was destroyed at the end of its life-cycle. It was demolished and the ruins levelled to make way for a new structure (Popovici *et al.* 2000, 17).

Moreover houses may have been intentionally burned (Haita 1997, 88: for the intentional burning of houses in Chalcolithic cultures see also Tringham 1992) and then demolished and levelled. Some fragments of the burned walls and floor were collected in pits (Comsa 1990, 90) together with ceramic fragments, bones, ashes and other inorganic and organic waste. This seems to have been strictly selective, and is also a common practice in other Neolithic cultures[3]. The material left was used to fill the space between the wooden screens of the palisade or to fill the space within the house walls (Marinescu-Bilcu 1996-1998, 111).

The Resuming of Growth

In many cases tells were totally abandoned for various periods of time, especially after flooding episodes. This is especially so in the communities of the Lower Danubian plain (see Dumitrescu 1986a). Total abandonment, involving the intentional or unintentional destruction of the palisade, forced the newcomers to reconstruct the site every time.

Up until the abandonment of the tell, or from the moment of the reconstruction of the settlement due to overpopulation or to population fission, the perimeter of the palisade had been constant. It had served like a belt to control the horizontal growth of the community. This is clearly visible from the superimposed occupation levels within this constant perimeter as demonstrated in the exhaustive excavations at Bulgarian tells (see Todorova 1982). The final levels of Bulgarian tells also show that with the increasing build-up of occupation layers the surface area of the palisade began to reduce (see Chapman 1991, 82: see also Comsa 1986, 61), compressing the inhabited area more. In the final levels the palisade and the houses lost their regular geometry.

The megaron house and the common rectangular house, both characteristics of the earliest levels of the tells, had in most cases a simple rectangular shape. Only in a very few cases did they contain additional small interior walls, although these did not affect the overall rectangular outline. Because of the repeated addition of material, the rotation of the axes of some buildings within the tell, and the growth of the families' sizes on the same built surface, it was necessary to subdivide the interior. As a result, new configurations of many interior and exterior walls emerged in the middle and final levels of occupation. A similar process of the transformation of the original geometrical pattern happened with the palisades' design.

A process of fusion, specifically a fusion between the palisade and the walls of the peripheral houses (see level IV at Poljanica tell, Todorova 1982; 212, fig. 165), emerged from the compressing and rotation phenomena mentioned above. A similar practice of locating the houses on the periphery of the settlement in order to form a defensive wall (Rowlands 1972, 456) may be observed in ancient Greece. In the succeeding levels of occupation the process of fusion was more obvious, as it altered the rites of passage, the former geometrically oriented entrances being now deviated from the original axis. The resulting spatial incoherence of the final levels of some tells might have been a factor in determining when the settlement was to be abandoned (Fletcher 1984, 222, cited in Chapman 1991, 81).

THE METAPHORS OF THE PALISADED TELLS

From the comparative examination of the additive and subtractive processes in the construction and utilisation of various objects such as the palisades, houses and vases, one can notice the existence of a persuasive analogy between the above mentioned processes. This produces a sort of symbolic equivalence between the significant components of a tell (i.e., the settlement's palisade or a house are built *like* a vase). It is possible that the symbols were determined by the hierarchical dimension of the signified objects, the order being the following: "the palisade *contains* the house that *contains* the vase". At the same time the metaphorical analogies already mentioned demonstrate a possible equality between them: "the palisade *is* the house that *is* the vase".

Some secondary metaphors may be added to this basic metaphorical structure. An example of this might be the "animal equated with the house". This recognition is probably the result of the perception of the palisade as a boundary between "Culture" and "Nature", its inner part being able to culturalise (or "domesticate") the wildness of earth, water, fire or animals.

The way in which prehistoric populations perceived their world is manifested in the material culture as iconography or as cognitive maps ("the way in which spatial information is organized and stored", Downs and Stea 1977, 62). This may be in the form of ceramic miniatures, or in the structure of processes, such as in the addition – subtraction instance mentioned above. This study reveals that one of the dominant metaphors of the past was 'the domesticated-Nature" (Gheorghiu 2000 b). This is generally expressed in the shape of ancillary objects with zoomorphic traits. From the analysis of building processes and miniature models that evoke architectural objects and animals, the present paper will discuss three variants of this metaphor with regard to the tell, the palisade, the houses and the vases.

Metaphor 1: "The palisaded tell as a domestication factor"

Throughout the controlled cyclical process of growth and shrinkage of its cultural material the life of the tell is similar to the cycles of life and the consumption of domesticated plants. The palisade controls the cyclical growth and decrease of clay and wooden objects that create the identity of a human group through "a physical and social expression of continuity with ancestors" (Chapman 1991, 93). The palisades, therefore, demonstrate the need for the protection of such a special space (Rowlands 1972, 448).

The mixture of old fragments into the fabric of new objects has a technical function (eg. tempering material) but it is also cognitive in ensuring the repetitive maintenance of memory (Malim 1994). This supports the concept of kinship and the continuity of group identity through maintaining links with the past. Not all the cultural material is included in the process of memory maintenance. The exits of the palisade allow a *part* of the cultural material to be removed while other parts of it are incorporated into the soil or into objects and yet other *parts* of the community's consumption are buried in pits. This control and selection of materials within the palisade can be perceived as a process of "domestication", as well as one of "transaction" with the Earth, through the sacrificial rituals and the continuous construction of memory.

Metaphor 2: "The house as animal"

One might infer that the miniature architectural models that have been discovered in tells could represent the images of actual houses built within the palisade (Bailey 1990) since their dimensions equate with those of the real houses. From amongst the corpus of these models, the type mentioned above with the horn-shaped façades evokes the image of a horned animal. Representations of bovine horns are frequent in the Gumelnita material culture and they are probably a metonym of domestication and value. The positioning of such an image on the entrance of a palisade or on a façade, could be interpreted as a symbol of "domestication" (by "incorporating" the animal into the human community - see Ingold 1996, 21), of "value" and of "defence". Thus the house and therefore the palisaded tell might be perceived as a "stable" or "corral" and its houses as a "flock" as the Vounous model of enclosure from Bronze Age Cyprus suggests (Peltenburg 1989, 115, fig. 15.4). Just such an example is the model from the Cascioarele Island tell (see Dumitrescu 1970, pl. III) (fig 6.13), that represents a high horned palisade with loop-windows in the trellis which shields four horned megaron houses. A more evocative model of the metaphor of the domestication of houses comes from Gumelnita itself (see Serbanescu 1998, 249, fig. 1) (fig 6.14). This model contains more selective and organised information and there is also a fragment from a similar model from the terrace tell at

***Fig 6.13**: Clay model from Cascioarele tell on the island.*

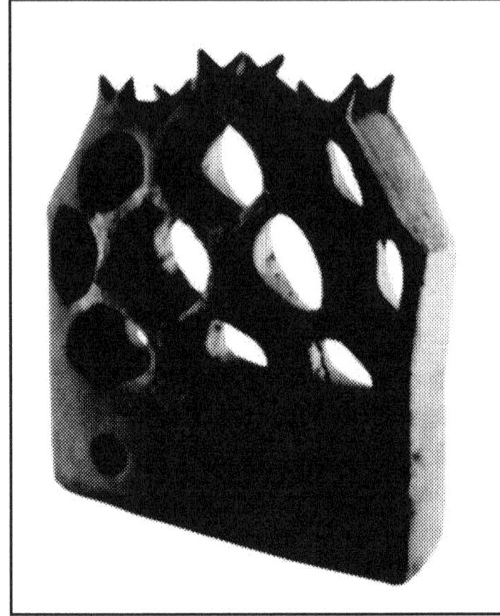

***Fig 6.14**: Clay model from Gumelnita tell (after Serbanescu 1997: 249, fig. 3/5).*

Cascioarele (Serbanescu 1997, 249, fig. 3/5). These models are, in my opinion, the most expressive prehistoric images of a human settlement. The site is enclosed by the palisade and the models evoke the emergence of an institutionalised, community-level authority (Halstead 1999, 90) through the hierarchy displayed in the positioning of the houses. A special characteristic of the images of these two models is their "selectivity" or "synthesis" (Down and Stea 1977, 96). In other words, they contain sufficient information to evoke three-dimensional images of the settlement (cf. Humphreys & Bruce 1995, 45), and subsequently to evoke the palisades as boundaries to control and contain objects and animals. The hierarchy of buildings on the model may well represent the real difference in the heights of the houses (cf. Halstead 1999, 90) which would otherwise be invisible in the archaeological record.

***Fig 6.15**: Gumelnita vase with a lid with an architectural handle from Pietrele tell (after Berciu 1956: 42, fig. 51).*

Metaphor 3: "The palisaded tell as a vase with a lid"

Vases are a rich medium of metaphorical information, especially when considering the analogies of their construction with other objects. Since all the significant objects discussed above and seen as defining the tells are containers, then the rhetorical analogies invite the metaphor of "the palisaded tell as a container". This metaphor reveals itself in the shape of vases with conical or domed lids and with architecturally modelled handles (such as at Izvoarele, Berciu 1956, 42, fig. 51; or at Bordusani, Marinescu-Bilcu *et al.* 1997, plate 33). The containing function of the vase might evoke the metaphorical function of the palisaded tell as a "container" and the single house would metonymically and synecdochically evoke the settlement. Additionally, the relationship between the spiralled patterns and miniature architectural objects on certain vases might evoke the process of the reorientation of the dwellings through time within the palisades.

CONCLUDING REMARKS: THE ADDITIVE-SUBTRACTIVE TELL AS A PRODUCT OF THE PALISADE

One can conclude from this comparative analysis of the founding, reorientation, and destruction of the representative objects that constitute a tell (*i.e.* the palisades, the houses (habitations, barns, or stables), the ovens and the vases) that the additive and subtractive processes are cyclical and metaphorical. The vertical rotating growth of the cultural material that characterises the tell formation is the result of controlled cyclical processes contained by the perimeter formed by the palisade. This also shapes the rituality of the settlement. Palisades, along with the "preconceived plan" and the rotating growth, in my opinion, represent dominant places through the prestige and efficiency of their original design. This resulted from the social differences and social control that surfaced with the emergence of Chalcolithic societies (for palisaded and two-storeyed buildings as indexes of a social difference see also Chapman 1991, 94). Moreover, palisades seem to have been the symbols of wealth with the tell, surrounded by a palisade, being perceived as a large stable.

The need to protect and emphasise the settlement was necessitated by factors such as the differential access to or control of resources (Bailey 1990, 43), the economic long distance networks for salt, metals and exotic goods (which linked the Balkans with the Carpathian-north-Pontic area), and the differences in soil occupation between different groups. By protecting its inner perimeter and by promoting symbolical accumulation and a stable relationship with the ancestors, by laying out the land, by controlling the movement of houses and objects, and by emphasising the community through the domination of landscape and of the imaginary of people, the palisade's role was simultaneously functional and symbolical (fig 6.16).

ACKNOWLEDGEMENTS

I am grateful to Dr. Alex Gibson for the invitation to contribute to his EAA session in Lisbon, and later for the improvement of the English of the present text. My gratitude goes also to Emilian Nicolae for showing me the Uzunu tell and to the Iordache family from Uzunu village whose household I used as an ethnographic model for my study. Many thanks also to Bogdan Danailescu for making and processing the illustration. Last but not least all my gratitude to Cornelia for her invaluable help in achieving this paper.

FOOTNOTES

1 The only exception is at Durankulak, where a "palace" structure and the bases of megarons were made of stone (Todorova 1989: Pernicka et al.1997, 59).

2 There are also examples of walls without any wooden structure (Marinescu-Bilcu 1997, 65).

3 For example in a Hamangia settlement at Techirghiol in Dobrodja, on the seashore of the Black Sea, the pits contained a small number of fragments of walls with slip, shards and bones of average dimensions. The rest of the material filling the cavity was crushed into very small fragments.

BIBLIOGRAPHY

Bailey, D. W. 1990. The living house: signifying continuity. In R. Samson (ed.), *The Social Archaeology of Houses*. Edinburgh: Edinburgh University Press, pp. 19-48.

Balteanu, A. C. 1997. Anthropology. *Cercetari Arheologice* X: 93-95.

Bem, C. 2000. Elemente de cronologie radiocarbon. *Cercetari Arheologice* XI, vol.I: 337-359.

Berciu, D. 1937. Sapaturile de la Petru Rares (1933–1935). *Buletinul Muzeului Judetului Vlasca* II: 1-30.

Berciu, D. 1956. Cercetari si descoperiri arheologice in regiunea Bucuresti. *Materiale* II: 1-80.

Chapman, J. 1991. The early Balkan village, in Ole Gron, Ericka Engelstad and Inge Lindblom, (eds.), *Social Space, - Human Spatial Behaviour in Dwellings and Settlements*, Odensee: Odensee University Press, pp. 79–99.

Chapman, J. 1994a. The Origins of farming in south-east Europe. *Prehistoire Europeenne* 6: 133–156.

Chapman, J. 1994b. Social power in the early farming communities of eastern Hungary – Perspectives from the Upper Tisza region, *Josa Andras Muzeum Evkonyve* XXXVI: 79-99.

Chernych, E. N. 1992. *Ancient metallurgy in the USSR. The Early Metal Age*. Cambridge: Cambridge University Press.

Comsa, E. 1955. Sapaturile de salvare si cercetari de suprafata in regiunea Bucuresti, SCIV, VI (3-4): 411-433.

Comsa, E. 1972. Quelques problemes relatifs au complexe neolithique de Radovanu, *Dacia*, NS XVI: 44-45.

Comsa, E. 1976. Quelques considerations sur la culture Gumelnita (L'agglomeration Magura Jilavei), *Dacia* NS, XX: 105-127.

Comsa, E. 1986. Santurile de aparare ale asezarilor neolitice de la Radovanu, *Cultura si civilizatie la Dunarea de Jos*, Calarasi, 2: 61-67.

Comas, E. 1990. Radovanu. *Cultura si civilizatie la Dunarea de Jos* VIII, Calarasi.

Dionysius of Halycarnassos, 1885. *Antiquitatum Romanorum que supersunt*, Lipsiae: Carolus Jacoby, Tenbnery, vol. I.

Downs M., R. &Stea D. 1977. *Maps in Mind. Reflections on Cognitive Mapping*, New York, Hagerstown, San Francisco and London: Harper and Row.

Dumitrescu, V. 1965. Principalele rezultate ale primelor doua campanii de sapapturi din asezarea neolitica tirzie de la Cascioarele, *SCIV* 16 (2): 215-238.

Dumitrescu, V. 1970. Edifice destinee au culte, decouvert dans la couche Boian-Spantov de la station de Cascioarele, *Dacia*, NS, XIV: 5-24.

Dumitrescu, V. 1986. A doua coloana de lut ars din sancturaul fazei Boian-Spantov de la Cascioarele (Jud. Calarasi), *Cultura si Civilizatie la Dunarea de Jos*, 2: 69-72.

Dumitrescu, V. 1986a. Stratigrafia asezarii-tell de pe ostrovelul de la Casioarele, *Cultura si civilizatie la Dunarea de Jos*, 2: 73-81.

Fletcher, R. 1984. Identifying Spatial Disorder: A Case Study of A Mongol Fort, in H. Hietala (ed.), *Intrasite Spatial Analysis in Archaeology*. Cambridge: CUP, pp. 196-223.

Gheorghiu, D. 2000a. The Rhetoric of People and Grains. In U. Albarella (ed.), *Environmetal Archaeology. Meaning and Purpose*. Dordrecht: Kluwer Academic Publishers.

Gheorghiu, D. 2000b. The Archaeology of Space: Ritual and Metaphor. In G. Malm (ed.), *The Archaeology of Buildings*. Oxford: British Archaeological Reports.

Gheorghiu, D. In press. Le passe comme oeuvre d'art, *Ipso facto*, Milan.

Gheorghiev, G. 1963. Glavni rezultati ot razkopkite na Azmatzkata celishna mogila pred g. 1961 . In *Bulletin de l'Institut d'Archeologie* XXVI: 157-176.

Gibson, A. 1998. *Stonehenge and Timber Circles*, Tempus, Stroud.

Haita, C. 1997. Micromorphological study. *Cercetari Arheologice* X: 85-92.

Haita, C. 2000. Sedimentologie. *Cercetari Arheologice* XI, vol. I: 48-55.

Halstead, P. 1999. Neighbours from Hell? The Household in Neolithic Greece. In Paul Halstead (ed.), *Neolithic Society in Greece*, 77-95. Sheffield Studies in Aegean Archaeology, Sheffield: Sheffield Academic Press,.

Hebbelynck, M. Th. 1905. En Roumanie, *Le Tour du Monde*, Tome XI, Nouvelle Serie, 33, 385-396.

Humphreys, G. W. & Bruce, V. 1995. *Visual Cognition. Computational, Experimental and Neuropsychological Perspectives*. Hove, London, Hillsdale: Lawrence Erlbaum Associates.

Ingold, T. 1996. Growing plants and raising animals: an anthropological perspective on domestication. In D. R. Harris (ed.), *The Origins and Spread of Agriculture and Pastoralism in Eurasia*. 12-24. London: University College London.

Ivanov, I. 1992. *El Nacimiento de la Civilizacion Europea*, Sofia: Borina.

Kostakis, K. 1999. What tells can tell: Social space and settlement in the Greek Neolithic, in Halstead Paul (ed.), *Neolithic Society in Greece*, 66-76. Sheffield: Sheffield Academic Press.

Laszlo, F. 1911. Haromzek Varmegyei praemykenali jellqutelepek – Stations de l'epoque pre-mycenienne dans le comitat de Haromszek. In *Dolgozatok – Traveaux*, Cluj.

Laszlo, A. 1993.Asezarea intarita de la Malnas Bai. In *Arheologia Moldovei* XVI: 33-50.

Leach, E. 1976. *Culture and Communication: The Logic by which Symbols are Connected.* Cambridge: Cambridge University Press.

Malim, T. 1994. *Cognitive Processes*, Houndsmill and London: The Macmillan Press.

Marinescu-Bilcu, S. 2000. Sur l'organisation interne des certaines stations des cultures Boian-Gumelnita et Precucuteni-Cucuteni. In *Cercetari Arheologice* XI, part I: 321-336.

Marinescu-Bilcu, S. 1996-1998. Santierul arheologic de la Bucsani (jud. Giurgiu). In *Buletinul Muzeului "Theohari Antonescu"*, (2-4): 93-111.

Marinescu-Bilcu, S. 1997. Archaeological research at Bordusani-Popina (Ialomita County) Preliminary report 1993-1994. In *Cercetari Arheologice* X: 35-39.

Marinescu-Bilcu, S. 2000. Sur l'organisation interne de quelques stations des cultures des complexes Boian-Gumelnitza et Precucuteni-Cucuteni. In *Cercetari Arheologice* XI, vol. I: 321-336.

Marinescu-Bilcu, S. & Ionescu, B. n.d. *Catalogul sculpturilor eneolitice din Muzeul raional de la Oltenita*, Sibiu.

Morintz, S. 1963. Oasezare Boian fortificata (Santurile de aparare ale asezarii de la Spantov), *SCIV* XVI (2): 265-282.

Nania, I. 1967. Locuitoarii gumelnieni in lumina cercetarilor de la Teiu. In *Studii si Articole de Istorie, Societatea de Stinte Istorice si Filologice din Romania* IX: 19-27.

Ovid 1933. *I Fasti.* A cura di Luigi Giuseppe. Milan: Sernini.

Peltenburg, E. 1989. The Beginnings of religion in Cyprus. In E. Peltenburg (ed.), *Early Society in Cyprus.* 108–126. Edinburgh: Edinburgh University Press.

Perles, C. The Distribution of Magoules in Eastern Thessaly. In Paul Halstead (ed.), *Neolithic Society in Greece,* 42-56. Sheffield Studies in Aegean Archaeology 2, Sheffield: Sheffield Academic Press.

Perniceva, L. 1978. Sites et habitations du Chalcolithique en Bulgarie. Studia Praehistorica 1-2: 163-170.

Pernicka E., Begemann, F., Schmitt-Strecker, S., Todorova, H. & Kulekk, I. 1977. Prehistoric copper in Bulgaria. *Eurasia Antiqua* 3: 41-179.

Plutarque, 1966. *Vies.* R. Laceliere (trad.), Paris: Les Belles Lettres.

Popovici, D., Randoin, B., Rialland, Y., Voinea, V., Vlad, F., Bem, C., & G. Haita, 2000. Les recherches archeologiques du tell de Harsova (dep. de Constantza) 1997-1998. *Cercetari Arheologice* XI, vol. I: 13-34.

Renfrew, C. 1997. Towards a cognitive archaeology. In C. Renfrew and E. Zubrow (eds.), *The Ancient Mind. Elements of Cognitive Archaeology.* 3-12. Cambridge: Cambridge University Press.

Rosetti, D. V. & Morintz, S. 1961. Sapaturile de la Vidra. *Materiale*, VII: 70-76.

Roman, P. 1962. O asezare neolitica la Magurele, *SCIV* XIII, 2: 259-262.

Rowlands, M. J. 1972. Defence: a factor in the organization of settlements. In P. Ucko & R. Tringham (eds.), *Man, Settlement and Urbanism*, 447-462. London: Duckworth.

Schalager, N. 1997. Mindful archaeology: unleashing the *chaine-operatoire* for an archaeology of mind. In C. Renfrew & E. Zubrow (eds.), *The Ancient Mind. Elements of Cognitive Archaeology*, 3-12. Cambridge: Cambridge University Press.

Serbanescu, D. 1997, Modele de locuinte si sanctuare eneolitice. *Prehistoire du Bas Danube*: 232-251.

Sherratt, A. 1972. Socio-economic and demographic models for the Neolithic and Bronze Ages of Europe. In D. Clarke (ed.), *Models in Archaeology*, 477-541. London: Methuen.

Sherratt, A. 1983. The Eneolithic period in Bulgaria in its European context. In A. Poulter (ed.), *Ancient Bulgaria*, vol. I, 188-198, Nottingham.

Theocaris, D. R. 1973. *Neolithic Greece.* Athens: National Bank of Greece.

Tringham, R. 1972. Territorial demarcation of prehistoric settlements. In P. Ucko & R. Tringham (eds.), *Man, Settlement and Urbanism*, 463-476. London: Duckworth.

Tringham, R. 1991. Households with faces: The challenge of gender in prehistoric architectural remains. In G. Joan & M. Conkey (eds.), *Engendering Archaeology*, 93-131. Oxford and Cambridge: Blackwell.

Tringham, R. & Krstic, D. 1990. *Selevac: A Neolithic village in Yugoslavia*, Monumenta Archaeologica 15, Los Angeles Institute of Archaeology, University of California.

Todorova, H. 1982. *Kupferzeitliche Siedlungen in Nordostbulgarien*, Muenchen: Verlag C. H. Beck.

Todorova, H. 1978. The Eneolithic period in Bulgaria in the V-th millennium BC, *BAR,* 49. Oxford: British Archaeological Reports.

Todorova, H. 1989. *Durankulak* 1, Sofia.

Whittle, A. 1996. *Europe in the Neolithic. The Creation of New Worlds*, Cambridge: Cambridge University Press.

APPENDIX 1

TELL[1]										
OBJECTS			**MATERIALS**							
LEVEL I										
Palisade	**House**	**Oven or fireplace**	**Vase**	**Human body**	**Inorganic refuse**	**Organic refuse**	**Clay from ditches**	**Clay from pits and foundations**	**Clay from flooding**	**Wood**	**Vegetal (cereals chaff) twigs, reed**
BEGINNING OF GROWTH											
Outlining the perimeter											
ENTRANCES AND PASSAGES Orientation and delimiting the areas of passage[2]; liminal zones marked by posts[3]										Procurement of tree beams of 30 cm average	Procurement of twigs
VARIANT: Digging of a contour ditch[4]							Addition of clay probably for houses				
VARIANT: contour with clay wall[5]											
Erecting the wooden palisade **VARIANT**: with regular posts [6]; **VARIANT**: with thick and thin posts[7], plaited with twigs											

1 The comments with Italics are the inferences of the author.

2 See Todorova 1982 :148, fig. 90.

3 For Boian: Spantov (Morintz 1963: 265-282), for Boian-Gumelnita: Radovanu (Comsa 1972: 44-45), for Gumelnita: Jilava (Comsa 1976: 105-127); for Vidra (Rosetti and Morintz 1961: 70—76); Magurele (Roman 1962: 259-262); Radovanu (Comsa 1972: 44-45); Teiu (Nania 1967).

4 Idem

5 Todorova 1982: 228, fig. 185; Gheorghiev 1963: 160.

The making of windows by leaving apertures in the trellis (see clay models)											
Covering the palisade with clay							*Addition of clay from ditches*				
THE CEASING OF THE PERIMETRAL GROWTH	**BEGINNING OF THE INTERIOR GROWTH**										
	Plotting[8] and orientation of houses[9]	*The foundation of ovens*	Mix of different clays with sand								
	Extraction of clay: digging of foundation ditch[10]	Building of ovens and exterior fireplaces[11]	Sacrifice of old vases	Frag-mentation of human skeleton				Accumulation from the extraction from the sacrificial pits and deposition pits		Addition of large and thin beams	Addition of twigs
			Selective addition of shards in tombs [12]	Addition through sacrifice[13] of children [14] or selective deposition of skulls							

6 Todorova 1982: 183, figs.114-115; 186, figs. 120-121; 188, figs. 124-125; 189, fig. 126; 190, figs. 128-129), Todorova 1982: 194, figs.135-137; 200, figs.147,149; 202, figs. 151, 153; 204, figs. 154-157); Todorova 1982: 218, fig. 71; 220, fig. 173; Gheorghiev 1963: 160.

7 Todorova 1982: 206-212, figs. 159-165; Todorova 1982: 222-226, figs. 175-183.

8 Todorova (1978: 48) and Marinescu-Bilcu (2000: 324) ; Todorova (1982: 206 ff.) and Marinescu-Bilcu (1997: 69).

9 Todorova 1982: 183-231: Comsa 1990: 72, fig. 33).

10 Marinescu-Bilcu et al. 1997: 68.

11 Marinescu-Bilcu 1996-1998: 96

12 Balteanu 1997: plate 42.

13 Marinescu-Bilcu 1996-1998: 111).

14 Marinescu-Bilcu 1996-1998: 111; Dumitrescu 1986: 78;

	FLOOR										
	Wooden floor[15]	Oven pedestals 16								Addition of layers of split beams or planks	
	Covering with clay and plastering		Addition of a layer of slip			Herbivorous faeces as plastering units[17]					Straw binder and clay[18];
	Covering of the floor with a vegetal mat 19		*Covering with a vegetal support (as with demi-johns)*								Vegetal mats plaiting
	WALLS										
	Erecting the structural posts	Building of walls									
	Erecting non-structural posts										
	Plaiting of twigs[20] Plaited barns added to houses[21]										

15 Comsa 1990: 85; Todorova 1982: 152-153, figs. 95-97.

16 Comsa 1990: 86.

17 Haita 1997: 88.

18 Haita 1997: 87

19 Haita 1997: 88

20 Marinescu-Bilcu 1996-1998: 111

21 Nania 1967: 7.

	Mix of clay with organic materials (straws[22] and dung or shards 23	Mix of clay with organic materials 24 and shards	Addition of crushed shards in clay		Addition of clay, shards, ash and charcoal	Mix of clay with organic materials (selective addition of osteological pieces					
	Addition of clay (sometimes as clods[25])		Clay prepared as clods			Soil covered with coprolites and vegetal remains[26] Organic remains in the ovens' clay[27]		*The use of the clay from deposit pits or sacrificial pits*			Straw binder in clay[28]
	The building of interior walls and of the ceiling		The building of the vase								
	The making of the windows	The making of the openings	The building of the vase								
	The plastering of the walls and columns 29		Addition of a slip layer			Herbivorous faeces as plastering units[30]					

22 Comsa 1990: 90
23 Marinescu-Bilcu 1996-1998: 111
24 Haita 1997: 87
25 Comsa 1990: 89
26 Haita 2000: 53
27 Haita 1997: 87
28 Haita 1997: 87
29 Dumitrescu 1986.
30 Haita 1997: 88

	The painting of interior[31] and exterior walls and interior columns[32]	*Painting*	Crusted ware, graphite, slip, incisions								
	Building the roof										
	The covering of the roof with reed and clay	Oven in the form of the house	Covering with lids; sometimes the handles are architectur al models		Pits filled with waste[33]	Pits filled with waste 34 (selective parts of animal skeletons)		Clay		Poles for fixing[35]	Reed
	Addition of successive layers of clay and painting[36] on architectural objects[37] (habitations and barns[38])	Addition of successive layers of clay[39]	*Probably crusted ware*		Accumulation of ashes and shards in pits; The levelling of the soil adding layers of ashes[40]	Accumulatio n of coprolits 41, bones on soil and pits	Levelling of the soil by adding layers of clay[42]		Layers of natural accumulation due to water drain 43		*Addition of cereals and fodder*
	THE END OF THE GROWTH; BEGINNING OF										

31 Comsa 1990: 81
32 Dumitrescu 1986
33 Haita 1997: 87
34 Haita 1997: 87.
35 Comsa 1990: 85.
36 Comsa 1990: 81.
37 Gheorghiev 1963: 160
38 Marinescu-Bilcu et 1997: 65-66.
39 Marinescu-Bilcu et al 1997: 65-66
40 Haita 2000: 53
41 Haita 2000; 53
42 Haita 2000:53
43 Haita 2000: 53.

	The intentional pull down of some unburned walls[44]	The destruction of the oven for levelling the foundation of a future building 45	The fragment-ation of vases *for ritual purposes*	The addition of shards near the human body in tombs							
	The transformation of the house in waste deposit or stable[46] Partial abandonment of the tell[47]										
	Intentional [48] or *accidental* burning of houses		Intention-ally or *accident-ally* burned vases		The filling of the deposit pits with shards and remains of fired houses 49	The filling of the deposit pits with vegetal remains, bones, shells					
VARIANT: The space between the palisade and interior filled with earth and rubbish from the destroyed houses[50]	The pulling down of burned walls and the crushing and leveling of remains[51]				The production of inorganic remains	The production of organic remains					
	END OF GROWTH										

44 Marinescu-Bilcu et al. 1997: 66.
45 Popovici et al. 2000: 17
46 Popovici at al. 2000: 17
47 Haita 1997: 88; Haita 2000: 53
48 Haita 1997: 88
49 Comsa 1990: 90
50 Todorova 1978: 49
51 Popovici at al. 2000: 17

Preserving the same perimeter	**VARIANT I: THE BEGINNING OF GROWTH** Addition of clay and ash layers and continuing dwelling							Digging pits				
VARIANT I: THE REDUCING OF GROWTH The filling of ditches[52] and the limitation of the surface of dwelling	The filling of ditches, the limitation of the surface of dwelling, and the increasing the number of houses				Accumulation in pits	Accumulatio n in pits						
VARIANT II: ABANDON The destruction of the palisade	**VARRIANT II:** Total abandon of the tell								Natural accumulation of sediments from flooding			
TELL LEVEL II												
The reconstruction of the old perimeter, or of a smaller one[53]	The reconstruction of houses on old foundations[54]		Selection and crushing of shards and architectur -al debris		Pits filled with fragments of burned houses			Digging of pits filled with fragments of burned houses[55]				
Emplecton walls made of the filling of palisade's wooden walls with clay mixed to waste	Floor prepared from destruction remains[56]; walls from clay with organic remains and shards[57]	Addition of shards or crushed architectural fragments	Addition of shards or crushed fragments	Addition of shards								

52 Comsa 1986: 61
53 Comsa 1986: 66.
54 Bailey 1990
55 Comsa 1990
56 Marinescu-Bilcu 1997: 69.
57 Marinescu-Bilcu 1996-1998: 111.

TELL LEVEL III	ditto	ditto	ditto	ditto	ditto	ditto					
LEVEL N The transformation of parts of the palisade into walls of houses 58	The transformation of parts of the palisade into walls of peripheral houses										
LEVEL N + 1 (with a smaller perimeter) The use of parts of the palisade as walls for peripheral houses[59], a change in the geometry of entrances	The use of larger parts of the palisade as walls for peripheral houses										
LEVEL N + 2 The identification of a large part of the perimeter of the palisade with the walls of houses; a complete disappearance in architecture of the rites of passage											

58 Todorova 1982; 212, fig. 165
59 Todorova 1982: 202, figs. 151, 153

www.ingramcontent.com/pod-product-compliance
Lightning Source LLC
Chambersburg PA
CBHW061003030426
42334CB00033B/3347
* 9 7 8 1 8 4 1 7 1 2 9 3 2 *